GARDEN DESIGN
with FOLIAGE

Ferns and Grasses, Vines and Ground Covers,
Annuals and Perennials, Trees and Shrubs

by Judy Glattstein

A GARDEN WAY PUBLISHING BOOK

STOREY

Storey Communications, Inc.
Schoolhouse Road
Pownal, Vermont 05261

Cover design by Judy Eliason
Text design and production by Judy Eliason, Cindy McFarland, and Carol Jessop
Edited by Gwen W. Steege
Garden watercolors by Carolyn Bucha
Black-and-white text illustrations by Judy Eliason
Front cover photograph by Richard W. Brown
Indexed by Little Chicago Editorial Services

Back cover photograph: *Acer palmatum* (Japanese maple), *Adiantum pedatum* (maidenhair fern)

Printed in the United States by The Book Press
Color text printed by Excelsior Printing
First Printing, October 1991

Library of Congress Cataloging-in-Publication Data

Glattstein, Judy, 1942-
Garden design with foliage : ferns and grasses, vines and ground covers, annuals and perennials, trees and shrubs / by Judy Glattstein.
p.   cm.
Includes bibliographical references and index.
ISBN 0-88266-687-8 — ISBN 0-88266-686-X (pbk.)
1. Foliage plants.   2. Landscape gardening.   3. Leaves.   I. Title.
SB431.G53   1991
715—dc20   91-55011
CIP

CONTENTS

To my husband, Paul, who gave me room to grow

$\mathscr{P}$REFACE

hy bother with leaves when plants have such beautiful flowers? This is a question people ask me over and over again. I have no simple answer for why I have become so enamored with foliage and its influence in the garden. So many memories have contributed to my fascination with this aspect of plants that no one incident can be said to be the proximal cause. A medley of impressions added up, and my addiction to gardening was the consequence.

I grew up as a city child in Chicago. The summer I was seven, my aunt bought a country place in Brookfield, Connecticut. Every year after that, my mother, father, older sister, younger brother, and I took a Pullman compartment on the overnight train to New York City, where we spent the night at my grandmother's. We then took another train to Brookfield. I can still remember my sense of wonder as the train moved from the world of pavement and tenements to green countryside. This country place was simple in the extreme — two attic bedrooms, a living room, kitchen/dining room, tiny bedroom, and screened porch downstairs. There was no bathroom, only an outhouse, and no electricity; the ice man came three times a week with the ice to keep food cold in an icebox. No one gardened, other than to mow a "lawn" in front of the house.

Entertainment was limited, with outdoor activities predominating. I remember walking two miles down to the lake to swim and bathe — for we had only a hand pump in the kitchen for water. We must have been a charming sight as we soaped up among the bulrushes—much more fun than a bathtub. We took many walks in the woods and fields, berry-picking and just exploring. One of my first plant identification lessons came when I was seven: "Leaflets three, leave it be." After several itchy encounters with poison ivy, I learned to spot the glossy, green leaflets. An area of wet woods had a small, gravel-bottomed spring that was surrounded by ferns as tall as I was then. I think they were probably either cinnamon fern *(Osmunda cinnamomea)* or interrupted fern *(Osmunda claytoniana)*. Even then, I was fascinated by a plant that had such enormous leaves.

A couple of years later, we moved to New York. My parents bought a large Victorian house in Brooklyn in a pleasant neighborhood with tree-lined streets. Dividing the traffic on 17th Street was a central island, or mall, where such homey shrubs as forsythia and spirea grew. It was fascinating to walk around the corner onto Foster Avenue, where there were no trees and no central mall. Not only did it look different, but once the trees had leafed out, the temperature on 17th Street was noticeably lower on sunny days. A neighbor had a mature female ginkgo tree. In the fall, we would all walk on the other side of the street to avoid the vomitus-smelling fruit that littered the sidewalk under the tree. This provided a lesson in plant selection — plant only male ginkgo trees.

Our house had two huge maples in front and flower beds edged in funkia (hosta). When the leaves emerged in the spring, I picked new shoots and uncurled them, intrigued by the way the leaf first appeared rolled up in a tube and then flattened out. Our desultory attempts at a lawn were doomed to failure from the start. After several years of an annual event called "seeding the lawn," we wised up and planted myrtle *(Vinca minor)*. This eventually thickened into a glossy, dark green carpet, which I thought was much prettier than the sparse grass and hard-packed dirt that had been there before. My brother and I were each given a garden of our own on the side of the house. My mother once said she had a nightmare that everything I ever planted in my spot came up, and it became a jungle. The only thing I remember growing was a castor bean plant *(Ricinus communis)*. This tropical annual with a large, speckled, beanlike seed grows rapidly in Jack-and-the-beanstalk fashion to an impressive height, over 6 feet, and has large, five- to eleven-lobed leaves, which are more than 18 inches across. Our cat used to loll in the shade underneath, and I imagined that *she* imagined herself to be a tiger in the jungle. Today, over thirty-five years later, I plant a castor bean cultivar with reddish leaves ('Gibsonii') for its foliage effect as an architectural accent in the summer garden. My current cats use it in the same manner as my childhood cat!

In college, I was required to take one botany course, but learning about photosynthesis as I looked at chlorophyll in *Elodea* leaves and geotropism as I turned pots of bean seedlings on their sides was all rather uninteresting to me. Fate plays many tricks, however, and I sometimes think a very slowly germinating seed was planted in me that has matured into my current passion for plants.

After marriage, babies, and apartments in Angola, Indiana; Lake Mohegan, New York; and Pittsburgh, Pennsylvania, we bought a house of our own in Norwalk, Connecticut. It was there that I began to take an interest in gardening. Thinking I should plant something, I put in a few annuals from the supermarket — annuals, because I was too impatient to wait for results. Most did rather poorly (I put sun-loving marigolds in too shady a place, for example), but I found it rather fascinating to plant and watch things grow.

The reason to create a garden is for its beauty and for the enjoyment — the evocative appearance, feel, and scents of the whole. The sight of dewdrops collected like moonstones on the leaves of lady's-mantle (*Alchemilla mollis*), the tender unfurling shoots on a fern, the architectural pattern of the leaves of bear's-breech (*Acanthus mollis*), the translucent colors of autumn foliage with sunlight streaming through the leaves, the furry feel of lamb's-ears (*Stachys lanata* or *S. byzantina*), and the strong scent of Corsican mint (*Mentha requienii*) as the leaves are gently stroked — all of these comprise the gestalt of a garden.

As I continue to accept the challenges of growing different kinds of plants — sometimes plants that are difficult, unsuitable, or not completely hardy — I realize a warm glow of accomplishment for my new successes. I also am convinced that whatever level of skill you possess, whether you garden in sun or shade, and no matter what the climate, you can use leaves to create a charming, attractive, and appealing garden with less effort than if you rely on flowers alone for effect.

PART ONE

Consider the Leaf

Leaves provide a whole range of visual effects in any garden. Their influence can be subtle — a peaceful, restful impression created by a play of shapes and textures in shades of green. They can also provide a bold, exciting dimension when colored and variegated foliage, from purple and yellow to copper and silver, is used to create vivid and striking designs. When their shape, pattern, color, and variegation are combined with flowers under the touch of an inspired gardener, the most desirable outcome in ornamental horticulture — the garden — is achieved.

In addition to visual effects, leaves serve a host of practical roles in a garden. When the flowers are gone, the leaves can continue to provide an attractive display, if they have been chosen with care. Perennials, annuals, and bulbs all present particular problems: Most perennials, the mainstays in the garden because they come back year after year, are in bloom for only a few weeks. Although annuals are in bloom for a longer period, they die each winter and need to be planted again the following year, and the numerous spring bulbs, like tulips and daffodils, go dormant in late spring or early summer, leaving a gap in the flower bed that is an invitation to weeds. Leafy plants also reduce maintenance chores in the garden, since they do not require the constant attention to deadheading and staking that flowers can demand.

There are also seasonal benefits of foliage effects. In many parts of the country, winter is a time of little growth and scanty, if any, bloom; evergreen plants can add interest and promise to a bare landscape. Likewise, in shady gardens that reach their flowering display in spring but have only a few kinds of annuals blooming in summer, leaves, with all of their diversity, can supply a handsome and effective display.

Learning How to Select Plants

Whether or not a plant has flowers, it has leaves, whose characteristics should be evaluated when plants are selected. Unlike the lilies of the field, which toil not, neither do they spin, leaves are the workhorses of the plant world, necessary for all life on earth. When we choose plants, however, we often use the romantic and subjective criteria of aesthetic appeal, and our artistic standards frequently measure only one component of the plant — its flowers. Overemphasis on flowers, to the neglect of foliage, often leads to disappointment in the overall appearance of the garden. Leaves, especially green leaves, are commonly regarded as a sort of neutral background against which flowers will be displayed. They are used to provide a pleasant backdrop, perhaps toning down harsh, contrasting flower colors, but they are generally not in and of themselves considered important except in a secondary role. All of us can recognize the fine texture of a grass, the intricate, lacy shape of a fern, and the bold simple form of a hosta or rhubarb leaf, but we tend to ignore, or not consider carefully enough, how these characteristics can be used to advantage in designing our gardens. Learning to look and appraise a plant for its foliage possibilities and using leaves as a significant design element in the garden can give splendid results.

No matter what kinds of plants you are using, there are, of course, pragmatic considerations. Of primary importance are environmental elements such as light, moisture, and temperature, which govern the growing conditions of the site. Plants that require full sun are not going to achieve healthy growth in the shade. Plants adapted to quick-draining, dry, sandy soil that is low in fertility cannot thrive in a rich, wet, muck soil but will probably die from root rot. Gardens composed of plants that are resistant to pests and diseases require less maintenance and have a more pleasing appearance. Thus, the physical conditions of a garden form a very important, pragmatic set of limits that govern the selection of a plant for inclusion.

Aesthetic choices, on the other hand, are as individual as the gardener. Like the practical considerations of site and climate, however, these preferences should be based on certain standards, including foliage texture, pattern, and color. A good foliage plant, for example, has leaves that are attractive alone as well as in combination with nearby plants. The leaves should be present, in good condition, for an extended part of the growing season. It might be desirable in a particular garden to use plants that are evergreen, or those that have good fall color. Specific gardens with their individual landscape conditions, as well as the personal taste of the gardener, dictate the variety of plant characteristics that can be used for successful design. In the following section are some criteria to consider when you plan your garden.

Extending the Season of Your Garden's Beauty

All gardens have a resting period, which may be during winter cold or summer drought. With careful attention to foliage you can create an aesthetically pleasing garden picture even at these slow times of the year. In Minnesota, for example, with its bitter winter temperatures of USDA Zone 3 or 4 (see map on page 210), only needled conifers will retain their leaves. On the other hand, in New Jersey and Connecticut in the more moderate Zones 5 and 6, broad-leaved evergreen trees and shrubs such as the American holly (*Ilex opaca*) and mountain laurel (*Kalmia latifolia*) provide additional winter interest to the garden, along with a few perennials such as the Christmas rose (*Helleborus niger*) and bergenia (*Bergenia purpurascens*). Broad-leaved evergreen, woody plants such as *Nandina* and the bull-bay magnolia (*Magnolia grandiflora*) thrive in the mild-winter areas of southeastern states like North Carolina. The subtropical climates of Florida and southern California permit the use of numerous evergreen perennials and vines as well as trees and shrubs.

On the other hand, some plants with beautiful leaves may have growing habits that make them unsuitable for certain situations. For example, bleeding-heart (*Dicentra spectabilis*) is an old-fashioned perennial that grows well in lightly shaded sites. Early in spring it sends up 30-inch high, arching stems with dainty leaves and dangling flowers that look like pink lockets. Soon after the weather gets hot, the entire plant goes dormant until next year. When a plant of this size turns yellow and collapses, it is unsightly, to say the least. Similarly, you may enjoy the crinkled silk petals of the Oriental poppy (*Papaver orientale*), but this plant presents a slightly different problem. In August, it sends up leaves that persist through the winter and expand in spring until its flowers appear in late spring. The plant then goes dormant for the summer, leaving a gap in the perennial border that is difficult to fill, since the poppy must resume its growth and reclaim its place again in late summer.

The growing habits of other kinds of plants also influence the appearance of the garden. The huge, rounded leaves of *Ligularia dentata* 'Othello' are flushed with purple on the reverse. They are very attractive, but only if you look at the plant early in the morning. Once the sun is on the leaves, they wilt like a broken umbrella, no matter how much moisture is available in the soil. On the other hand, sometimes a plant can do *too* well in the garden. Variegated goutweed (*Aegopodium podagraria* 'Variegatum'), with its attractive, white-patterned leaf, is often sold as a ground cover. It will certainly cover ground: unless it is confined between a concrete sidewalk and an asphalt roadway, it will spread despite determined efforts to halt it.

In a shady garden, flowering is concentrated in spring before the trees leaf out and shade the ground below; very few plants flower in a shady location in the summer. Many early-blooming, shade-tolerant plants, such as Virginia bluebells (*Mertensia virginica*), and the majority of early bulbs, such as snowdrops (*Galanthus* spp.) and daffodils (*Narcissus* spp. and hybrids), go dormant and disappear after flowering. If flowers were the only criteria used for selection, the garden would be of little interest in summer and early fall.

Most perennials are in bloom for approximately two or three weeks. Once the flowering portion of their growing cycle is completed, it is the foliage that will be visible in the garden. A six-month growing season includes thirteen two-week periods. Even if the garden is large enough for multiple groupings, it is still the foliage that is present and apparent most of the time. For the most unbroken results, the foliage should be as attractive as possible, both before the plants come into bloom and after the flowers have faded. For example, herbaceous peonies (*Paeonia officinalis*) have lovely flowers as well as exquisite foliage from the time the shoots first appear in the spring until the plants go dormant in the fall, thus making peonies a first-class choice. Multi-useful peony leaves can conceal the yellowing leaves of nearby narcissus that were in bloom earlier, complement their own flowers, contrast wonderfully with the Siberian iris (*Iris sibirica*) that flowers at the same time, and often turn a beautiful orange shade in autumn. Now *that* is a plant that really pays its rent in good measure.

Using Plants in Combination

It is not sufficient, however, to appraise plants separately, since plants are used in combination in the garden. While it is important that each plant has neat and attractive foliage, we must consider how it will look with its neighbors. The lemon lily (*Hemerocallis flava*) is an early-blooming daylily with sweetly fragrant, clear yellow flowers and attractive fountainlike clumps of grasslike leaves. Siberian iris has wine-purple, blue, or white, beardless flowers with reflexed falls and erect standards. The combination of 'Caesar's Brother', an old cultivar with velvety, deep purple flowers, and spiderwort (*Tradescantia* 'J.C. Weguelin'), with its large, three-petaled, clear blue flowers, and the lemon lily, makes a pretty, late-May/early-June flower display. The complementary color harmony of the flowers is attractive, but after flowering — a haystack! All three plants have grasslike leaves with no distinction, no play of pattern and form for visual interest. If in the preliminary plant selection we had looked beyond the flowers to examine the foliage as well, a more satisfactory combination could have been developed. A creamy ivory peony (*Paeonia* 'Harvest Moon') used with the Siberian iris and a peach-leaved bellflower (*Campanula persicifolia* 'Telham Beauty'), with its spikes of large, light blue flowers, would create a similar color scheme. In addition, after the flowering period in late May/early June, the plants would look attractive for the rest of the season. Using these concepts, each of us can find his or her own way to create gardens that will be easy to care for and beautiful to look at throughout the year.

CHAPTER ONE

LEAF FORM AS A DESIGN CONSIDERATION

Summers in Brookfield, Connecticut, were well supplied with snakes, and I always found them fascinating. Some black snakes once used the woodshed under the living room as a communal nursery, and hundreds (or so it seemed) of shoestring-sized babies came wriggling up through the ash pit in the fireplace. In college, I took a graduate course in herpetology, and we spent one session examining live specimens. I can still remember the feel of a reticulated python, steel-cable muscle wrapped in a beautifully patterned hide. But when I mentally compared this exotic serpent to the black snakes of my youth, the model was basically the same. Think of how the scales on a snake are arranged. The configuration on a black snake and a python are quite similar, yet one is uniformly colored black and the other is beige-brown with handsome markings of yellow, black, and white. So it is with plants — shape and color are two different aspects of design.

To use another, nonreptilian, analogy, think of the garden as a photograph. First, examine it in black and white, a photographic medium that has often been used to create great works of art. In black-and-white photography the shape and outline of objects and their relationship to each other is important. In contrast, the vibrancy of color photography can sometimes mask inherent weaknesses. My college courses in black-and-white photography and in Oriental brush painting taught me more about harmony and spatial relationships than any color workshop would have done. If the first-stage shapes are incompatible, this cannot be corrected by an overlay of color. In our gardens, only after we decide which leaf shapes to combine can we advance to the second level of choices — color — and conclude our aesthetic decisions.

The Vocabulary of Leaf Form

Every specialized area of knowledge has its own vocabulary, and certainly botany is no exception. Learning this language changes incomprehensible jargon to helpful precision. The seemingly complex vocabulary is merely a more accurate way to describe the form of a leaf.

Leaves are green due to the pigment *chlorophyll*, which converts carbon dioxide and water to carbohydrates. This conversion using sunlight for energy is called *photosynthesis*. All life on earth depends on this process. Chlorophyll is contained in leaf tissue and green stems.

Leaves are categorized in several different ways: by their shape, by their arrangement on a branch, and by their life span. If a characteristic is important enough to describe, it probably has some relevance for the gardener. When you read a book or catalog description of a plant that is new to you, the terms that are used can help you visualize it.

Leaves are made up of a *blade* and a *petiole*; the petiole is the means by which the leaf is attached to the twig. In its overall shape, a leaf may be *oblong*, like an elongated circle; *ovate*, like an egg, with the broader portion closer to the petiole; *obovate*, also like an egg, but with the narrower portion closer to the petiole; or *oval*, with the broadest part of the leaf blade in the middle. In addition, there are the exceptions, leaves that do not fit any of the categories listed above: a leaf may be *ensiform*, swordlike with a pointed tip; *hastate*, shaped like an arrow with flaring basal lobes; *lanceolate*, lance-shaped; *linear*, elongated with nearly parallel sides; *peltate*, with the petiole attached on the underside of the leaf; or *sagittate*, arrowlike with basal lobes pointing downward.

Simple leaves have only one blade; *compound leaves* have more

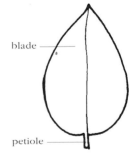

blade

petiole

LEAF FORMS

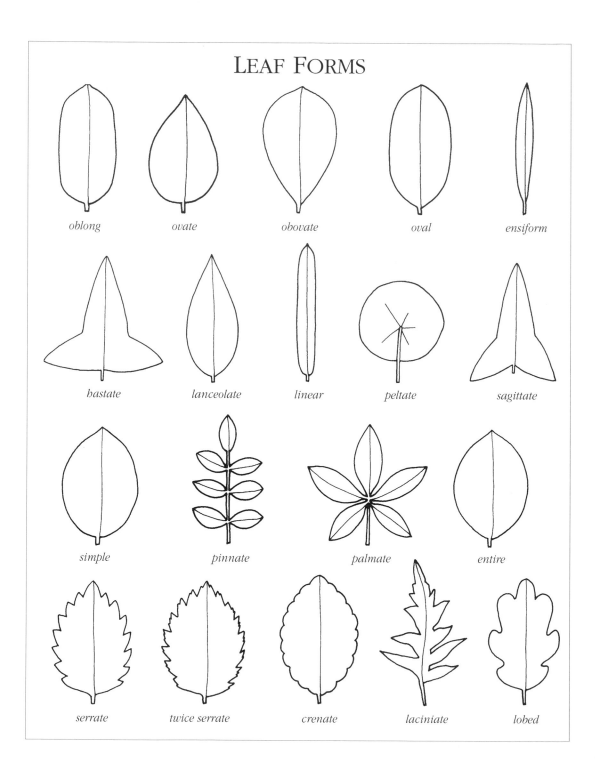

oblong ovate obovate oval ensiform

hastate lanceolate linear peltate sagittate

simple pinnate palmate entire

serrate twice serrate crenate laciniate lobed

than one blade (usually referred to as leaflets) attached to each petiole. The arrangement of the leaflets can be *pinnate*, arranged along a central axis like the barbs on a feather, or *palmate*, arising from a central point like the fingers on your hand. A *pedatisect* form consists of leaflets palmately arranged with the side lobes cut into two or more segments.

The edge of a leaf may be anything from simple to toothed to lobed. An *entire margin* is smooth; *serrate* is like a saw, with pointed teeth often curving forward; *twice serrate*, with the edge coarsely toothed and these teeth additionally serrated; *crenate*, with small, rounded teeth on the margin; *laciniate*, cut into narrow, pointed lobes; or *lobed*, with the space between the serrations or waves extending at least one-third of the way toward the center of the leaf.

Generally, the leaves that first emerge upon germination, the *seed leaves* or *cotyledons*, are different from the mature foliage. Plants are classified into two categories by their seed leaves. If they have only one seed leaf, they are called *monocots*. These plants, which include all the grasses and sedges, irises, lilies, cannas, and palms, have veins that are parallel. Plants with two seed leaves are called *dicots*. The veins in the leaves of dicots are usually branched or netlike. Most familiar seed-bearing plants (including trees and shrubs) are dicots. Sometimes the juvenile leaves, too, are different from those on a mature plant. This is generally true of woody plants, such as junipers and eucalyptus, which may have larger leaves on young shoots than on more mature wood.

monocot

dicot

Leaves are *deciduous* when they naturally separate from the plant after the growing season. Deciduous woody plants drop *all* their foliage; herbaceous perennial plants have no woody parts but die to the ground during their resting period. *Evergreen* plants keep their leaves for several seasons, never dropping all of them at the same time. Some plants are in-between, or semideciduous— they remain green during the winter but lose their leaves at the beginning of the second growing season; an example is the stinking hellebore (*Helleborus foetidus*). Semievergreen plants lose their leaves in response to harsher conditions; one example is bayberry (*Myrica pensylvanica*), which keeps its leaves in the milder area of its range and loses them where winters are more severe.

Using these terms to describe familiar plants, we say that liriope has an evergreen, simple, linear leaf with an entire margin. Ivy (*Hedera helix*) has an evergreen, simple, entire leaf with a wavy margin. Japanese

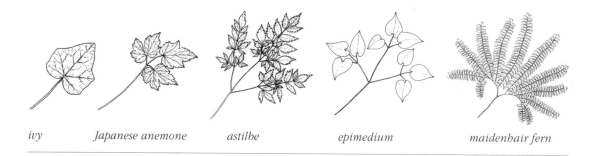

ivy   *Japanese anemone*   *astilbe*   *epimedium*   *maidenhair fern*

anemone (*Anemone japonica*) has a deciduous, simple, lobed leaf with a twice-serrate margin. Astilbe has a deciduous, palmately compound leaf with a serrate margin. Epimedium has a semievergreen, twice-palmately compound leaf with an entire margin. Maidenhair fern (*Adiantum pedatum*) has a pedatisect arrangement of its leaflets — the leaflets are palmately arranged with the lobes at the side cut into two or more segments. Plants as diverse as staghorn sumac (*Rhus typhina*) and Jacob's-ladder (*Polemonium caeruleum*) have pinnately compound leaves.

Using Leaf Shape as a Design Feature

Gardeners select favorite plants for a variety of valid, but personal reasons. Perhaps you adore peonies, dislike the color orange, or prefer annuals for instant gratification — all legitimate criteria for choosing plants for your garden. Sometimes you act on impulse, not on plan. All of us have fallen in love with a plant at a nursery, bought it on a whim, and then wandered in the garden, pot in hand, wondering where to plant it.

Whether you have followed your fancy or an overall garden design, your newest acquisition needs an appropriate location. Just as the conditions of sun and shade, dampness or dryness, winter cold and summer heat must be taken into account, aesthetics must also be considered. Although a tree might be placed as an isolated specimen, plants such as shrubs, perennials, grasses, and annuals are generally grown in association with other plants. Wherever cultural conditions are suitable, plants can be randomly associated or the location of each plant can be selected as part of a purposeful, aesthetically motivated design. The first approach results in a collection; the latter, in a garden. A collection may contain superbly grown specimens, but it is not as delightful and appealing in appearance as a garden. Careful attention to detail lifts the medley out of the ordinary and transforms it into a garden.

A garden needs pattern and balance, and leaves exist in all sizes and shapes as well as a range of complexity of form. Some perennials, such as rhubarb (*Rheum* spp.), umbrella plant (*Peltiphyllum peltatum*), and false hellebore (*Veratrum viride*), have bold, architectural foliage. Ferns, even large ferns such as the 5-foot-tall cinnamon fern (*Osmunda cinnamomea*), retain a daintiness through their lacy texture that balances their stature. The fine, linear texture of the grasses provides gracefulness no matter what the scale of an individual species. Some combinations are obviously appropriate. Anyone can place a fern near a hosta and enjoy the results, but a bit more thought and effort are required when working with leaf patterns on a broader scale. Enchantment and appeal in the eye of the beholder are built upon the creative use of plants in combination. Such creativity makes use of leaves and flowers, color and shape, to establish a beguiling picture that is attractive not only at the moment but also later in the season. An effective garden is one that calls you back again and again to enjoy its unfolding.

If you are just beginning to plan your garden design around foliage, choose plants with leaves that are quite simple in form. Perhaps the simplest are the thin, linear leaves of the grasses, sedges, and rushes. Very similar to these are the grasslike leaves of lilyturf (*Liriope*), daylilies (*Hemerocallis*), and Siberian and Japanese irises (*Iris sibirica* and *I. ensata*). Bearded iris (*I. germanica*) has a stiffer, more swordlike leaf, as does yucca (*Yucca glauca*). But too many plants with analogous form placed near one another make a boring design, so for your next selection, use a plant with a rounded, heart-shaped leaf, such as hosta

A simple garden design using two plants with contrasting leaf shapes: (left) Siberian bugloss and (right) lilyturf.

or Siberian bugloss (*Brunnera macrophylla*). Contrasted with this bold shape, the grassy-leaved, linear pattern then assumes a more delicate appearance, and the aggregate is visually more distinctive (see illustration).

Relative size is another important consideration when choosing plants for each combination. The grouping must display a sense of proportion, of relative scale. If you use small, dainty plants, a greater quantity will usually be needed for them to have sufficient effect in the landscape. For instance, a dwarf grass like the blue sheep's fescue (*Festuca ovina* 'Glauca'), with its threadlike texture and 10-inch height, needs to be grouped as several plants to produce an adequate effect. On the other hand, a massed planting of giant Eulalia grass (*Miscanthus sinensis floridulus*), with its 8- to 12-foot-tall plumes, requires a landscape on a heroic scale to support it, even though it has a relatively fine-textured leaf.

Another effective leaf combination is created when a simple shape, such as that of a grass or a hosta, is combined with a complex leaf with compound structure, such as that of a fern, an astilbe, or an epimedium, which have lacy patterns. One of many possible combinations is bearded iris with herbaceous peonies and columbines, a lovely grouping both in bloom and beyond (see illustration). Or, try using Siberian iris with the white-flowered bleeding-heart (*Dicentra spectabilis* 'Alba'), the foliage of which persists longer than that of the more common pink form. For shady areas, consider a combination such as *Liriope muscari* 'Majestic', which has 10-inch-long, straplike, dark green leaves, with a hosta such as *Hosta fortunei*

An effective design combining plants with a simple leaf shape and those with compound leaves: (left) peonies, (middle) columbine, and (right) bearded iris.

'Hyacinthina', which has pointed, glaucous, ovate leaves; these two, combined with the evergreen Christmas fern (*Polystichum acrostichoides*), create an effective, texturally rich foliage display.

The most attractive plantings often result from grouping several specimens of a few plants rather than one each of many. Suppose in a shady corner there is room for a dozen plants. If you use one each of twelve different kinds of plants, the result will look cluttered and disorganized. Instead, if you plant six liriope, three medium-sized hosta, and three astilbe, the resulting design will be stronger and more attractive. Be sure, too, that the astilbe are all of the same variety; three different astilbe will disrupt the unity, especially when they are in bloom. (Most *Astilbe* x *arendsii* hybrids have similar foliage.) Three different hosta would be even more awkward, since hosta cultivars can vary greatly from leaf to leaf. *Hosta venusta*, for example, has a dainty green leaf the size of your thumbnail, while *Hosta sieboldiana* has enormous leaves 12 to 15 inches across and 18 inches long. Another different but equally interesting hosta/astilbe/liriope combination would consist of one large hosta, three astilbe, and eight liriope. In this instance, the greater number of liriope balances the increased mass, though smaller quantity, of hosta.

In all of these combinations, the effect is created by the form, or outline, of the leaf. By making judicious use of the play of shape upon shape — simple to bold, plain to complex — you can create a pleasing richness of design. As you become increasingly aware of possibilities, you may wish to try combining several different leaf patterns — a more intricate, palmately compound leaf, such as a rodgersia (*Rodgersia aesculifolia*) or a pinnately lobed fern, with the bold silhouette of a hosta and simple, linear, grasslike leaves to further enhance textural contrast. In abandoning uniformity, your only risk is going to the opposite extreme and having too much contrast.

PLANTS FOR SPECIFIC SHAPE

Latin Name	Common Name	Plant Type[1]	Sun/ Shade	Soil Type[2]	Hardiness Zone	Features
BOLD, ARCHITECTURAL FOLIAGE						
Acanthus mollis	bear's-breech	P	sun	2	8–10	Coarse-toothed foliage
Arum italicum	lords-and-ladies	P	shade	2	6–10	Summer dormant
Bergenia cordifolia	bergenia	P	lt. shade	2	3–8	Winter burns
Canna x *generalis*	canna	P	sun	2	8–10	Tropical appearance
Cynara cardunculus	cardoon	P	sun	2	8–10	Coarse-toothed foliage
Echinops ritro	globe thistle	P	sun	3/4	4–9	Thistlelike foliage
Hosta spp.	hosta	P	shade	1/2	3–8	Available in many sizes
Paeonia lactiflora	peony	P	sun	3	3–8	One of the best
Rheum officinale	rhubarb	P	sun	2	3–8	Huge
LINEAR, SWORDLIKE FOLIAGE						
Acorus calamus	sweet flag	P	sun	1	4–10	For wet places
Carex spp., *Luzula* spp.	sedges and rushes	G	shade	1/2	varies	Looks grasslike in shade
Hemerocallis spp.	daylily	P	sun	3	3–8	Easy to grow
Iris sibirica and others	iris	P	sun	1/2/3	3–8	Elegant foliage
Liriope muscari	lilyturf	GC	shade	3	6–9	Specimen/ground cover
Miscanthus spp., *Pennisetum* spp., etc	grasses	G	sun	3	varies	Many available in a range of size
Ophiopogon spp.	mondo grass	GC	shade	3	6–9	Specimen/ground cover
Phormium tenax	New Zealand flax	P	sun	3	8–10	
Yucca filamentosa	yucca	P	sun	4	4–10	
LACY, FINE-TEXTURED FOLIAGE						
Artemisia	'Silver Mound' artemisia	P	sun	4	4–10	Lush growth leads to rot
Aruncus dioicus	goatsbeard	P	shade	2	3–9	Like bugbane and astilbe
Astilbe x *arendsii*	astilbe	P	shade	1/2	4–8	
Cimicifuga racemosa	bugbane	P	shade	2/3	3–10	Leaves similar to astilbe
Dryopteris spp., *Polystichum* spp., etc	ferns	F	shade	1/2	4–10	Varied growth habit depending on species
Foeniculum vulgare	fennel	P	sun	3	4–10	Herb
Myrrhis odorata	sweet cicely	P	shade	3	4–9	Herb
Paeonia tenuifolia	fernleaf peony	P	sun	3	4–9	Summer dormant
Thalictrum spp.	meadow rue	P	shade	2	5–10	Elegant leaves

[1]PLANT TYPE: A – annuals, F – ferns, G – grasses, GC – ground covers, P – perennials, S – shrubs, T – trees, V – vines
[2]SOIL TYPE: 1 – wet, 2 – moist, well-drained, 3 – average loam, 4 – dry
NOTE: *Zone ranges are approximate and apply to winter lows only. Please see "Plant Dictionary" for more detail about the temperature range for the plants in which you are interested.*

CHAPTER TWO

Color as a Design Consideration

Plants and the color green are nearly synonymous. In fact, part of the definition for the word "green" in the dictionary is leafy herbs and green vegetation. This color, somewhere between blue and yellow in the spectrum, is the calm, refreshing shade of grassy meadows and shady forests. But within this one color are found a range of hues — greens such as aqua, celadon, and viridian have a bias toward blue; chartreuse and pea green, toward yellow. There are deep somber greens, such as olive and yew, and clear ones, like cucumber and moss green. A beautiful garden can be created by using variations of only this one color and the textural contrasts of shape — grassy, swordlike leaves; broad, rounded leaves; and lacy, fernlike leaves.

At one time in England, a vogue for the green garden relied only on green foliage to create a peaceful, shady garden. The Japanese garden, too, severely restricts the use of flowers to a scant few — azaleas and peonies, iris and chrysanthemum — and relies on the green of trees and shrubs and ground-carpeting moss to create a serene landscape. This use of leaf shape and the monochromatic color range provided by greens is the first level of design, the most basic aspect of gardening with foliage. We can go beyond this, however, to explore other possibilities, because not all leaves are green. Some plants may have colored leaves as a seasonal aspect in spring or fall; this will be discussed in chapter 3. Some plants have colored leaves throughout the growing season. The color may cover all or only a portion of the leaf. Use of this color, with foliage as with flowers, can be subtle or blatant.

With so many possibilities available, it is easy to go overboard. It is just as important to achieve a balance when adding foliage color to the garden as it is selecting flower color. Most familiar plants have green leaves, and we accept this as the norm. It is difficult to avoid an artificial look in a garden that goes to the other extreme and uses every leaf color *except* green. Since green is the most characteristic hue of leaves, I will use the word "color" to describe leaves that are other than green.

Let's look at some examples of how color should and shouldn't be used. Hostas are common in gardens, and one could expect to find either of the following examples: A long sweep of a plain green variety, perhaps the old-fashioned *Hosta ventricosa*, might line a driveway. Or, several cultivars might grow under a tree in close proximity to each other — one with a green leaf; the next, glaucous blue; yet a third, variegated; a fourth, golden; and there might well be others. In both examples, the basic leaf shape is the same. The first, a mass planting of a single cultivar, is simple and rather plain. The monotony would be alleviated if a variegated cultivar, rather than a plain green one, were selected. The effect of color and pattern would enliven the planting. The second example has variety, but it is a collection rather than a garden because there is no design, only a random association. Order needs to be created out of chaos. At one end of the planting bed, you could use a glaucous blue hosta (*Hosta sieboldiana* 'Elegans'), followed by a cultivar with a gold variegation, an edging on a glaucous leaf (*Hosta* 'Frances Williams'); the other end of the bed could be finished with a golden-leaved hosta (*Hosta* 'Golden Sunburst' or 'Piedmont Gold'). Now an orderly, logical progression has been developed.

Another example. Ferns grow well in the same sort of dappled light and moist, organically rich soil that hostas prefer. The association of shape of these two is pleasing as well. Having envisioned a green fern with a green hosta, it is time to turn to color effects. One of the smaller, glaucous blue hostas ('Blue Cadet', 'Blue Moon', or 'Hadspen Heron') can be planted with the silver Japanese painted fern (*Athyrium goeringianum* 'Pictum'). The blue and silver leaves are in equilibrium in both shape and color and are thus quiet and balanced. White impatiens (*Impatiens wallerana* 'Accent White') can then be added so that foliage, flowers, shape, and color are all well utilized.

Analogous, Monochromatic, and Complementary Color Combinations

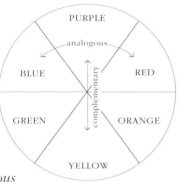

Colors within the same quadrant of the color wheel — combinations such as red/orange/yellow or blue/violet/purple — create a simple harmony, subtle and quiet. These are known as *analogous color harmonies*. On the other hand, a *monochromatic* color harmony, a combination of different yellows, for instance, can be created by using a small, yellow hosta (*Hosta* 'Wogan Gold') and Bowle's golden grass (*Milium effusum* 'Bowles Golden'), one of the few true grasses for shady conditions. If forget-me-not (*Myosotis sempervirens*) is used for a third plant, its transitory blue flowers will enliven the combination. We can also use *complementary* colors (two colors that are nearly across from each other on the color wheel) in combining the hosta with a grass for livelier effect. Blue *Hosta* 'Halcyon' with Bowle's golden grass pairs plants of complementary colors. Other examples of complementary colors are red and green, purple and yellow, blue and orange. Making use of the strong contrast provided by these combinations allows us to create a dramatic impression. Such potent colors must be used with restraint, for when random colors are placed together the results may look chaotic, abrupt, restless.

A stronger, more pungent effect is achieved with the use of purple/bronze and chartreuse foliage. However, this type of powerful contrast should be used in moderation since the effect is so vibrant. An interesting possibility to use is *Heuchera micrantha* 'Palace Purple', which has a reddish-brown, lobed leaf with serrate edges, in combination with *Hosta* 'Wogan Gold', which has a small golden leaf. *Hosta* 'Kabitan', which has a small golden leaf with a narrow green edge, paired with *Ophiopogon planiscapus* 'Ebony Knight' makes a strong gold and black pairing. Or try ophiopogon with Japanese painted fern for a cool, yet sophisticated, black and silver combination.

Using Solid-Colored Leaves

Some plants have leaves that are bronze, red, or purple, colors produced by *anthocyanin* (a kind of pigmentation). The strongest color, especially in trees and shrubs, is generally produced under sunny conditions. Crimson pygmy barberry (*Berberis thunbergii atropurpurea nana*) has small, oval, red-purple leaves if it is located in full sun but dark green leaves if it is grown in shade. The best color in the purple smokebush (*Cotinus coggygria* 'Purpureus') occurs in well-drained soils low in nitrogen. Red, bronze, and purple leaf colors are usually most intense in the spring and in young leaves. If the smokebush is pruned hard each spring, the new shoots will have a wonderful, glowing impact. (This technique of severe cutting back, known as *stooling*, also produces larger, showier leaves.) Herbaceous peonies have lovely red shoots in the spring, and many of the red-flowered astilbes, such as 'Fanal', 'Feur', 'Glut', and 'Red Sentinel', have coppery or bronze, compound, fernlike leaves early in the season; however, as these plants mature, their color fades and the leaves turn green.

Many tropical plants have a red pigmentation that disappears when they are grown under low-light conditions as indoor houseplants. Some of these make great summer bedding plants. For example, *Setcreasea pallida* 'Purple Heart' is an old-fashioned plant that roots easily from cuttings; its silvery purple, pointed oval leaves with a few hairs are superb in combination with chartreuse leaves or blue flowers.

Purple and chocolate-colored foliage can appear somber, especially if used in the shade. Here, plants like *Heuchera micrantha* 'Palace Purple' need to be paired with the bright yellows of some kinds of hosta or the chartreuse of yellow feverfew (*Chrysanthemum parthenium* 'Aureum'), yellow lamium (*Lamium maculatum* 'Aureum'), or the billowy flowers of lady's mantle (*Alchemilla mollis*). A lively combination would be *Coleus* 'Red Velvet' and Japanese painted fern (*Athyrium goeringianum* Pictum'). The coleus echoes and reinforces the red color in the center of the silvery fern frond; in addition, the lacy fern and the blockier coleus provide an interesting contrast of shape. The same silvery fern used with white impatiens creates an entirely different effect. Coleus, fern, and impatiens — and a garden (rather than a collection) begins to take shape.

In sunnier locations, perennials such as catchfly (*Lychnis x awkrightii* 'Vesuvius'), with its chocolate-colored leaves, can look stupendous paired with red flowers like nasturtiums (*Tropaeolum majus*) or pale lemon yellows like the Ozark sundrop (*Oenothera missourensis*). Check catalogs for plants with the species names *atropurpurea*, *cupreus*, or *sanguineus*, for foliage that is purple, coppery, or red, respectively.

Silver coloration is most often found as a response of plants to intense sunlight and dry soil conditions. Hairs on the leaves produce a silvery appearance. Many herbs, such as various sages (*Salvia* spp.), lamb's-ears (*Stachys lanata*), and wormwoods (*Artemisia* spp.), fit into this category. A few plants with silvery, smooth, glaucous leaves tolerate shady conditions; the two most notable examples are the Japanese painted fern (*Athyrium goeringianum* 'Pictum') and the lovely ground-covering lamiums (*Lamium* 'Beacon Silver' and 'White Nancy').

When silver foliage is used with silver foliage, form and shape are important elements of the selection process; plants with different leaf textures should be combined. For instance, both lavender-cotton (*Santolina chamaecyparissus*) and *Artemisia* 'Silver Mound' have a rather fine, threadlike leaf; it is difficult to distinguish one from the other. But if one of these plants is combined with lamb's-ears (*Stachys lanata*), which has a broader, more oval shape, the proper contrast of shape will be obtained (see chapter 1).

Silver can be used with any color. It produces delightfully cool, frosty results when used with white flowers: the effect of the silver leaves of *Artemisia* 'Silver Queen' and white shasta daisies (*Chrysanthemum maximum* 'Alaska') is delectable on a hot summer's day. Such a combination is especially eye-catching in the evening, since white and silver seem to gather and reflect the last of the light and show to great effect at dusk. Another superb combination is silver used with blue and violet flowers, such as asters, campanulas, delphinium, or geraniums. These colors often have a certain luminosity just before twilight, and paired with silver foliage they seem especially rich. Silver can also look sensational in full daylight, providing a very contemporary look when used with purple-foliaged plants and flowers.

Frosty foliage can also be used to tone down hot, bright, vivid flower colors. *Artemisia* 'Powis Castle', with its mound of fine-textured gray foliage, grown near the bright orange flowers of butterfly weed (*Asclepias tuberosa*) is pleasing to the eye. Look in catalogs for plants with species names of *argenteus, cinereus, dealbatus,* and *incanus,* all of which denote gray or silvery foliage.

Using Variegated Leaves

blotched

spotted

veined

If color is found in only part of the leaf, the leaf is said to be *variegated.* The species names of plants often indicate the different kinds of leaf variegations: blotched (*maculatus* or *variegatus*), spotted (*guttatus*), veined with color (*marmoratus*), edged (*marginatus*), striped (*fasciatus* or *pictus*), or zoned (*zonatus*) in different colors.

Variegation patterns are usually white (as in *Iris pallida* 'Albomarginata') or yellow (as in *I. pallida* 'Aureo-variegata') on a green ground, but they may also be red, as in the polka-dot plant (*Hypoestes sanguinolenta*). Variegation may result from an absence of chlorophyll in portions of the leaf, leaving them white. Plants with white-edged leaves include perennials, such as hosta cultivars (*Hosta* 'Thomas Hogg', for example) and variegated Japanese Solomon's-seal (*Polygonatum* x *hybridum* 'Variegatum'), as well as woody shrubs, such as variegated Siberian dogwood (*Cornus alba* 'Elegantissima') and variegated kerria (*Kerria japonica* 'Picta'). Because the white portion of the leaf does not produce food for the plant, variegated leaves and generally the plant as a whole do not grow as vigorously as nonvariegated forms. (A plant with entirely white leaves cannot produce any food and will die when past the cotyledon stage.) In some cases, the plant *reverts,* producing a branch or shoot with plain green leaves which will grow more vigorously and crowd out the slower growing variegated portion. This frequently happens with the double tawny daylily (*Hemerocallis fulva* 'Kwanso'), which should have attractive green-and-white, variegated leaves. However, a reversion to the more vigorous, plain green leaf is common, and it is this form that is most often offered for sale. In order to keep the patterned leaf predominant, watch for and remove these reversions.

The absence of chlorophyll also results in yellow variegation. The yellow leaf pigments, *carotene* and *xanthophyll* (which also give carrots and egg yolks their color) are usually masked by the deeper color of chlorophyll. When chlorophyll is absent, the yellow color is revealed. Since this accessory pigment is capable of photosynthesis, the plant can survive even if the leaf is entirely yellow. For example, numerous hosta cultivars, such as 'Piedmont Gold' and 'Wogan Gold', are entirely golden. Others, such as *Hosta sieboldiana* 'Frances Williams', are considered variegated forms because their green leaves have a golden edge. A grasslike plant with golden foliage is Bowle's golden sedge (*Carex stricta* 'Bowle's Golden'), which has a very narrow, green edge and a golden center. Yellow variegation may be transient; many of the older chartreuse-yellow variegated cultivars of hosta turn all green as summer progresses, although newer cultivars remain variegated. In the variegated yellow flag iris (*Iris pseudacorus* 'Variegata'), the leaf turns completely green in mid-summer. If the soil is particularly rich in nitrogen, the variegation may disappear, even though a plant is normally variegated throughout the growing season. When you are interested in using yellow or yellow-variegated leaves in your garden, look in catalogs for plants named *aureus*, *citrinus*, *flavescens*, or *luteus* (but be sure it refers to their leaves and not the flowers).

edged

striped

zoned

Yellowed leaves are not, of course, always a normal, healthy occurence. Plants that grow in acid soil — for example, mountain laurel (*Kalmia latifolia*), rhododendrons, pachysandra (*Pachysandra terminalis*) — may exhibit a yellowing of the leaves if the pH of the soil is too high. This condition is called *chlorosis* and is a symptom of ill-health that requires attention.

E. A. Bowles, a noted English plantsman of the early twentieth century, grew all of his variegated plants together in one section of the garden, which he referred to as his "lunatic asylum." Most of us, however, find it difficult to focus on many different variegations all at once. One of this plant and one of that plant results in a "child-in-a-penny-candy-store" design. Variegated *Iris pallida* 'Aureo-variegata' is charming with Johnny-jump-ups (*Viola tricolor*), which have yellow-and-purple, pansylike flowers, but a combination of the iris and a white-edged grass like gardener's-garters (*Phalaris arundinacea* 'Picta') would look confusing. *Yucca* 'Bright Edge', with its stiff, swordlike, yellow variegated leaf is a good choice to combine with bright yellow gloriosa daisies (*Rudbeckia pulcherrima*) but would be a poor choice in combination with porcupine grass (*Miscanthus sinensis* 'Stricta'), which has horizontal yellow bars across the leaf. These examples using combinations of differently colored or patterned variegation but similar leaf shape are exaggerated but still present my point.

Variegated Leaves for Shady Gardens

A variegated plant can be used as a focal point or as a counterpoint to solid greens or glaucous blues. Generally, the best results occur when one or two kinds of distinctively variegated plants are used as an accent with green-leaved plants. Plants with white or yellow variegated leaves, as well as completely yellow leaves, are particularly useful in a shady garden. These colors lighten and brighten an area that might otherwise appear dark and somber. Even gardeners uninterested in variegation for its own sake often grow a couple of variegated hosta for just this reason. The many variations include hosta with a green leaf and a white edge ('Crispula' or 'Louisa') and hosta with a green edge and a white center (*Hosta undulata*). Yellow patterning on the leaf may either be on the edge ('Gold Edger' and 'Frances Williams'), in the center ('Gold Standard' and 'Kabitan'), or as an overall golden yellow with no green at all ('Golden Sceptre', 'Piedmont Gold', and 'Wogan Gold'). There is even a golden-leaved hosta with a white margin ('Lunar Eclipse'), though it may not be to everyone's taste. One very effective combination is *Hosta* 'Piedmont Gold' with *Liriope muscari* and Christmas fern (*Polystichum acrostichoides*). This combination works well when both shape and color are considered: The linear leaf shape of the liriope, the bold, rounded form of the hosta, and the lacy fern frond are excellent in association. In addition, the dark green of the liriope and fern contrast with the bright light yellow of the hosta leaf.

Another way to lighten a shady corner is to plant August lily (*Hosta plantaginea*) with *Caladium* 'Candidum' and an annual, white-flowered impatiens. Through most of the growing season the combination relies on the white leaf of the caladium, the glossy, light green leaf of the hosta, and the white flowers of the impatiens. The fragrant white flowers of the hosta appearing in August are a bonus.

A third grouping for dark areas in the garden would combine the native ginger (*Asarum canadense*) with maidenhair fern (*Adiantum pedatum*); a white-flowered astilbe, such as *Astilbe* 'Bridal Veil'; and a hosta with a white edge to the leaf, perhaps *Hosta sieboldii albomarginata*. This simple yet effective grouping makes use of the low, rounded form of the ginger, the fernlike pattern of the astilbe, the bolder, roundish shape of the hosta, and the delicate, pedatisect fronds of the maidenhair fern to create a charming combination on the primary level of shape. The white edge on the hosta leaves adds a light touch to the different shades of green, while at the same time reinforcing the effect of the white astilbe flowers when they are in bloom.

A different type of patterning is found in the lungwort (*Pulmonaria saccharata*). These low-growing plants have leaves pleasantly spotted with silver, reminiscent of dapples of sunlight through tree branches. The cultivars 'Margery Fish' and 'Sissinghurst White' are exceptionally spotted, while 'Argentea' has a nearly all-silver leaf. An attractive planting results when lungworts are combined with the Lenten rose (*Helleborus orientalis*), which has large, glossy, serrate, palmate foliage, and the little, glaucous, ferny leaved *Dicentra* 'Luxuriant'.

Shrubs as Part of the Garden

It is important to explore beyond herbaceous perennial plants. All too often we relegate shrubs to the foundation planting and isolate herbaceous perennials in the flower border. The English cleverly mix the two types of plants with abandon and call it a shrub border. Small shrubs such as the dwarf purple barberry (*Berberis thunbergii atropurpurea nana*) can be combined with flowering plants such as pale yellow lupines to add structure to the flower border. The erect, vertical spires of the lupine are a pleasant contrast to the mounded form of the shrub. Dwarf conifers such as golden mop chamaecyparis (*Chamaecyparis filifera aurea*) can be used in the same manner. This chamaecyparis would be especially nice early in the season combined with the Siberian squill (*Scilla siberica*), whose incandescent blue flowers make a vivid spring contrast to the yellow shrub. Blue ageratum (*Ageratum houstonianum* 'Blue Mink') can be planted to continue the yellow/blue theme during summer, or orange marigolds (*Tagetes* 'Inca Orange') can be planted instead for a rich yet subtle effect. Variegated kerria (*Kerria japonica* 'Picta') is cool and pleasing with white impatiens in the shady garden, with ajuga and a blue-leaved hosta to complete the display.

The time spent in deliberation and planning — consideration of leaf color as well as leaf shape — results in an attractive garden, as opposed to the jumbled effect that is produced by placing plants in the garden without thinking about these relationships. Colored or variegated leaves can, when wisely used, accent and offset both the leaf shape and flower color of adjoining plants.

PLANTS FOR SPECIFIC COLOR

Latin Name	Common Name	Plant Type[1]	Sun/ Shade	Soil Type[2]	Hardiness Zone	Features
PLANTS WITH GOLDEN FOLIAGE						
Berberis thunbergii 'Aurea'	barberry	S	sun	3/4	4–10	
Coleus 'Pineapple Wizard'	coleus	A	shade	3	10	Useful for summer color
Helichrysum petiolatum 'Limelight'	licorice plant	S	sun	4	9–10	Useful for summer color
Hosta cultivars, like 'Kabitan', 'Piedmont Gold'	hosta	P	shade	2/3	3–9	Superb for brightening shady areas
Lamium maculatum aureum	spotted dead nettle	GC	shade	3	3–10	Ground cover
Milium effusum 'Aureum'	Bowle's golden grass	G	lt. shade	2/3	6–9	Comes true from seed
Salvia officinalis 'Kew Gold'	sage	S	sun	3/4	5–10	Herb
PLANTS WITH SILVER FOLIAGE						
Achillea x *taygetea* 'Moonshine'	yarrow	P	sun	4	3–10	
Artemisia, several	artemisia	P	sun	4	6–10	Individual species vary
Athyrium goeringianum 'Pictum'	Japanese painted fern	F	shade		25–10	Best forms propagated by division
Calluna vulgaris 'Silver Queen'	heather	S	sun	3/4	5–8	Susceptible to winter burn

THE SEASONAL GARDEN

 he best thing about gardening is that it is truly the never-ending story. Gardening is the cultivation of living plants that grow and respond to changing conditions. It is this aspect of transformation in their outward appearance that signifies the cycle of the four seasons. I think of time not as a circle but a helix — an ever-rising coil, with a constant diameter. We come around again and again to spring, summer, autumn, and winter, but never to one that is identical to another. Each spring is different from those that preceded, just as it is different from those that will follow. There are sufficient similarities that we know "This is spring," yet the variations resulting from the previous season's influence and current conditions make each one unique. Thus, a summer drought has not only an immediate effect but also one that influences the autumn appearance of the plants. To feel that you know a plant simply because it has been in the garden for a season is hasty judgment. The deepest pleasure of a garden is its changing aspect over time.

In one sense, the Brookfield memories that I described earlier are flawed, for I knew it only in summer; spring, autumn, and winter remained mysterious to me. But my perception of summer was deep and

Latin Name	Common Name	Plant Type[1]	Sun/ Shade	Soil Type[2]	Hardiness Zone	Features
Dianthus, several species	dianthus	P	sun	3/4	4–10	Likes lime
Santolina chamaecyparissus	lavender-cotton	S	sun	4	6–10	Herb
Senecio cineraria	dusty-miller	A	sun	4	8–10	Often used as annual

PLANTS WITH RED OR PURPLE FOLIAGE

Berberis thunbergii atropurpurea	Japanese barberry	S	sun	3/4	5–10	
Canna 'Wyoming'	canna	P	sun	1/2	8–10	Tropical
Coleus 'Red Velvet', 'Othello'	coleus	A	lt. shade	3	10	Useful for summer bedding
Cotinus coggygria 'Purpureus'	smokebush	S	sun	4	6–10	Prune hard for best color
Foeniculum vulgare 'Bronze'	fennel	P	sun	3	4–10	Self-sows; can use as annual herb
Heuchera americana 'Palace Purple'	heuchera	P	sun or lt.shade	3	4–10	Winter mulch in cold areas
Malus 'Evelyn'	crab apple	T	sun	3	4–10	Resists scab
Prunus x *cistena*	sand cherry	S	sun	3/4	3–10	Very hardy
Ricinus communis 'Gibbsoni'	castor bean	A	sun	2/3	8–10	Large; used for summer interest

PLANTS WITH VARIEGATED FOLIAGE

Aegopodium podagraria 'Variegatum'	goutweed	GC	shade	3	5–10	Invasive!
Caladium 'Candidum'	caladium	P	shade	2	8–10	Summer bedding
Cornus alba 'Elegantissima'	variegated Siberian dogwood	S	lt. shade	1/2	3–9	Periodically prune hard
Euonymus fortunei 'Silver Queen'	euonymus	V	shade	3	6–10	Semi-evergreen, vine/shrub
Hedera helix, such as 'Cavendishii','Glacier'	ivy	V	shade	3	6–10	Can winter burn
Hosta, numerous cultivars	hosta	P	shade	2/3	3–9	Many choices
Liriope 'Silvery Sunproof'	lilyturf	GC	shade	3	5–10	Ground cover; cut back in early spring
Pulmonaria saccharata	lungwort	P	shade	2	3–9	Slugs are a problem
Thymus aureus 'Gold Edge'	thyme	GC	sun	4	5–10	Herb
Yucca filamentosa 'Bright Edge', 'Golden Sword'	yucca	P	sun	4	4–10	Elegant

[1]PLANT TYPE: A – annuals, F – ferns, G – grasses, GC – ground covers, P – perennials, S – shrubs, T – trees, V – vines
[2]SOIL TYPE: 1 – wet, 2 – moist, well-drained, 3 – average loam, 4 – dry
NOTE: *Zone ranges are approximate and apply to winter lows only. Please see "Plant Dictionary" for more detail about the temperature range for the plants in which you are interested.*

rich, as could only be achieved through the ten years we spent June, July, and August there. I quickly learned to recognize certain constant landmarks, such as the mature oaks at the bottom of the driveway leading to the dirt road. I was fascinated by changes, like the growth of the red cedars (*Juniperus virginiana*) that were dug from a nearby field our first summer; they were a foot and a half high when we planted them along the driveway and grew taller year by year. The blueberries were especially large and sweet the year after a grass fire in the field where they grew; and each summer more transitory changes were produced by rainfall or the lack of it.

The Garden in Summer

Just as flowers are a brief and passing aspect of plant growth, leaves also are of limited duration. They grow, mature, and then are discarded by the plant. We use them In their youth and maturity, contrasting shape and color for decorative effect. When we speak of leaves and their utility in the garden, the luxuriance of summer first comes to mind — the shady canopy of trees, the lavishness of perennials and annuals at their peak. It is easy to have an opulent display; easy, that is, compared to the slow stirring of spring, the gradual decline of autumn, and the spartan simplicity of winter. In summer, the garden is roaring along as plants reach their full growth and create a grand display of foliage and flower. Perennials, annuals, trees, and shrubs are all responding to longer days and the intensity of sunlight with vibrant panoply.

Overlooked in this exuberance is the task leaves accomplish in the summer garden, in addition to pattern play of shape and display of color. For instance, they compensate for deficiencies in the growth habits of many early-blooming plants. Imagine a perennial border that provides an inaugural spring display of tulips and daffodils. Once their growth is completed, these plants retreat underground until the following year, leaving lacunae in the border. As the flowers go by, the leaves must be allowed to grow in order to provide nourishment for the following spring's performance. This necessary work must proceed unhampered, so tidying up in the form of folding and rubber banding, braiding, or otherwise mutilating bulb foliage is a poor idea. If, however, these groups of bulbs are planted between perennials such as peonies (*Paeonia lactiflora* hybrids) and daylilies (*Hemerocallis* cultivars), the expanding foliage of these later-appearing plants will hide such gaps. Similar conditions exist in the shady garden, where daffodils, snowdrops, and scilla bloom early. Native woodland plants such as Dutchman's-breeches (*Dicentra cucullaria*), dogtooth violets (*Erythronium* spp.), and Virginia bluebells (*Mertensia virginica*) also provide early color. All of these go dormant early and are absent in summer. Here in the shady woodland garden, unrolling fern fronds and the broad shapes of hosta can distract the eye from yellowing leaves, mask empty spaces, and provide summer interest.

The Garden in Autumn

Leaves are useful, too, in their decline and decay. In autumn, the time of leaf raking, the trees seem to shed more leaves than ever grew on them in summer. Huge heaps accumulate for children to jump into. Canny gardeners always let the leaves be broken down a bit in this fashion and then cart them off to a compost heap to rot and decay into the organic matter so necessary for a healthy garden.

Leaves are spectacular as they undergo a magical transformation before they fall, turning deciduous woodlands into a brilliant array of gold and orange, red and purple in the seasonal spectacle of color. However, this unequaled display occurs only in certain geographical areas, for particular physical conditions are needed to trigger the change from green to flame and allow leaves on some woody plants to turn resplendent colors. My friends who moved to Colorado were surprised to learn that the "autumn foliage display" announced on the radio consisted of the golden hues of aspen amid the evergreens. Coming from Massachusetts, they had expected more diversity, a variety of those bonfire hues of orange, red, scarlet, and purple that is typical of the northeastern United States and Canada, as well as central and northern Japan. In the United States — unless you go up into the mountains where elevation compensates for latitude — the further south you go, the less brilliant the display. It may seem that this doesn't make much sense. After all, to paraphrase Gertrude Stein, a tree is a tree is a tree. If a maple tree turns a brilliant color in Connecticut, why not in California?

Unlike evergreens, on which some leaves remain green while others on the same plant turn yellow and drop, deciduous trees and shrubs drop all their leaves and go through the winter with bare branches. Vivid color is inherent in some deciduous trees and shrubs, such as those high in tannins, like oaks (*Quercus* spp.) and sumacs (*Rhus* spp.), which have the potential to turn red and scarlet. But growing conditions — climate and rainfall — actualize the mechanisms that produce the color. In tropical or temperate regions with a pronounced wet or dry season (as in California), the trees drop their leaves near the end of the dry season. Because the leaves dry up before they fall, they just turn brown.

The brilliant reds and splendid scarlets that delight the eye do not appear every year because the growing conditions that allow the production of the necessary pigments may not be present, but good yellow leaf color is consistent from year to year. In the late summer or early autumn, when the production of chlorophyll slows (see page 7), the natural breakdown of the old chlorophyll removes the green coloration of the leaf and reveals yellow pigments that were previously masked. The leaves of most herbaceous plants that die back each winter turn yellow or gold. The cinnamon fern (*Osmunda cinnamomea*), hosta (in autumn, they *all* look like 'Piedmont Gold'), and balloon flower (*Platycodon grandiflorus*) are only a few. Peony (*Paeonia lactiflora*) is an exception in that it often turns a warm orange-red. But for the best displays of orange, red, and scarlet, we must turn to the woody plants, and the production of these colors is more complex.

Anthocyanins (see page 18) are produced as a result of accumulated sugars and tannins in the leaf. Maples, which are noted for their sugar (sugar maples), and oaks, which are high in tannins (tanbark), are renowned for their autumn color. The first step toward coloration occurs during warm, bright sunny days, when the trees and shrubs produce sugar. If these bright days are followed by cool nights with temperatures below 45°F, the sugars are trapped in the leaves. Anthocyanins then form and give the leaves the brilliant flaming hues of autumn. This occurs only if the plant is growing in a sunny place, for sunlight is necessary for the best production of color. Leaf color naturally changes at the end of the growing season, but the quality of the display varies. A warm, rainy, cloudy autumn produces a dull display. The production of sugars decreases with reduced sunlight; with warm temperatures at night, the sugar that is produced does not remain in the leaf but moves to the trunk and roots.

A woody plant growing in a shaded site will never turn as brilliant a red as one growing in full sun. Leaves at the tips of the branches will have a brighter color than those closer to the trunk. Some plants will exhibit a more pronounced color on the side exposed to afternoon sun, which is stronger than morning light. Plants growing in a low spot will color earlier than those on a ridge; because cold air moves downhill, on still nights the temperature will be lower in the hollows than on level ground or in higher elevations. And, even when the site has been carefully chosen, the weather has to cooperate.

As gardeners we have no control over the weather, but we can choose plants with a potential for good color. A combination of colorful foliage with late-flowering perennials makes the best possible use of seasonal foliage color. For example, complement woody plants that have yellow, orange, or red autumn foliage with yellow, gold, bronze, pink, and wine-red flowers, such as chrysanthemums, which blossom late in the year. (In many parts of the country, chrysanthemums are treated as annuals.) A number of truly perennial composites, daisy-flowered plants, such as sneezeweed (*Helenium autumnale*) and goldenrods (*Solidago* spp.), as well as the blue and lavender Michaelmas daisies (*Aster novae-angliae* cultivars), also flower late enough to combine with fall foliage.

The ornamental brassicas — flowering cabbage (*Brassica oleracea*) and flowering kale (*Brassica acephala*) — are excellent cool-season choices. Often grown for their foliage, these annuals grow best in autumn, producing frilly leaves attractively marked with rosy pink or creamy white. If used for the cool, spring season, they will bolt to seed as soon as the weather turns warm. This is one annual that is much more satisfactory if grown for autumn use. Used as carpet bedding, the ornamental brassicas combine beautifully with chrysanthemums and shrubs for fall display.

Fall-blooming bulbs are another unusual source of color for the autumn garden scene. They are a good choice to plant under deciduous azaleas, such as the Knaphill and Exbury hybrids, the leaves of which turn soft rosy-pink at this time of year. Colchicum and fall-blooming crocus send their flowers up on naked stems in September and October when much of the rest of the garden is going dormant; the leaves come up the following spring. Colchicum have very coarse, bright green leaves that turn yellow, slump, and smother smaller plants when they go dormant in June; like the species that bloom in spring, fall-blooming crocus also have narrow, grasslike leaves that quietly wither away in May. Because these plants have no foliage of their own when they are blooming, it is important to combine them with foliage plants, so that the leaves of the companion plants "dress" the bulbs and prevent the flowers from becoming mud-splattered when it rains. It is visually more appealing, too, when flowers are clothed with leaves, even if the leaves are not their own. Additionally, the companion plants use moisture in the summer as they grow, and this helps to provide the drier conditions the bulbs prefer when they are dormant at this time. Colchicum and fall crocus usually have lavender, mauve, or pinkish-purple flowers; look for *Colchicum speciosum* and *Crocus speciosus*. Use ground-cover plants such as glossy, dark green myrtle with the colchicum or small hosta in a lightly shaded site. Crocus prefer a sunny place and look good appearing from under a carpet of thyme (*Thymus serpyllum*). Another late-flowering bulb that can be used to enhance a shrub border is the resurrection lily (*Lycoris squamigera*); it has lilylike pink flowers on 2-foot-tall stems and straplike leaves in spring, very similar to daffodil leaves. It makes a charming display when interplanted with hosta.

Gardens *can* be interesting after Labor Day. It takes a little more thought, planning, and care. But, if well done, the glory of the garden will continue with brilliant foliage during the balmy days and cool nights of Indian summer, the bright colors of autumn providing a fitting conclusion to the seasonal cycle in the garden. As summer turns to autumn and winter, it is foliage that really enhances the garden and provides interest when flowers are absent.

The Garden in Winter

Winter in the city is more of a nuisance than a pleasure: streets are hazardous as the pristine white snowfall becomes a compacted, slushy, dingy gray. My gardening is such a consuming passion, however, that I am reluctant to surrender any time to a dormant season. Winter may be quiescent for the plants, but there is still much to enjoy in their appearance. This fourth season of a garden is all too often ignored, yet it is at this time of year that foliage can play a dominant and especially rewarding role.

When considering the winter garden and its foliage, it is imperative to keep the other seasons in mind. A winter garden created entirely of conifers and broad-leaved evergreens results in a static appearance throughout the year, presenting little change no matter what the season; furthermore, it will have a rather somber, somewhat formal structure. Evergreens should be thought of as a framework, with individual plants selected for their mass, for the height and bulk they add during the growing season, as well as for the prominence they achieve when all else is bare. The use of evergreens in conjunction with deciduous woody plants and herbaceous perennials will produce the most exciting results year-round as the seasons change.

Deciduous woody plants drop their leaves in autumn as a strategy to conserve moisture and then expend energy in the spring to completely re-foliate. Evergreen trees and shrubs use a different strategy and retain their leaves in winter. The leaves are either reduced and needle-like, as on such conifers as yews (*Taxus* spp.) and pines (*Pinus* spp.), or are broad-leaved, as on such shrubs as mountain laurel (*Kalmia latifolia*) and bull-bay magnolia (*Magnolia grandiflora*). The harsher the winter climate, the fewer the evergreens. In fact, one "evergreen" native in Minnesota and Maine, the coniferous larch (*Larix laricina*), drops its needles completely in the fall. The milder climates have more broad-leaved evergreens than do colder climates.

For the winter garden, foliage pattern should be considered with the same focus and attention given when selecting perennials for the summer garden. Similar textures are inherently less interesting than diverse patterns, and so a combination of both needle-leaved evergreens and broad-leaved evergreens is naturally more appealing than if only one or the other type is planted. A grouping of pines, spruces, and hemlocks may result in the trees being lost in a forest.

All evergreens are not the same color green. Some, for example, like gold thread cypress (*Chamaecyparis filifera aurea*), are a brighter, yellower-green. Boulevard moss cypress (*Chamaecyparis pisifera* 'Boulevard') is a soft steely blue. Others, like Hick's yew (*Taxus* x *media bicksii)*, have very dark green needles. Some evergreens change color in the winter with the advent of cold temperatures. Creeping junipers (*Juniperus horizontalis* cultivars), for instance, often turn a plum-purple in winter and then change back to steely blue-green in the spring. Broad-leaved shrubs such as leucothoe (*Leucothoe fontanesiana*), the ground-carpeting wintergreen (*Gaultheria procumbens*), and the little-leaved rhododendrons such as *Rhododendron* P.J.M. hybrids turn red to purple if grown in somewhat open situations. A planting of a white-barked canoe birch (*Betula papyrifera*) with these rhododendrons, along with evergreen myrtle (*Vinca minor*) as a ground cover, would present a pleasing winter aspect of green leaves, purple leaves, and bare twigs. Spring brings tender new leaves on the birch and flowers on the rhododendrons and myrtle, while in autumn, yellow leaf color on the birch provides new interest.

Arrange these plants where they may be readily seen from a window, for inclement winter weather confines all but the most ardent gardener indoors. The large scale of trees and shrubs makes it possible for them to be enjoyed at a distance.

In the winter garden, special care must be taken to protect plants from *winter burn*, in which the tips and edges of broad-leaved evergreens turn brown and look scorched. This is caused by the loss of water from the leaves; the moisture cannot be replaced by the roots because the ground is frozen. Plants located in exposed, windy areas are particularly at risk. For this reason, be cautious when planting at the corner of a building where the wind comes whipping around. It is worth the effort to select an appropriate location where the plants can grow without additional protection beyond their natural hardiness. After all, looking at a shrub swaddled in burlap is hardly of interest, even in winter! If possible, site broad-leaved evergreens where they are not exposed to early morning sun. When the air has a chance to warm even slightly before sunlight reaches the plants, damage is reduced. More protected locations, such as under the shelter of taller deciduous trees or on the north side of a building, are suitable for the winter garden. Be sure, too, that all plants, but especially evergreens, go into the winter with adequate supplies of water. If rainfall is scanty, supplement it before the ground freezes. Once the ground is frozen, a mulch of pine bark or similar material is helpful. If an anti-transpirant is used, remember that it should be reapplied during the

January thaw; this type of artificial coating wears off in heavy rain or snow.

When you begin planning your foliage-based planting, think of it as a shrub border, and instantly the scope of material to be utilized seems wider than the ubiquitous azalea and forsythia. You can use broad-leaved or needled evergreens such as the blue-silver, dwarf globe blue spruce (*Picea pungens globosa*), which is rounded and densely branched and grows only 1 to 3 inches a year. This can be combined with drooping leucothoe (*Leucothoe fontanesiana*), which has a more arching, moundlike form and bronze-purple leaves in winter; a deciduous dwarf Korean lilac (*Syringa palibiniana*); and an ornamental grass like eulalia grass (*Miscanthus sinensis* 'Gracillimus'), which, at 5 feet, will be the tallest plant in the grouping. The winter aspect of the grass, contrasted with the twiggy lilac, a broad-leaved evergreen, and a conifer, is a more exciting use of the space generally given to shrubs.

Another simple, yet effective, winter garden consists of a specimen pin oak (*Quercus palustris*), with its downward drooping branches, underplanted with creeping yew (*Taxus baccata repandens*), whose dark green needles provide contrast to a ground cover of myrtle (*Vinca minor*).

In a woodland now lightly shaded by an overhead tracery of bare branches, evergreen perennials provide winter interest. Evergreen Christmas fern (*Polystichum acrostichoides*) has tapering, pinnately divided evergreen fronds growing in a cluster from a central point. A group of these planted near the stinking hellebore (*Helleborus foetidus*), with its dark blackish green, finely divided pedatisect foliage, and a ground cover of European ginger (*Asarum europaeum*), with round, glossy evergreen leaves, would provide a fine aspect to an otherwise barren landscape. Or, use the hellebore and fern with bergenia (*Bergenia purpurascens*), which has cordate, glossy evergreen leaves that turn purple in winter. Even in winter there are options.

PLANTS FOR SEASONAL INTEREST

Latin Name	Common Name	Plant Type[1]	Sun/ Shade	Soil Type[2]	Hardiness Zone	Features
TREES AND SHRUBS WITH RED FALL FOLIAGE						
Aronia arbutifolia	red chokeberry	S	shade	3	4–9	
Cornus florida	flowering dogwood	T	sun/shade	3	5–9	
Euonymus alata	burning bush	S	sun/shade	3	4–8	Best color in sun
Hydrangea quercifolia	oak-leaf hydrangea	S	shade	3	5–9	Fall color a deep purple
Prunus pensylvanica	pin cherry	T	sun	3	3–9	Short-lived native tree
Quercus rubra	red oak	T	sun	3	4–8	Transplants easily
Rhus typhina	staghorn sumac	S	sun	3/4	4–9	Best used for mass planting
Vaccinium corymbosum	highbush blueberry	S	sun	3	4–9	Needs acid soil
TREES AND SHRUBS WITH YELLOW FALL FOLIAGE						
Amelanchier laevis	Allegheny serviceberry	T	lt. shade	3	4–9	Fall color yellow to orange
Betula spp.	birch	T	sun or lt. shade	3	4–8	Clear golden yellow in fall
Chionanthus virginicus	fringe tree	T	sun	3	5–8	Bright yellow
Ginkgo biloba	ginkgo	T	sun	3	5–8	Fan-shaped leaves; female trees have smelly fruit
Hamamelis virginiana	witch-hazel	S	lt. shade	3	5–8	Bright yellow
Lindera benzoin	spicebush	S	shade	1/2/3	4–8	Clear yellow
Sassafras albidum	sassafras	T	shade	3/4	4–8	Brilliant orange color
TREES AND SHRUBS FOR WINTER INTEREST						
Erica carnea & *Calluna vulgaris* cultivars	heaths and heathers	S	sun	3/4	6–8	Can winter-burn; need acid, peaty, sandy soil
Ilex crenata	Japanese holly	S	sun or lt. shade	3	6–9	Lustrous, dark green leaf; dwarf forms available
Ilex glabra	inkberry	S	shade	2/3	4–9	
Juniperus spp.	juniper	T/S	sun	3/4	4–9	Diverse needled evergreens
Leucothoe fontanesiana	leucothoe	S	shade	3	5–9	Lustrous oval foliage
Pieris japonica	andromeda	S	shade	3	5–9	Broad-leaved
Taxus cuspidata	yew	T	sun or lt. shade	3	4–9	Dark green needles, dwarf forms available
PERENNIALS FOR WINTER INTEREST						
Arum italicum	lords-and-ladies	P	shade	3	5–10	Arrow-shaped leaves
Bergenia cordifolia	bergenia	P	shade	3	4–10	Can winter-burn
Cyclamen coum, *C. hederifolium*	cyclamen	P	shade	3	6–9	Leaves from September to June
Hedera helix	ivy	V	shade	3	6–10	Ground cover

(CHART CONTINUES OVER)

PLANTS FOR SEASONAL INTEREST
(CONTINUED)

Latin Name	Common Name	Plant Type[1]	Sun/ Shade	Soil Type[2]	Hardiness Zone	Features
PERENNIALS FOR WINTER INTEREST (CONTINUED)						
Helleborus orientalis	Lenten rose	P	shade	2	4–10	Palmate leaves
Pachysandra terminalis	pachysandra	GC	shade	3	5–10	Ground cover
Polystichum acrostichoides	Christmas fern	F	shade	3	4–9	Elegant
Vinca minor	myrtle	GC	shade	3	5–10	Ground cover
Yucca filamentosa	yucca	P	sun	4	4–10	

[1]PLANT TYPE: A – annuals, F – ferns, G – grasses, GC – ground covers, P – perennials, S – shrubs, T – trees, V – vines
[2]SOIL TYPE: 1 – wet, 2 – moist, well-drained, 3 – average loam, 4 – dry
NOTE: *Zone ranges are approximate and apply to winter lows only. Please see "Plant Dictionary" for more detail about the temperature range for the plants in which you are interested.*

CHAPTER FOUR

Bringing It All Together — Designing with Foliage

Designing with plants often takes on the aspects of a juggling routine. What does the plant require in order to achieve its most decorative potential? What does it look like? And critically important, what effect do you want to realize? Each style of garden — a romantic garden, a formal scheme, the cottage garden, or an informal, naturalistic planting — has a pattern, a coherency. If this is not followed, a planting will look disorganized and confused. It is thus most important that you work toward a definite goal. As you select plants for a particular design, think of the specific effect you intend to achieve. This effect will be accomplished through a blending of style and technique. Perhaps there is a shady corner that you would like to brighten up. Or, instead, in a similar location you might wish the effect to be a cool and tranquil one. Perhaps plants will be selected for their winter aspect, to provide interest near a front entry at a slack time of year in the garden. Plants may be chosen for a foliage effect that will enhance flowers in a sunny border and thus create a garden picture that will be effective throughout the growing season. As you gain familiarity with your plants and an understanding of their response to sun and shade, moisture and dryness, and the cycle of the seasons, some of this will become second nature to you. Whatever the desired goal, select a combination of plants that will provide a cohesive and effective composition.

Many garden books provide complete garden plans. This is useful if your garden is identical in size and layout to the one depicted, and if you are starting with bare ground. However, it is unlikely that your garden and the paper garden are twins. Such idealized plans are thus not always useful to the readers. In hopes that the information in this chapter will provide more serviceable features, I have set up scenarios that describe a situation, set a design goal, and then suggest plants that will accomplish the desired result. The exercise of examining a site and determining a goal is an important step that must precede plant selection. Beginning with the plants, on the other hand, and attempting to assemble them into a garden is a difficult, backward approach that is unlikely to succeed. Each garden described here provides an example you can follow and will enable you to see how a particular design evolved. You can then personalize the results, perhaps selecting only a portion of those plants suggested and choosing others more to your liking.

Shady Garden 1 *(color page 41)*

For this design, as well as the one that follows, it is assumed that shade is provided by deciduous trees, which shed their leaves in autumn.

Rather than begin with beech or Norway maples, which present the difficult challenges of poor soil and surface roots, let us design under the dappled shade of an oak. These large-canopy trees have deep taproots and are easy to work with. They can be pruned to increase the amount of light that reaches the ground below, either by raising the canopy or by thinning the branches, or a combination of both. Oak leaves provide an excellent mulch, unlike maple leaves, which can mat into a good imitation of roofing felt.

In such a site, we would have success with bulbs for early season color. Foliage, then, is needed to conceal yellowing bulb leaves in late spring and to hide bare ground after the bulbs are completely dormant. Since the area is fairly shaded, a bright sunny effect is wanted, which suggests the use of gold and yellow foliage. If only perennials were used, there would be a great disparity in scale between the canopy tree that is providing the shade and the lower herbaceous plants. Thus, some smaller tree or large shrub is indicated. In order to enjoy this garden when viewed from the house, plants must be used in sufficient quantity to have an effect when seen at a distance; it will also help to use contrasting colors, like a dark green against the lighter yellow foliage. Since there is a path near the garden, some interest — foliage shape and texture — must also be provided for close viewing. Additionally, we want to select plants that require little maintenance once they are established.

The shape of the bed, too, is important. All too often planting beds under a tree are perfectly circular, with the tree at the center like a compass point. A more interesting planting bed is a 27-foot-long oval, with the oak tree at its widest point, about 15 feet. Because the oak casts most shade to the north, it is sunniest at the south end of the bed.

An excellent understory tree with golden foliage is the Japanese full moon maple (*Acer japonicum aconitifolium* 'Aureum'). It has a lovely leaf shape and a fresh chartreuse leaf color. Unlike Norway or sugar maples, its roots do not compete with the herbaceous plants.

Golden-leaved hosta are available in a wide range of sizes. We use two different ones. By planting the smaller one, perhaps *Hosta* 'Wogan Gold', near the full moon maple, and the large one, *Hosta* 'August Moon' or 'Piedmont Gold', near the oak, we maintain a sense of scale and balance. In a planting of this size, five to seven of the large hosta and eighteen of the smaller one are appropriate quantities.

Another plant is needed — something that contrasts with the hosta but still has a simple leaf shape and may also be used in a mass as a ground cover and as a contrast with the hosta. Liriope, sometimes called lilyturf, has a straplike leaf, and it is available in both dark green and gold variegated forms. To remain in scale with the arrangement of hosta, the liriope is used in groups of eighteen of each variety.

A plant with a more intricately cut, lacy leaf can be used to complement what we have selected. The evergreen Christmas fern (*Polystichum acrostichoides*) is an excellent choice. Its dark green leaves provide a color balance to the golden hosta, and the shape of the fern complements that of the hosta.

Flowers add transient, colorful interest to this planting scheme. While evergreen foliage still persists and before the new growth on dormant plants begins, early bulbs add the first color. Groups of snowdrops, ten to twenty-five in a colony begin the display. This flowering is fol-lowed in April by dwarf yellow daffodils. Cultivars with bright yellow flowers and suitable height include 'February Gold', 'Tete-a-tete', and the May-flowering jonquil 'Quail'; these are planted in groups of ten. By late June their foliage is gone, but the yellowing foliage of the snowdrops and the daffodils is concealed by the expanding hosta leaves. Toward the edge of the planting bed where there is sun, blue columbines (*Aquilegia* hybrids) add a pleasant color, complementary to the golden foliage of the other plants. Columbines are short-lived perennials and therefore need to be replaced every few years. In June, perennial foxglove (*Digitalis ambigua*) displays its spikes of creamy yellow flowers. Happy in light shade, this plant will probably self-sow and multiply, so we can start with just a few. After the foxglove blooms, the foliage plants we have selected will carry the display through the rest of the summer.

Shady Garden 2

Working with the same shady conditions under the oak, we will design the next garden with a different goal in mind. Rather than creating a warm, sunny effect, we will choose plants to bring about a cooler, more subtle effect — a calm and restful oasis in the summer heat.

A white-variegated shrub provides a starting point. One excellent choice is variegated red-twig dogwood (*Cornus alba* 'Elegantissima'). The white edging on its leaves is clean and crisp, and in winter, the red bark on younger branches provides additional interest. To control the height, prune the shrub back hard every three or four years in early spring.

In this garden, blue and silver are our foliage colors, for this combination has a cool and frosty effect. Thus, we turn again to hosta, some of which have excellent glaucous blue leaves. Perhaps the best are Eric Smith's *tardiana* hybrids, introduced from England. 'Halcyon', 'Serendipity', and 'Hadspen Heron' are small-leaved hosta that can be used in a ribbon or band, curving out and around the shrub. The silver-splashed leaves of false lamium (*Lamiastrum* 'Herman's Pride') are also used in a drift. This plant grows in a clump, so it is not invasive, as many of the lamiums can be. It has charming yellow flowers along the length of its

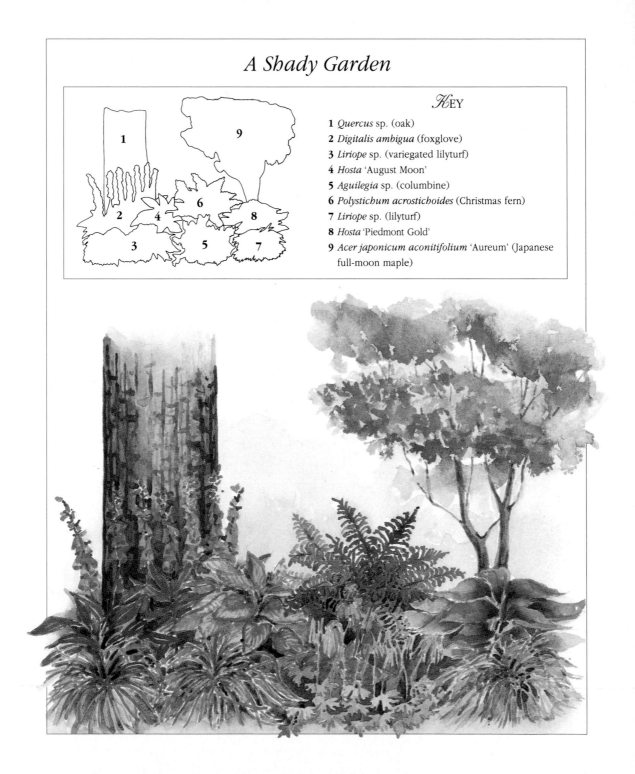

A Shady Garden

KEY

1 *Quercus* sp. (oak)
2 *Digitalis ambigua* (foxglove)
3 *Liriope* sp. (variegated lilyturf)
4 *Hosta* 'August Moon'
5 *Aguilegia* sp. (columbine)
6 *Polystichum acrostichoides* (Christmas fern)
7 *Liriope* sp. (lilyturf)
8 *Hosta* 'Piedmont Gold'
9 *Acer japonicum aconitifolium* 'Aureum' (Japanese full-moon maple)

A Dry, Sandy Garden

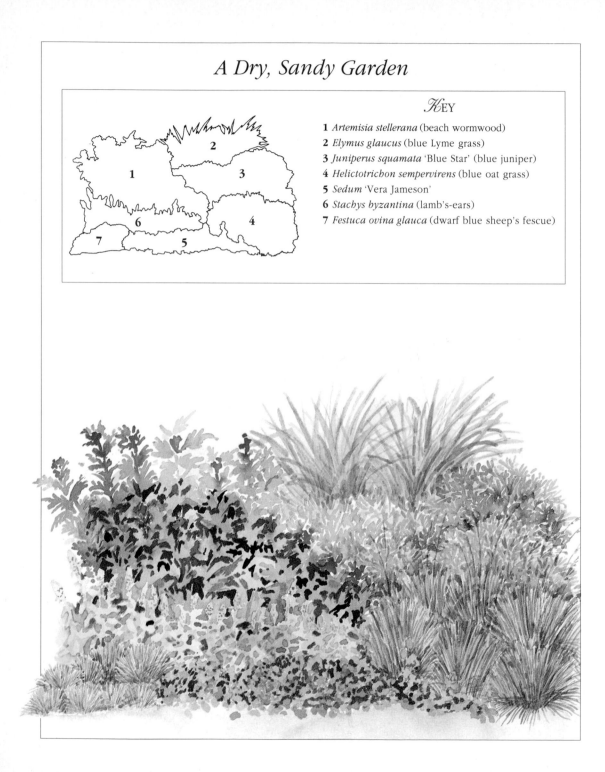

A Sandy, Infertile Garden

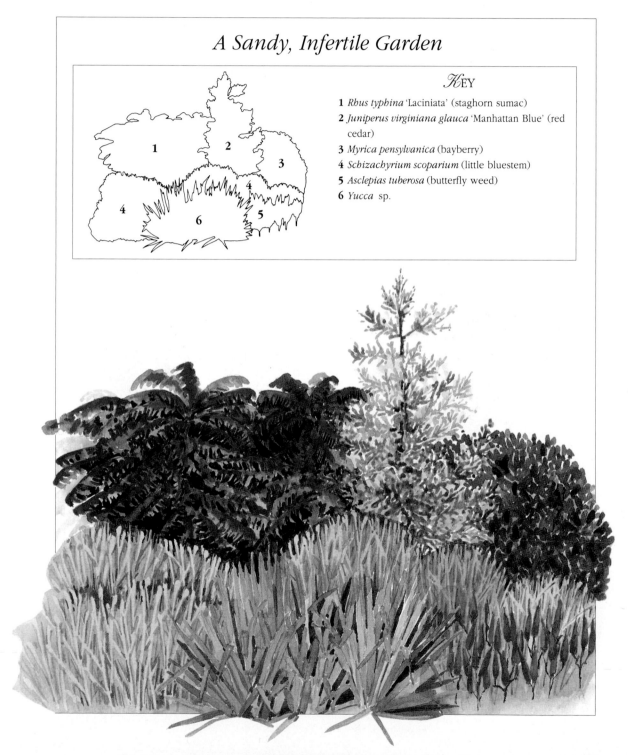

KEY

1 *Rhus typhina* 'Laciniata' (staghorn sumac)
2 *Juniperus virginiana glauca* 'Manhattan Blue' (red cedar)
3 *Myrica pensylvanica* (bayberry)
4 *Schizachyrium scoparium* (little bluestem)
5 *Asclepias tuberosa* (butterfly weed)
6 *Yucca* sp.

A Wetlands Garden

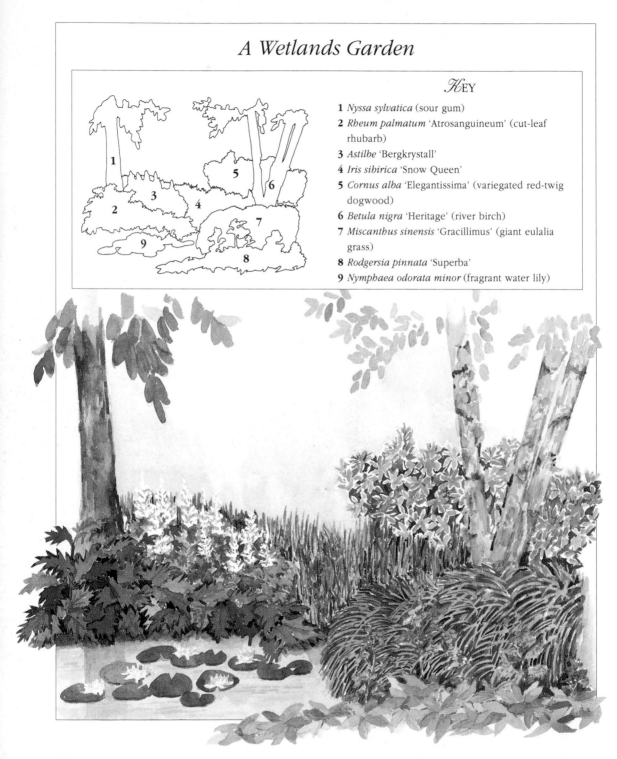

Key

1 *Nyssa sylvatica* (sour gum)

2 *Rheum palmatum* 'Atrosanguineum' (cut-leaf rhubarb)

3 *Astilbe* 'Bergkrystall'

4 *Iris sibirica* 'Snow Queen'

5 *Cornus alba* 'Elegantissima' (variegated red-twig dogwood)

6 *Betula nigra* 'Heritage' (river birch)

7 *Miscanthus sinensis* 'Gracillimus' (giant eulalia grass)

8 *Rodgersia pinnata* 'Superba'

9 *Nymphaea odorata minor* (fragrant water lily)

stems in midspring, but the foliage is its most striking feature. In addition, it is as easy to root from cuttings as coleus (to which it is related). Next, the Japanese painted fern (*Athyrium goeringianum* 'Pictum') adds another silver leaf with a delicate, lacy pattern, opposed to the simple, more solid appearance of the hosta. This fern can be planted in groups, on the other side of the band of hosta. Thus, the blue hosta has two separate companion plants, each with a very different appearance. Because the fern and the false lamium are both silver, however, they contrast less strongly with each other, even though their shapes differ. With the hosta located between them, all three plants are most effectively displayed.

Using plants with only colored foliage creates an artificial situation — we expect to see green in a garden. Thus, in addition to variegated, glaucous, and silver-leaved plants, we will use others with a strong shape and green foliage. Astilbe are choice plants for a shady garden. Staying with our intent to create a cool and restful garden, we will consider only cultivars with white flowers, such as 'Bridal Veil', 'White Gloria', and 'Deutschland'; all have the typical, lacy, fernlike astilbe foliage plus white flowers in July. If the astilbe and Japanese painted fern are used in proximity, the result is weak, since their leaves have similar shapes. We need to provide the contrast of a bolder, stronger leaf shape. A good choice is bergenia (*Bergenia* hybrids), which blooms in early to mid-spring, well before the weather warms up. For consistency, we will select among those with white flowers rather than pink. The two best whites available are 'Bressingham White', and 'Silberlicht' ('Silver Light'), whose pure white flowers develop a pinkish tinge as they age. Both flower in April/May, and then, for the remainder of the gardening season, their bright green foliage provides a foil for other leaves. It also continues into winter, adding evergreen interest to the bare red twigs of the dogwood.

Here, again, columbines (*Aquilegia* hybrids) can be introduced as flowering plants. We can select either blue-flowered plants to intensify the blue of the hosta foliage or white-flowered ones to increase the cool and frosty effect. The addition of bergenia flowers in April/May, with perhaps a brief overlap as the columbines bloom in May, and the astilbe in June/July, supplements a display that relies very strongly on foliage. The subtle diversity of shapes and colors of the variegated dogwood, variegated false lamium, silver Japanese painted fern, glaucous hosta, green bergenia, and astilbe provide a cooling effect on hot summer days.

A Shady Slope

An extensive area such as a shady slope needs an interesting informal, naturalistic effect. Because slopes are somewhat difficult to maintain, we will select only those plants that require little assistance; thus, if we are unable to carry out such maintenance procedures as deadheading spent flowers, the overall appearance will not be seriously affected.

To carry a design of this type, we need large, bold plants. Two of the best are goatsbeard (*Aruncus dioicus*) and bugbane (*Cimicifuga racemosa*). Both have ferny, astilbelike foliage. The goatsbeard approaches 4 feet in height, with creamy white, astilbelike plumes of flowers in June/July; the bugbane has tall, wandlike flower spikes that reach 5 feet tall in July/August, but its foliage is lower.

The goatsbeard and bugbane have very similar leaves, so we must select additional plants with simpler, stronger shapes. The hosta cultivar 'Krossa Regal', has leaf stalks that emerge close together and spread out in an elegant, vaselike shape. The cool grayish-green leaves are 3 feet in height; flower stalks can reach 5 feet under ideal conditions. This hosta can be used to separate the too-similar leaves of the bugbane and goatsbeard, yet it is regal enough to provide interest of its own.

Giant Solomon's-seal (*Polygonatum canaliculatum;* sometimes *P. commutatum* or *P. giganteum*) offers additional diversity. Although it is often listed as 5 feet tall, it is more commonly seen in gardens at 3 feet, still a respectable size. The stem is arching, with pairs of horizontal, oval, fresh green leaves that turn a pretty yellow in autumn.

Mayapple (*Podophyllum peltatum*) is a coarse, spreading ground cover. Each stem extends from the roots to about 2 feet tall and carries one large, coarsely lobed leaf with a serrate edge. The flower is difficult to see because it is carried beneath the leaf, so this plant's decorative value is negligible. Furthermore, if the soil is not moist enough, mayapple will go dormant in midsummer. However, all of the plants suggested for this combination do best in dappled shade in a moist but not sodden soil that is high in organic matter.

Foxgloves (the taller *Digitalis purpurea* rather than *D. ambigua*) add their 3- to 4-foot-tall wands of flowers and coarse, wrinkled, basal rosettes of leaves. The flowers are typically a crushed-raspberry pink, but the white-flowered form is well worth searching out. White displays well in the shade, for it stands out in poor light, whereas raspberry pink dims and fades. Lasting only two or three years, this foxglove species is even shorter lived than the creamy yellow *D. ambigua*, but like other foxgloves, it will establish as a self-sowing colony in filtered shade.

All of these plants are winter dormant, and because a large expanse of mulch is unappealing in the winter, additional foliage is needed for seasonal interest. A glossy, evergreen ground cover of myrtle (*Vinca minor*), which winds inconspicuously at the feet of the dominant plants in summer, creates a prominent display of its own in winter. Use it over only a portion of the area, for too much myrtle can be as bad as none at all. To further relieve winter's bareness, we will locate a colony or two of the evergreen Christmas fern (*Polystichum acrostichoides*) at the edge of the planting area, where the larger plants won't overwhelm it.

A Small Spot of Shady Drama

In a small, lightly shaded area, we can be playful and use foliage in an extreme manner. Here the potentialities of leaf color can be explored. For instance, bronze, black, and gold create a striking avant-garde effect. With such extremes of color, however, foliage shape should be kept simple. If there is too much going on at once, the elements distract from one another and the total impact is confusing. Black is the least common leaf color, so it makes a good starting point from which to build, rather than attempting to fit it in with previous choices. The best of the black-leaved plants is a liriope relative, *Ophiopogon planiscapus* 'Arabicus', usually offered as 'Ebony Knight'. It has a narrow, grasslike leaf that is truly black. Small, inconspicuous flowers in late June and July are followed by blue-black, beadlike fruits. It grows in clumps and spreads slowly by underground stolons. Along with this slow-growing plant, it may be desirable to use one with more vigor, as long as it is not allowed to overrun the ophiopogon. *Heuchera americana* 'Palace Purple' has large (for a heuchera), moderately lobed leaves; they are coppery red when first emerging in the spring but change to a rich and somewhat somber olive green in summer shade. Their color will be more intense if they are grown in sunlight. This heuchera is often raised from seed, and thus the intensity of color can vary from plant to plant.

The colors of these two plants lack vitality — the spark that golden foliage will provide. Several possible selections exist: First is any of the small, golden hosta. Cultivars such as 'Wogan Gold' or 'Kabitan' have narrow lanceolate leaves of a beautiful golden yellow; they grow less than a foot tall. Their leaf shape contrasts simply to the ribbonlike leaf of the ophiopogon and the lobed leaf of the heuchera. Another possibility is a bright chartreuse-yellow coleus cultivar, such as 'Pineapple Wizard'. This option allows flexibility and change the next growing season.

Perhaps these simple shapes provide too simple a combination; we can achieve a stronger effect with a more complex shape. The golden feverfew (*Chrysanthemum parthenium* 'Aureum') has a compound, lobed, serrate-edged leaf in a lovely shade of chartreuse. Often treated as an annual, it has single, white, daisylike flowers. The feverfew can be used in conjunction with the hosta to provide a stronger yellow component, which brightens the plant grouping.

On the other hand, we may find the impression created by the yellow foliage is too vivid, too overwhelming for our taste. The heuchera and ophiopogon could be used as a starting point for other interesting combinations. Bronze, black, and red, for example, can look very striking, although darker than the combinations using golden foliage. Caladium are tender bulbs often used for summer bedding in cold-winter areas, year-round in warmer parts of the country. They have a simple, heart-shaped leaf and are available in such cultivars as 'Ace of Hearts', which has transparent, crimson red leaves with a soft green margin, and 'Frieda Hemple', which has bright red leaves with a green border. Red-leaved coleus such as 'Red Monarch', which has large, savoyed leaves, can also be included, and red-flowering impatiens add a pleasing touch.

Bronze, black, and red combinations are effective in areas that receive little or no direct sun but are open to the sky — a situation found on the north side of a building — or in sites with good dappled light at the edge of a shady planting bed. A heavily shaded area, however, will be too dim to effectively display the darker leaf colors. The shadier the site, the more important it is to use white, silver, or golden foliage to brighten it up. Remember, too, that the darker the site, the greener the leaf of the heuchera, so it may not be suitable either. In such a spot, black and silver are elegant and arresting. Because most silvery leaved plants need sun in order to grow well only a small selection is available for shady sites. Japanese painted fern (*Athyrium goeringianum* 'Pictum'), lamium (*Lamium* 'Beacon Silver' with pink flowers or 'White Nancy' with white flowers), and false lamium (*Lamiastrum* 'Herman's Pride') are possibilities. If only a few ophiopogon can be obtained, then lamium or lamiastrum would be a good choice, since all these plants have leaves that are relatively in scale with one another. However, if ten or more ophiopogon are to be used in the design, then the fern, which is both taller and more complex in shape, could be considered. With the addition of some small, blue hostas, such as 'Blue Moon' or 'Buckshaw Blue', a cool, sophisticated grouping will add flair to a dark corner. If light is adequate for flowering, white impatiens could be added with good effect.

The Sunny Garden of Blues and Purples

In a sunny garden, foliage can add a certain enduring beauty that goes beyond the transient charm of flowers. Since leaves are present over an extended period, they provide a continuity, a smooth flow that carries the garden from month to month. Leaves furnish a backdrop for the flowers and thus enhance the attractiveness of the blossoms, and colored foliage can contribute an exciting display of its own.

Longwood Gardens, in Kennett Square, Pennsylvania, is an inspiring place to visit at any time. In the summer, however, the long border reaches a peak. One segment makes especially effective use of purple and silver foliage with blue flowers. The tall, common rose-mallow (*Hibiscus sabdorffii* 'Coppertone'), with its lobed, deep coppery purple leaves, adds a strong architectural accent. Purple-heart (*Setcreasea pallida* 'Purple Queen'), is a lower growing plant, almost a ground cover; it may be more familiar as a houseplant than in an outdoor setting. It has slightly hairy leaves that are purple with silvery overtones; and it roots at the joints and spreads like the inch plants, making a nice carpet. Silver foliage, an effective foil for the deep colors of these plants is provided by dusty miller (*Senecio cineraria* 'Silver Cloud'). This powerful combination is striking to see stretching along the path with the deep blue, narrow spikes of mealy-cup sage (*Salvia farinacea* 'Victoria') accenting the foliage fantasia.

Sunny Garden 2

Purple foliage provides an excellent backdrop to flowers of many different colors. Let us imagine a site in full sun with well-drained soil. One excellent shrub for such a place is purple smokebush (*Cotinus coggygria purpureus*), with its rounded leaves of a deep plum color that is most intense (and the leaves larger) on young branches. Each spring before growth begins, the shrub must be pruned to a deformed-looking framework of stubs. Soon buds begin to arise along the bark and slender erect shoots will appear, reaching 6 feet tall or more in one season. Smokebush creates a vivid, contrasting backdrop for pale yellow flowers, like the bearded iris cultivars 'Kentucky Derby' (lemon yellow with some white near the center of the falls) or 'Showcase' (yellow and maroon bicolor). An entirely different result is obtained with blue to purple or red iris, such as 'Inferno' (ruby red) or 'Sapphire Hills' (with medium blue, ruffled, flaring flowers) or 'Interpol' (unique purple-black color). Pinks like 'Beverly Sills' (clean coral-pink) or 'Glenbrook' (light pink with a tangerine beard) produce still a third effect in combination with smokebush. The crisp, strong, swordlike iris leaves nicely contrast with the shrub foliage once the flowers are past. With the color scheme selected, we can add more plants.

For sites with a rich, somewhat moist loam, we can consider the strong shape of canna (*Canna* hybrids). Most have green leaves, but some, such as 'Wyoming', have a rich red-purple coloration; its orange flowers can be removed, if desired. For a strong, late-summer effect, a tall, red, single-flowered dahlia (*Dahlia* 'Japanese Bishop') provides an elegant display. If we add tall, clear red snapdragons (*Antirrhinum majus* 'Rocket Red'), we'll see color earlier in the season. Japanese blood-grass (*Imperata cylindrica rubra* 'Red Baron') is approximately 18 inches tall and is blood red from the middle of the leaf to the tips. These four plants would provide an outstanding foliage display until the annuals and tender bulbs begin to flower.

A Dry, Sandy Garden (color page 42)

We'll work next with a dry, sandy, rather barren site, the type left after construction when all the topsoil has been scraped away and only subsoil remains. It is difficult to establish plants, especially flower gardens, under such conditions. An attractive grouping can be created, however, by working with foliage effects and selecting plants that prefer a lean soil. Some of the best shrubs for dry places are the junipers. Naturally found along beaches, upland meadows, and similar locations, their needlelike foliage resists desiccation. A number of species and cultivars are available, ranging from trees to shrubs to ground covers. Many are green; others have a blue coloration. One of the best of the blue junipers is *Juniperus squamata* 'Blue Star'. It is low growing and slowly spreads into an intense steely blue mound.

A linear texture can be played against the shape of this juniper, and several grasses provide an assortment of sizes from which to choose. Blue sheep's fescue (*Festuca ovina glauca*) is the littlest, growing a mere 6 to 8 inches high and forming a dense tussock of needle-fine blades colored a steel blue similar to that of the juniper. Blue oat grass (*Helictotrichon sempervirens*) is taller, about 18 inches high, and forms a clump of very narrow, slightly arching blades; it is also a very glaucous blue. Blue Lyme grass (*Elymus glaucus*) is a 24-inch-tall, spreading plant with wide, arching, pale blue blades.

Herbs are an excellent source of silver foliage and can provide a broad, silver leaf to contrast with the needle-leaved shrub and linear form of the grass. Another source of silver-leaved plants for sandy soil are those that grow along beaches, such as the familiar beach worm-wood (*Artemisia stellerana*), which grows 18 to 30 inches high and can get leggy. The cultivar 'Silver Brocade', introduced by the botanical garden of the University of British Columbia in Canada, has a spreading habit that makes it more suitable for ground-cover use. Its silver, felted, deeply lobed leaves make an excellent, cool contrast to the blue plants.

These three plants make a pleasing, if somewhat subtle combination. The design can be strengthened by adding a deeper tone, a darker color, to offset the cool and frosty blue/silver. Succulent plants like sedum (*Sedum maximum* 'Atropurpureum'), with fleshy, swollen leaves that store water, are found in sandy, dry places. However, the purple-maroon foliage and sprawly 2-foot-long stems of 'Atropurpureum' combine awkwardly with the refined character of the other plants we have selected. This sedum is thought to be one of the parents of *Sedum* 'Vera Jameson', which has dark purple leaves with grayish overtones, and it is only half as tall as 'Atropurpureum', thus making it more suitable for the relatively small scale and close-up viewing this combination suggests.

It is important to remember that even though these plants are tolerant of dry conditions once they are established, they are not equally adaptable when first planted. Some watering will be required the first season if rainfall is limited.

A Large, Sandy, Infertile Garden *(color page 43)*

But what if the backhoe *really* scraped and leveled, and you need to plant a large area of sandy, infertile soil to protect it from erosion. Foliage plants naturally adapted to such difficult conditions can provide an excellent, long-term display. Working on a larger scale requires the use of sizable plants that need to be massed and grown in greater numbers in order to be effective. This type of naturalistic landscape should be planned so that it provides visual beauty at several seasons.

Once again, junipers provide an evergreen accent, and there are two choices, depending on where you live. In the East, the native Eastern red cedar (*Juniperus virginiana*) will do well. The silver red cedar (*J. virginiana glauca*) is a narrowly columnar tree with silvery blue needles, brightest in spring and turning silvery green in summer; 'Manhattan Blue' is a compact pyramidal tree with bluish green needles. J. C. Raulston of the North Carolina State University Arboretum has been working on selection of the Eastern red cedar, and new introductions are being made. West of Illinois, the Western red cedar, also called Rocky Mountain juniper (*Juniperus scopulorum*), grows well and is very drought resistant. Desirable forms include *J. scopulorum argentea*, which has a narrow, pyramidal shape and silvery-white needles; 'Gray Gleam', which has a very pronounced gray color, especially in winter; 'Kansas Silver', which is pyramidal in growth with an upward twist at the end of the twigs and silvery blue foliage; and 'Platinum', which has brilliant silvery foliage year-round and is especially good in the Southwest and Great Plains. With all of these choices it is clear that a fine starting point for our grouping is a medium-sized tree with a blue or silver color that is generally strongest in spring, perhaps turning greener in summer.

With an evergreen tree as the first component, the next choice will be another woody plant, but one that is smaller in scale — a shrub rather than another tree. Bayberry (*Myrica pensylvanica*) has semievergreen leaves that are aromatic when crushed. As the weather gets cold in autumn, its leaves turn from olive-green to bronze. Although hardy to −35°F, this bayberry loses its foliage where winter temperatures approach zero. Growing to about 9 feet tall, it forms a substantial, rounded, billowy mass. The suckers that it produces help stabilize the loose sandy soil in which it grows best. Plants are male or female; the small, gray berries of the female are the source of bayberry wax for candles, provide good food for birds in winter, and are decorative after the leaves have dropped. The rounded form and dense mass of foliage contrasts the juniper in summer; and in cold regions where it drops its leaves, it emphasizes the evergreen aspect of the juniper in winter.

To add interest in autumn, we need a shrub with excellent color — a brilliant red to contrast with the juniper and bayberry — and one that will perform well in poor soil. Given these requirements, one of the best choices is the staghorn sumac (*Rhus typhina*). While it would not ordinarily be selected for specimen treatment, it is excellent when planted in a group on poor, dry soil. Massing is easy, since staghorn sumac, like bayberry, is a suckering plant. There is a cut-leaf form, *R. typhina* 'Laciniata', with deeply divided leaflets that add a feathery, fernlike texture to the planting. The fall color of staghorn sumac is a rich orange-red that is quite outstanding. At Wave Hill, a public garden in the Riverdale section of the Bronx, New York, this plant is the focal point of the wild garden in autumn. Some plants are male, some female, some both. Female plants have fuzzy, pyramidal trusses of fruit in winter, so it is worth trying to secure a fruiting clone.

The next selection should be a plant that is smaller than the shrubs but still has enough mass to make a balanced contribution to the display. Something evergreen would be especially effective in winter, but the selection is limited. Fortunately, we have the yuccas. Although, like the other plants we have chosen, yuccas are actually woody plants, they are generally lumped with perennials because their stems are underground. The clustered, swordlike, linear leaves of yucca provide an architectural effect. In addition, they are extremely drought resistant, heat resistant, and cold tolerant—ideal for our purpose. Great Plains yucca (*Yucca glauca*) has narrow gray spears that fan out from the crown. Adam's-needle (*Yucca filamentosa*) has gray-green, rigid, pointed leaves about 2 feet long, edged with curling marginal fibers. While variegated forms of Adam's-needle exist, such as 'Bright Edge', 'Golden Sword', and 'Variegata', the naturalistic aspect of this plant grouping suggests the simple, nonvariegated form as more appropriate.

Herbaceous plants should be chosen next, once the woody plants that will provide good textural interest in summer, fall, and winter are in place. The bulkiness of the woody plants demands that the herbaceous plants be used in quantity in order to balance the design. Something with a fine texture, a delicate appearance (which will belie a rugged constitution) is indicated. Grasses offer these characteristics.

Because of the yucca's linear form, a grass with a relatively wide blade, such as the blue Lyme grass (*Elymus glaucus*), would not have sufficient contrast. One with a finer texture would be more suitable, but it needs to be taller than the dwarf blue sheep's fescue (*Festuca ovina glauca*). Mosquito grass (*Bouteloua gracilis*) is one possibility. It is a densely tufted grass that grows 1 to 2 feet tall and has beautiful seed heads. Native to the Great Plains, mosquito grass grows best in light, sandy soil. My favorite choice, however, is the little blue stem (*Schizachyrium scoparium*, formerly named *Andropogon scoparius*). It also has a clumping habit, somewhat looser than mosquito grass, and reaches 2 to 3 feet tall. It is excellent when grown in the light, sandy soil it prefers, turning a lovely, warm tawny color in autumn.

With this supporting framework of foliage, grace notes in the form of flowers can be added for transient color in summer. Perennials such as blanket flower (*Gaillardia aristata*) with yellow-and-red, daisylike flowers, butterfly weed (*Asclepias tuberosa*) with brilliant orange umbels, and rattlesnake master (*Eryngium yuccifolium*) with its clusters of small, gray, thistlelike flowers are some possibilities.

A Wetlands Garden *(color page 44)*

If the garden-to-be is located in wet soil, we must choose plants appropriate to this situation. If the planting is along the banks of a pond or stream it will require a large-scale design.

The pepperidge or sour gum (*Nyssa sylvatica*) tree is often found naturally growing adjacent to water. Reaching 90 feet tall and spreading 50 feet wide, it is an imposing feature in the landscape, especially when the lustrous, oval leaves turn an absolutely spectacular red in autumn. Reflected in the mirror surface of a pond, it will dominate the scene.

Along with this, a select form of another native deciduous tree, the Heritage river birch (*Betula nigra* 'Heritage'), will be impressive, for it has yellow fall color to contrast with the red of the sour gum. The river birch is native to stream banks and lowlands, so the damp soil we are working with is ideal. Additionally, it has an exfoliating off-white bark that peels away to show tones of tan and pink. This is a particularly important feature in winter when the tree is bare, and as the tree matures to its 50-foot height, the trunk is revealed more and more.

For our next selection, a shrub with white-variegated leaves would echo the interest of the river birch trunk. The variegated red-twig dogwood (*Cornus alba* 'Elegantissima') has several points to recommend it: During the growing season its green leaves have an elegant, crisp white edge; its stoloniferous habit helps to hold the pond bank, protecting it from erosion; and its young branches have bright red bark and will develop a thicket of dense, brightly colored twigs for winter interest if cut back hard every third year in the spring before leaf growth begins.

When planning this wetland site, just as with the dry site, we begin by choosing the framework of woody plants and then turn to the herbaceous plants. Here, too, a grass may be utilized for its graceful linear texture, but in this case it must naturally thrive in wet conditions. (It is essential to remember that the key to successful design is appropriate plant selection; if the physical conditions are not considered, the design is useless.) Maiden grass (*Miscanthus sinensis* 'Gracillimus') is an excellent grass that grows over 4 feet high; it has a very finely textured leaf less than ½ inch wide that adds a delicate grace. Growing in an upright and strongly arching fashion, it adds mass to the landscape and is thus considered for placement before smaller plants. When dormant in winter, it has a pinkish beige color, complementing the bark of the river birch.

Against the fine texture of the grass, a large, bold leaf will provide strong architectural contrast. Rhubarb (*Rheum rhabarbarum*), a familiar culinary plant, has robust foliage that does double duty as an ornamental. Since rhubarbs grow to their mightiest dimension in deep, moist soils high in organic matter, a pond bank provides suitable accommodations.

Of the rhubarbs used only for ornamental purposes, perhaps the best is the cut-leaf rhubarb (*Rheum palmatum* 'Atrosanguineum' or 'Rubrum'). The leaves are 2 to 3 feet long, palmately lobed and jaggedly toothed. The young leaves are strongly flushed red, while the mature leaves are green above, red beneath. With an overall height of 6 feet or more, this, too, is a prominent plant in the waterside planting.

Rodgersia (*Rodgersia pinnata* 'Superba') provides a different form to contrast with the rhubarb while still adding a bold texture. It is much more modest at 3 to 4 feet tall and has five to nine oblanceolate, serrate, pinnately compound leaflets flushed with bronze.

Something still large in scale but finer in texture than the rhubarb and rodgersia should be introduced in order to provide a transition to the delicate texture of the grass. Goatsbeard (*Aruncus dioicus*) was previously discussed as suitable for use on a shady bank, but this adaptable plant can also grow in full sun if there is adequate moisture. It has two to three pinnate, obovate, twice-serrate leaflets and compound leaves and thus provides the desired characteristics. Astilbes also have ferny, compound leaves and will grow in sunny places if given moist soil such as that on the banks of a pond. Select only from among the taller cultivars so the plants are not dwarfed by those we have already chosen. Be aware that the height given in books and catalogs includes that of the flower stalk, but the foliage also grows higher on the following cultivars: 'Bergkystall', which grows 42 inches tall and has white flowers; 'Professor van der Wielen', which grows 48 inches tall and has white plumes; 'Betsy Cuperus', which is a pale pink counterpart to the 'Professor'; and 'Ostrich Plume' ('Straussenfeder'), which is a deeper pink and grows 36 inches tall. These last three cultivars all have large and open plumes and a graceful arching form, which complements their handsome foliage.

To complete our planting of the pond bank, we need another linear, grasslike texture, somewhat broader than the maiden grass. Possibilities include cattails (*Typha* species) and iris. The following iris tolerate or even enjoy wet "feet": Siberian iris (*Iris sibirica*); Japanese iris (*Iris ensata*, formerly called *Iris kaempferi*); blue flag iris (*Iris versicolor*); yellow flag iris (*Iris pseudacorus*); and Louisiana iris, which are hybrids of several species including *Iris brevicaulis*, *I. fulva*, and *I. hexagona*. All of these iris have thin, linear, rich green leaves that create a lovely susurrus when a breeze passes by. The flowers are of various colors and bloom at different times, depending on the species and cultivar. Out in the water, we can float the broad pads of hardy water lilies (*Nymphaea odorata* hybrids), providing suitable resting places for a meditating bullfrog.

The Container Garden

Containers can add vital decorative notes to the garden. They are a focal point in a general garden scene, provide interest on a terrace or deck, and allow apartment dwellers to grow plants on a balcony.

Containers can be extremely simple, and they offer opportunities to use otherwise problematic plants. For instance, a half whiskey barrel, in a location where it gets good sun at least four or five hours a day, can be planted with gardener's-garters grass (*Phalaris arundinacea* 'Picta'). The nearly 1-inch-wide, bright green leaf blades are striped lengthwise in white. In the garden this plant can be invasive, but the container controls it. If conditions are dry, it tends to turn brown; it will need less water if you add polyacrylamide crystals to the potting mix.

The important consideration in container gardening is size. Only if the container is large enough can a mixture of plants be used. Individual plants can be grown in smaller containers that are then grouped together, but this is rarely as successful as a mixed planting. A dwarf red banana (*Ensete ventricosum maurei*) might be grown in this manner, thus displaying its red stems and bold leaves suffused with red, with only a narrow green band in the center. In most cases, however, it is much better to use containers no less than 18 inches in diameter — and the bigger the better. Larger containers not only allow more plants to be grown, but they also do not dry out as rapidly as smaller ones.

By starting with a goal in mind, such as the number and size of the containers and their location, you can select plants that work well together even if they are in separate but adjacent pots. All containers should be of similar material so as not to distract from the plants displayed in them; use either clay, plastic (of a suitably neutral color), or wood. With large containers, weight can be a concern, especially on a city terrace. One way to reduce weight is to use a half-and-half mix of sterilized potting soil with one of the peat-lite blends of peat moss, vermiculite, and perlite. In very large containers it is unlikely that perennials and annuals will need to use the entire depth for root run, so you can fill the container one-third to one-half with Styrofoam packing chips or a similar lightweight, inert material; this, too, will cut down on the weight. Cover the fill material with a water-permeable soil barrier, such as one of the nonwoven landscape fabrics, and then add the soil mix. If you use one of the polyacrylamide super-absorbent polymers in the soil mix, the need for frequent watering will also be reduced. These saltlike crystals swell to transparent little nuggets, providing water as plants need it; they then reabsorb more water when it is available. Expand the crystals in a bucket of water before adding them to the potting mix, and do not use more than 15 percent expanded volume to 85 percent soil mix or you may experience problems with root rot.

Fertilize the container plants on a regular schedule (at all or alternate waterings) with a half-strength liquid fertilizer for even growth. Or use a slow-release pellet fertilizer mixed into the soil at planting time (these are formulated for a three- or five-month effective period).

It is also a good idea to mulch in order to reduce evaporative losses before the plants have grown enough to cover the surface. Possible mulch materials include crushed red brick or red shale, especially suitable in terra-rossa pots; ⅜-inch traprock, a gray-blue color, effective in cement or lead urns; or a fine grade of pine-bark chips, which is practical in half whiskey barrels or other wooden containers. If plastic pots are used, try to find something suitably neutral in color to use as a mulch.

A Focal Point for a Woodland Path

It is important to plant something colorful at the start of a path. Since the location is partly shaded, only those plants adapted to low light levels should be considered. A tall pot may feel too imposing in such a position, so use a squat pot, half as tall as it is wide. An 18-inch-diameter pot fits nicely without crowding the path; the style called a rolled-rim terra-rossa is somewhat more decorative than a standard clay pot.

Cover the drainage hole so that water can drip out but the soil mix will stay in, and fill the pot with a mix containing added organic matter. Most shade-tolerant, woodland-dwelling plants, including the tropical species often used as houseplants, prefer a soil high in organic matter.

Excellent choices for container plants to be used as garden ornamentals in mild winter areas can be found among the common tropical houseplants. For the dominant plant, consider ti plant (*Cordyline terminalis* 'Imperialis'). Its young leaves open in a neon fuschia pink, then slowly age to a plum-green color. Given sufficient time, this plant will grow fairly tall in a subtropical garden, but it grows more slowly in a pot. In any event, if it becomes leggy, it can be rejuvenated by cutting off the top, rooting it, and discarding the base.

To carry on the hot pink color, associate the ti plant with a couple of rex begonias (*Begonia* x *rex-cultorum*), whose leaves are marked in silver and pink. Because both of these have simple leaves, complete the container with plants whose leaves have a more complex shape. In addition, the hot colors of the two tropical plants need to be combined with something cool. Shade tolerance and a complex, silver leaf is offered by the Japanese painted fern (*Athyrium goeringianum* 'Pictum'). Two or three of these can be tucked in with the begonias, their fronds reaching out from among the begonia leaves. This hot pink-and-silver combination will look even more attractive if the planting in the garden around it also reflects this color scheme. Groups of the Japanese painted fern can be planted as a permanent feature with caladiums such as 'Lord Derby', which has almost transparent rose-pink leaves with green veins and edging, or 'Rio', which has transparent rose-pink leaves splashed with green in the center and a green margin dotted pink. Wax begonia (*Begonia semperflorens*) cultivars in appropriate colors, such as 'Brandy' with deep bronze foliage and clear pink flowers or 'Linda' with green leaves and deep rose-pink flowers, would add more seasonal color to the display, and, in addition, would integrate the container and the garden.

A Container for a Sunny Terrace

Container plantings can bring color and vibrancy to an outdoor living area such as a sunny terrace. If the backdrop is primarily green, or if the terrace is secluded by a fence, you can be as creative as you wish with the container combinations. If the garden and its colorful display are clearly visible from this location, however, then care must be taken that the color schemes in the containers harmonize with those in the garden.

Suppose the garden has flowers in shades of lavender, purple, and blue. The terrace containers might use associated colors, like rose, as well as a little complementary color contrast, like creamy yellow. We can use several large, terra-rossa pots planted in similar color schemes. Repeat some plants from one container to another, but make sure no two pots are alike, so that the overall effect is harmonious but not repetitious.

Our first selection will be New Zealand flax (*Phormium tenax*), a tender perennial that is widely used in mild winter areas. Similar in shape to yucca, the leaves of some modern cultivars are strikingly variegated in pink, yellow, and cream. The olive-green and bright pink striped leaves of 'Maori Sunset', for example, are edged in olive-green; 'Maori Maiden' has olive-green leaves around a light pink central band; 'Maori Queen' is a reverse of the others, having a central olive green band edged with pinkish red; and 'Rainbow Warrior' has dark pinkish red leaves striped deep olive-brown. Most New Zealand flax plants grow 3 to 4 feet tall and are hardy only to about 20°F; if they are exposed to continuous low temperatures, they will look pretty ugly by spring. Potted flax grow a bit more slowly and are also easier to bring indoors for the winter.

Containers not only are a good way to use plants that are not winter hardy in your area, but also provide an opportunity to grow scarce, rare, or unusual material, since you are more apt to keep an eye on the plant and see that it is not overlooked than if it is in the garden. As you become familiar with its cultural requirements, you can propagate it to obtain the number of plants you will need for garden use. One such plant is the black-leaved sweet potato (*Ipomoea batatas* 'Blackie'). Many of us grew sweet potatoes in our childhood by using three toothpicks to suspend one in a jar of water. The trailing vines with palmate, green leaves were a decorative addition to the windowsill collection. The black-leaved sweet potato with leaves handsomely colored a dark greenish black is a sport — an unexpected variation. Early one spring, I was given some cuttings from such a plant in the greenhouse at Wave Hill. They rooted with such tremendous ease, within a week, that it was almost scary. Trailing down from a pot with the New Zealand flax, black-leaved sweet potato adds good contrasting color and shape. It will be necessary to take cuttings in late summer to carry the plant through winter. (It may not root as easily in fall, however, because the lengthening days of spring may have had something to do with my success.)

What are summer containers without geraniums (*Pelargonium* x *hortorum*)? These familiar inhabitants of window boxes and urns are grown for their flowers, but other geraniums, which are slower growing and less decorative in flower, are enjoyed for their decorative foliage.

Some of these fancy-leaved geraniums are marked in white and include such cultivars as 'Flower of Spring' and 'Foster's Seedling', both with a white border, and 'Happy Thought', which has a cream-colored butterfly variegation in the center of the leaf. Other geraniums have yellow- or gold-edged leaves with the horseshoe zone in the leaf colored red to orange; some examples are 'Miss Burdette Coutts', 'Mrs. Cox', and 'Skies of Italy'. They make a very striking effect as a foliage component in a container, whereas they would easily be overwhelmed in the garden.

With the addition of some pink-flowered New Guinea impatiens and perhaps yellow-and-pink-flowered lantana (*Lantana camara*), the basic container mix is established. It can be varied by substituting a fuchsia pink-flowered geranium ('Better Times') for the New Guinea impatiens, by adding purple-heart (*Setcreasea pallida* 'Purple Queen') to accent the black-leaved sweet potato, or by making other small changes that add a touch of freshness and individuality to the different containers.

An Easy-Care Container Planting

Perhaps you want a no-nonsense container, without exotic plants, that will provide some simple color and interest throughout the summer in response to a little care. Foliage plants are easier to care for than flowering annuals because there is no need to pick off the spent flowers in order to keep things neat.

One uncomplicated scheme would combine a red-leaved coleus (*Coleus* x *hybridus* 'Fiji Red' or 'Red Velvet') with dracaena (*Dracaena tricolor*), a grassy-leaved accent plant. The red coleus will echo and intensify the red-edged green leaf of the dracaena. The edge of the container can be softened by a trailing plant such as ivy (*Hedera helix* 'Pettipoint'), which has a small, dark green leaf.

A Container for a Shady Corner

If you need something to lighten and brighten a shady corner or for special effect toward dusk as you relax at the end of the day, the colors to use are white and silver, since they are most visible under low light conditions. A caladium such as 'Candidum', which has a white leaf with dark green veins and border, or the similar 'White Princess', could be used in conjunction with the Victorian brake fern (*Pteris cretica*), which has a silver, very narrow, almost skeletal leaf. Some white impatiens (*Impatiens wallerana* 'Dazzler White' or 'Blitz White'), with their green leaves and white flowers, can add the final touch.

Conclusions

As we have seen, foliage can be used to create simple or complex patterns on both large and small scales. In the most memorable gardens the plants are selected with a particular purpose in mind. Whether the design is on a small scale intended for close-up viewing or on a grand scale, with plants used in bold sweeps, the same attention to detail is required.

Knowledge is gained by observing plants as they grow. Although photographs are informative, they are static. It is necessary to visit gardens and see what plants do over the fourth dimension of time. The more you familiarize yourself with a diversity of plants, the wider will be your "palette" of choices. The sincerest sort of flattery is to recreate in your own garden a pleasing combination seen elsewhere. Often the design cannot be transported intact but will need some adaptation to fit your needs. Through this process of adjustment, you will familiarize yourself with plants and their possible associations and will learn to create combinations the easy way. The hard way — rearranging the plants in your garden — is laborious for you and difficult for the plants. Learn to assess what you see and determine why you find one combination appealing and dislike another. Try to imagine "what if" — what if I use a different plant? another color? remove one? change the cultivar? Look for the design that is balanced and harmonious — one that creates a garden rather than a collection.

PART II

Plant Dictionary

A good garden design consists of two key elements: the concept and the plants. The concept is the most creative. Above all, you must know what you want to achieve in terms of pattern, scale, and color. With this firmly in mind, select plants with suitable qualities — those attributes that actuate the design concept. To select plants first and then attempt to fit them into a design is a backward approach. Once you know in broad terms what you want, you can use a reference list to find specific plants to fill those needs. Perhaps you want a medium-sized tree with purple leaves, or a spreading fern that will grow in the sun, or an annual with bronze architectural foliage. If you are unaware of a plant's existence, it is worthless for your purposes, since you will not consider it. My young niece matter-of-factly acknowledged this truth in response to the question, "Does everybody like you, Sara?" "Oh no!" she replied. "Why, there are some people who don't even know me."

Some individual plants become favorites, based on their appearance and good behavior in the garden, as well as the imponderables of personal taste. They are usually reliable performers that contribute to the display. Then there are the host of unknowns. More fascinating plants exist than any of us can ever hope to cultivate in a single lifetime. In the following listing, I have concentrated on garden-worthy plants and their variant forms, especially cultivars with colored, variegated, or otherwise exceptional foliage. Standard plants in their typical forms are widely available at local garden centers and nurseries or through mail order. Even small trees and shrubs can be purchased through the mail; indeed, this is the only way in which rare or scarce cultivars may be obtained.

Use your ingenuity when seeking out the plants you want. Each plant nursery is likely to offer some plants that are unique. When you travel, go treasure hunting — if you live in Connecticut, for instance, bring plants home from your trip to California. Protect those that cannot survive a New England winter outdoors, by putting them in a greenhouse or under grow lights. Next summer, in containers or in the ground, they will augment the palette of material with which you create the foliage garden. Dahlia, canna, caladium, geranium, and coleus, for example, are not winter hardy in most of the United States, but all can be used as summer bedding plants.

This chapter presents a diversity of plants for consideration. Trees and shrubs, the backbone of the garden, are important for the structure they provide. Herbaceous perennials are a widely cultivated plant group. Ground covers are treated separately from other perennials because they are used en masse, rather than as individual plants or in a small grouping. Ferns and grasses are also listed separately in order to give more thorough descriptions of their diversity. The listing for annuals contains both botanical and horticultural examples. Botanically, annuals germinate, grow to maturity, and die in a single season; biennials take two years. Horticulturally, annuals are used for a single season and then discarded, usually killed by winter temperatures; coleus, begonia, and impatiens are familiar examples. If a plant is commonly used as an annual, it is included here, even though in mild winter areas it is perennial.

The list of foliage plants in this chapter is intended to be introductory. Some plants will be readily procurable and the availability of other selections will be quite limited. As you become more attuned to foliage plants, you will find additional ideas in other books, as well as in gardens that you visit. The discerning gardener unites concept and availability to develop potential imagery into practical reality.

Note: Entries are arranged alphabetically by botanical name. For common names, see pages 195-209.

REES

TREES ARE LARGE PLANTS WITH WOODY TRUNKS, which support the plant and transport water. Single-trunk trees are most common, but some trees have more than one trunk, with branches and lateral shoots on the main axis. Trees are evergreen or deciduous. As a general rule, more broad-leaved evergreen species are found in mild-winter areas; deciduous species, in temperate areas; and coniferous, needled-evergreen species, in cold-winter regions. Trees can be featured as a specimen, to be enjoyed as an individual plant in the garden, or they can be used to shade and shelter smaller trees, shrubs, and perennials. Trees can also function as a backdrop against which to display shrubs and other, smaller trees, resulting in a display of foliage with foliage on a grand scale. In sum, trees provide a permanent framework in the landscape and a sense of structure to the garden.

Acer spp.
MAPLE

This group consists of approximately 200 different species, including large trees, small trees, and shrubs; most are deciduous, but a few are evergreen; most have simple, lobed leaves, but a few have compound leaves. With such diversity it is possible to find a maple for almost any purpose, whether as a street tree or an ornamental specimen. Many have a dense habit of growth that provides heavy shade; this, coupled with their shallow root system, makes it difficult to grow other plants beneath them. Most have outstanding autumn color.

The tall maples grow to 90 to 120 feet, depending on the species. Usually quick growing,

they require adequate room for the development of a full, symmetrical crown. Their shallow, fibrous root system makes them easy to transplant, but it is difficult to grow grass or other ground covers beneath them. A mulch is often the simplest solution.

NORWAY MAPLE **(*Acer platanoides*)** is a 90-foot-tall tree at maturity. It is hardy to −25°F; in severe winters, frost-cracking of the trunk may be a problem at the northern limits of its range. The leaves of 'Albo-marginatum' and 'Drummondii' are light green in the center and have a silvery-white variegation at the margin. As might be expected, these variegated forms are slow growing, hardy only to about −10°F. Both of these cultivars will occasionally revert, and the branches of such all-green leaves must be removed to preserve the unusual effect the white-variegated leafed forms present in the landscape. 'Albo-variegatum' is similar but the young leaves are tinged with pink. 'Crimson King' (dark maroon leaves, broad oval crown), 'Faasen's Black' (darker than 'Crimson King' and has a more pyramidal form), and 'Royal Red Leaf' (dark red, glossy leaves) are superior to the older cultivar 'Schwedleri' in that these three have dark plumred foliage throughout the growing season whereas 'Schwedleri' fades to bronze and then green. 'Green Lace' has very finely cut, dark green leaves, giving the tree a more delicate texture; it has a moderate growth rate and a smaller size, maturing at 40 feet. 'Laciniatum' has cuneate leaves with the lobes ending in curved, slender, clawlike points. 'Walderseei' has leaves very densely speckled with tiny white dots.

RED or SWAMP MAPLE **(*Acer rubrum*)** is tolerant of a wider temperature range than Norway; it can be grown from the northern tier of states with winter temperatures of −30°F south to Texas and parts of Florida, where it barely freezes. Certainly an individual tree could not be expected to thrive under such diverse conditions, but with selection, suitable material can be obtained. However, some ice and storm damage can be expected, because red maple is larger (to 120 feet) and somewhat weaker-wooded than the Norway and sugar maples. Red maple is valuable for its tolerance of wet, swampy conditions and excellent, brilliant red, scarlet, and orange autumn color on its simple, three- to five-palmately lobed leaves. 'Autumn Flame' has smaller leaves in profusion and is valuable for relatively early and persistent color on a compact, rounded tree. 'Bowhall' has good autumn color on a full-sized, compact, upright, and pyramidal tree; and 'Morgan' has consistently brilliant autumn color. 'October Glory' has persistent, bright crimson autumn foliage; it colors very late in the fall, indicating its late adjustment to dormancy and winter. As might be expected, it is susceptible to winter damage in northern areas and is better suited for coastal areas of the Deep South. 'Schlesingeri' has unusually early autumn leaf color, often by as much as two weeks or more. 'V. J. Drake' has unique autumn coloration, beginning with purple mottling and changing to red margins and a green center, which turns yellow; it colors well even in mild winter areas.

SUGAR MAPLE or ROCK MAPLE **(Acer saccharum)** is one of the most common large shade trees, reaching over 100 feet tall with a spread of more than 50 feet, but usually less in cultivation. Even as young specimens, they make excellent shade trees. They are hardy in winter temperatures from –30°F to 0°F. The sturdy wood breaks less easily than Norway or swamp maple, resulting in less damage from ice and snowstorms. This is the tree that blazes across the woodlots of New England; the simple, usually five-lobed palmate leaves turn golden yellow, orange, and red in the autumn.

'Bonfire' is a heat-tolerant cultivar that turns a brilliant carmine color. 'Laciniatum' (also known in the trade as 'Sweet Shadow') has a deeply cut, dark green leaf that gives a foliage effect similar to the Norway maple cultivar 'Green Lace'.

The smaller maples (15- to 30-foot tall) evolved as understory woodland species. They can therefore tolerate light to medium shade, and their root structure is less fibrous and competitive for moisture and nutrients than that of the larger maples. They provide some of our loveliest small trees either as specimens or grouped for a naturalistic effect. Some have multiple trunks that give them a shrublike character. Best autumn color results from at least half-day sun.

AMUR MAPLE **(Acer ginnala)** is a hardy (to –35°F) small tree (to 20 feet) or large multistemmed bush, best adapted to areas with cool summers. The leaves are nearly 4 inches long by almost 3 inches wide with three (sometimes five) lobes, with the middle lobe always much longer than the laterals; all are doubly serrate. The foliage is glossy, dark green in summer and changes to brilliant hues of fiery scarlet and deep red early in autumn. 'Flame' is a cultivar with orange-red coloring in the autumn. With the natural variation to be found, selection of other clones should be possible.

FULL-MOON MAPLE **(Acer japonicum)** grows slowly to 25 feet tall. Although it is hardy to –5°F, in the colder part of its range it needs some protection from winter winds, such as can be found under the canopy of taller deciduous trees like oaks. It has green, almost circular leaves with seven to thirteen lobes that turn crimson in autumn. Cultivars include 'Aconitifolium', or fern-leaf full-moon maple, with each leaf pinnately cut almost to the base with nine to thirteen segments turning ruby-crimson in autumn; and 'Aureum', or golden full-moon maple, which has pale golden yellow leaves throughout the growing season.

JAPANESE MAPLE *(Acer palmatum)* can be quite variable in size, from 10 to 25 feet tall, depending on the individual cultivar selected. These are usually seen as multitrunk specimens. Some, especially the thread-leaf forms, have a rounded, moundlike appearance; most of these are so slow growing that an 8-foot-tall specimen is quite mature. Japanese maples are hardy to –5°F but not if this temperature is sustained. Avoid planting in frost pockets; these maples have a tendency to leaf out early enough in spring so as to be damaged by late frost. Cultivate in a similar fashion to azaleas: in filtered shade and with protection from drying winds, especially in the colder areas. A moist but well-drained soil high in organic matter is best. This species produces some of the most airy and fine-textured small trees. The leaves are 2 to 4 inches long, deeply cut into five to nine lobes. Foliage color throughout the season is quite variable — young leaves are often a glowing red, turning green in summer, and then changing to scarlet, orange, or yellow in autumn. Some are red or burgundy throughout the growing season, and a few are variegated. The leaves may be so strongly dissected as to be threadlike. Numerous cultivars are available, generally as grafted specimens. Cultivars with green leaves include 'Bonfire', with dissected leaves that are red when young; 'Heptalobum Osakazuki', with large green leaves that turn bright scarlet in autumn; 'Linearilobum', with green leaves divided into very fine, narrow, threadlike segments that turn yellow in autumn; 'Lutescens', with yellow foliage in autumn; 'Ukon', with leaves that are yellow as they unfold, turning green in summer and then gold with a red flush in autumn; 'Viride', with bright, soft green foliage; and 'Yatsufusa', which has very small leaves with a red margin in the spring, turning all red in autumn. Cultivars with red leaves include 'Atropurpureum', with doubly serrate, palmate, dark red leaves; 'Beni Kagami', with deeply cut orange-red foliage; 'Bloodgood', with new foliage of brilliant red deepening to dark red; 'Burgundy Lace' and 'Crimson Queen', both with dissected leaves in their respective colors; 'Garnet', with dissected deep red leaves; and 'Nigrum', with very large, dark purplish-black leaves. One cultivar with yellow leaves is the aptly named 'Aureum'. Cultivars with variegated leaves include 'Aochanishiki', with nine-lobed leaves variegated in green, cream, rose, and white; 'Asahi zuru', which has green leaves with crisp pink-and-white variegation; 'Aureo-variegatum', with green-and-yellow leaves; 'Butterfly', with bluish-green leaves edged with white; 'Reticulatum', which has leaves with green veins on a yellowish white ground; 'Roseo-marginatum', which has green leaves with a pink margin (watch for reversion); 'Tricolor', with leaves that are green, pink, and yellow; and 'Versicolor', with green leaves spotted pink, fading to white. The variegated cuttings especially need light shade to prevent leaf scorch in the summer.

PAPERBARK MAPLE *(Acer griseum)* is a favorite small tree with the cognoscenti. It is hardy to –5°F and grows a little taller than Japanese maples, slowly maturing to 25 feet tall. The leaf is unlike that of most maples, consisting of three, coarsely toothed, elliptic to ovate leaflets, palmately arranged. In the spring, when they first appear, they are bronze-red, turning medium green above and silvery beneath in summer before changing to a brilliant red in autumn. Paperbark maple is scarce and expensive because most seed does not develop an embryo; it has been suggested that the tree is infertile unless cross-pollinated.

VINE MAPLE *(Acer circinatum)* is a small tree native to moist sites along the Pacific Coast from British Columbia south to northern California. In the shade it is multistemmed, sprawling, and weak-stemmed but will grow as a single-trunked small tree (to 30 feet tall) in sunny sites. The leaves are 2 to 6 inches long and wide, with five to eleven lobes. Leaf color is reddish in spring when unfolding; it turns to light green in summer before changing to scarlet, orange, or yellow in autumn. Vine maple is lovely with conifers as a background to display the autumn coloration. Here, especially, a contorted, twisting character can be an advantage.

Aesculus hippocastanum
HORSE CHESTNUT

No longer as popular as it was in the past, the horse chestnut is a large, bulky tree that grows 60 feet or more tall and 40 feet wide, is hardy to −25°F and has dense foliage, providing heavy shade. It needs to receive adequate water in summer if conditions are dry. The palmately compound, obovate, serrate leaflets, five to seven in number, grow up to 10 inches long. Both the shape and the length of these leaves provide a very coarse texture. It is susceptible to a rust disease that can spoil its appearance in late summer. Ohio buckeye, *Aesculus glabra,* is perhaps more desirable but is less frequently seen. This smaller tree grows only 30 to 50 feet tall and is narrow — half as wide as it is tall. Leaf color is a pleasing lime green in spring and dark yellow-green in summer, turning orange to red in autumn.

Amelanchier laevis
ALLEGANY SERVICEBERRY, SHADBUSH

Native chiefly to North America, the shadbush or serviceberry is well known for its attractive white flowers, which appear early in spring when the shad swim upstream to spawn. The simple, oval leaves with finely serrate margins begin to unfold as the flowers bloom. The leaves are a red-bronze color when they emerge, but turn bluish green in summer. Allegany serviceberry is notable for its rich fall colors of yellow-orange to red. Growing up to 35 feet tall, it is hardy to −20°F. It is tolerant of moist soils and is thus useful for naturalistic plantings at the edge of a pond or woodland. The tasty, blue-purple berries are quickly eaten by birds.

Arundinaria. See Bamboos, page 69.

Bamboos *(Bambusa* spp., *Phyllostachys* spp., *Pseudosasa* spp.)
(See also under "Ground Covers," p. 120.)

Although considered in this section, bamboos are more correctly classified as grasses. Long-lived and often quite tall, "bamboo" includes a diverse array of plants that differ from other grasses in that they have persistent woody stems, called *culms.* The better-behaved, clump-forming species tend to be tropical and thus more frost-tender, although some are hardy to 15°F. *Bambusa,* for example, consists of a single, dense clump of stems, with new shoots appearing at the beginning of a rainy season, generally in summer or autumn after a relatively dry period. The cold-hardy species are more invasive and can spread impressive distances. Some of the latter are grown as far north as Massachusetts, where low winter temperatures serve as a check on their invasive tendencies. *Phyllostachys* has rhizomes that spread far and wide to produce open colonies, with new shoots appearing in the spring.

Bamboos are heavy feeders and, as might be expected for grasses, nitrogen is especially important. The nutrients stored in the rhizomes that grew the previous season more directly affect the growth rate than fertilizer supplied in the current season. For this reason, do not expect full-sized culms to grow until after several seasons. Once a culm achieves its height, it grows no taller, although it should become leafier. A culm lasts several years and then dies; at this point, it should be cut off at ground level with lopping shears.

Bamboos like a moist but well-drained soil, even along a pond or stream, where the mat of bamboo roots can help to control erosion. Some bamboos are shade-tolerant; others grow in full sun. It is necessary to provide bamboos with protection from drying winds, especially in winter in colder regions, or leaf scorch will result.

Bamboos are readily associated with the Orient as a garden ornamental, in art, as a craft and building material, and as a food, and they also contribute much to occidental gardens. Bamboos add a graceful linear pattern and fine texture to the garden, and hardy varieties are breathtakingly elegant in the snow. The susurrus of a breeze through their leaves is a delight to hear. Nomenclature is constantly undergoing revision, and, as elsewhere, I have used *Hortus III* as the standard.

ALPHONSE KARR BAMBOO *(Bambusa glaucescens 'Alphonse Karr')* is a clump-forming bamboo hardy to 15°F. It reaches a height of 15 to 35 feet and has a graceful, fountainlike pattern of growth. The new stems are pinkish and green, changing to brilliantly striped green on yellow as they mature.

ARROW BAMBOO *(Pseudosasa japonica; syn — Arundinaria japonica)* has large, rather pointed leaves and widely spreading rhizomes; the culms reach 15 to 20 feet high, though usually only 6 to 12 feet in cold-winter climates, where it spreads more slowly to form dense, erect clumps. In milder areas it can be used as a hedge. One of the hardier bamboo species, it will survive to 0°F. It grows best with some shade rather than in full sun.

BLACK BAMBOO *(Phyllostachys nigra)* generally grows 10 to 15 feet tall in gardens but has been reported to be as tall as 26 feet. New canes are green but turn black the second year. It will grow better if given afternoon shade, especially if summers are hot. Hardy to 5°F, black bamboo is a favorite ornamental species, long in cultivation, and is often used as a container plant. This is a running species.

FERN-LEAF BAMBOO *(Bambusa glaucescens 'Fernleaf'; B. disticha)* is a clump-forming bamboo that grows 10 to 20 feet tall and is hardy to 15°F. The dense leaf growth — ten to twenty closely spaced leaves to a twig — gives this bamboo a fernlike look. The weight of the leaves may cause the cane to arch, since branches occur only on the upper two thirds of the cane. Do not confuse this with the dwarf fern-leaf bamboo listed under Ground Covers (page 120).

FOUNTAIN BAMBOO *(Sinarundinaria nitida)* is a clump-forming bamboo that grows 15 to 20 feet tall and is hardy to 0°F. It is highly prized for its beautiful, greenish purple stems, which mature to a deep, purplish black. The stems are erect when they first appear and arch as they mature. Delicate, narrow, linear evergreen leaves persist except in cold winters.

GOLDEN BAMBOO *(Phyllostachys aurea; P. bambusoides* var. *aurea)* grows 10 to 20 feet tall and is hardy to 0°F. The canes are bright green when they first appear and become a dull golden yellow, especially in sunnier sites. Although it is somewhat drought tolerant it has a better appearance if given abundant water. Its dense foliage makes a good screen. This is a running species.

GOLDEN GODDESS BAMBOO *(Bambusa*

glaucescens 'Golden Goddess'), hardy to 15°F, is a clump-forming bamboo with golden stems, and an elegant, arching habit of growth; it thus needs room to spread out at the tops of the canes. It makes a graceful container plant.

JAPANESE TIMBER BAMBOO *(Phyllostachys bambusoides)* usually reaches 25 to 45 feet tall in gardens, although this species has been reported growing as much as 72 feet tall with culms nearly 6 inches in diameter. It is most attractive with its lower branches clipped off, better displaying the canes as a dominant yet graceful landscape plant. It will not thrive in tropical regions and may be damaged at cold temperatures (0°F). This is a running species.

OLDHAM BAMBOO or CLUMPING GIANT TIMBER BAMBOO *(Bambusa oldhamii; Sinocalamus oldhamii)* is a clump-forming bamboo that grows 20 to 40 feet tall and has stems 3 inches wide: it is hardy to 20°F. This bamboo is elegant on a grand scale, for its vigorous, upright habit of growth provides a majestic vertical mass.

PALMATE BAMBOO *(Sasa palmata; Sasa senanensis; Bambusa palmata)* is a running bamboo that grows 8 to 12 feet tall and is hardy to 0°F. Although it is a notorious spreader and must be curbed in its attempts to take over, it is welcome for its handsome, broad leaves that can be as much as 14 inches long and 4 inches wide. The leaves are bright green above and glaucous below and spread, fingerlike, from the stem and branch tips. A related species is *Sasa tessellata*, which is lower growing (3 to 5 feet high) and has leaves to 2 feet long. Best in shade, it is also slow growing. Rare.

SILVER-STRIPE BAMBOO *(Bambusa glaucescens* 'Silver-stripe')* is a clump-forming bamboo, hardy to 15°F. It grows 40 feet tall, making it one of the most vigorous bamboos for hedge or screening use. Stems are usually narrowly striped with yellow, but the cultivar name ('Silver-stripe') refers to the leaves, which are striped with white.

YELLOW-GROOVE BAMBOO *(Phyllostachys aureosulcata)* is the hardiest of the bamboos — to −20°F. At this temperature it dies back to the rhizomes but will regenerate each year. Its normal culm height of 15 to 25 feet is not attained when it is exposed to very low temperatures. In appearance it is like a slender form of golden bamboo. New growth is green, maturing to olive green with a pronounced yellow groove. The dark green leaves are up to 6 inches long. A rampant spreader, it must be contained in some manner. New shoots are edible when they first appear. It will grow in full sun but needs protection from strong winds.

Bambusa. See Bamboos, pages 68-70.

Catalpa bignonioides
CATALPA, INDIAN BEAN TREE

This cold-tolerant (to −20°F) tree presents a subtropical appearance; it has coarse heart-shaped, 5- to 8-inch long leaves and upright flower panicles, which grow as much as 7 inches long. Growing 45 feet tall, this tree has a broadly rounded form. It is adapted to extremes of heat and cold, tolerates both drought and wet soil conditions, and makes very quick growth. On the other hand, because of these characteristics, it is somewhat weak wooded and not especially long lived. 'Aurea' is a cultivar with golden yellow leaves throughout the growing season.

Cedrus atlantica 'Glauca'
BLUE ATLAS CEDAR

This moderately slow-growing, large tree, can grow over 60 feet tall and as much as 40 feet wide. It is hardy to −5°F. Best as a specimen plant with room to spread, the Atlas cedar has an open, angular growth habit when young, less open as it matures. It is deep rooted and will be drought tolerant once it is established in a sunny site with good drainage. Its short, 1-inch-long needles in dense clusters along the branches present a stiff appearance; in the cultivar 'Glauca' they are a beautiful silvery blue. These trees are elegant when used with deep reddish-purple foliage for contrast.

Cercis canadensis
JUDAS TREE, EASTERN REDBUD

This is a common understory tree in the eastern United States. It is hardy to –15°F, grows 35 feet tall and 35 feet wide, and has vivid cerise-pink, pealike flowers on bare twigs before leafing out in spring. The Judas tree grows well in a moderate- to well-drained soil; it prefers moist conditions but will tolerate dryness once it is established. The heart-shaped simple leaves with an entire margin provide a somewhat coarse texture, emerging light green in the spring, presenting a rather glaucous appearance in the summer, and then turning a lovely clear yellow in autumn. 'Forest Pansy' has purple leaves in the spring which turn purplish green in summer if grown as an understory tree; it has better summer color (more purple) in sunny sites.

Chionanthus virginicus
FRINGE TREE

This is a small tree that grows 20 to 35 feet tall and as wide; with multiple trunks, it has the character of an outsize shrub. Its coarse lateral roots can lead to problems in transplanting, but it can be moved in spring as a balled-and-burlapped specimen. It is hardy to –10°F, and is shade tolerant, though it does better with at least half-day sun. It requires moist soil which

can be either poorly or well drained as long as it does not dry out. In June, it has numerous sweetly scented clustered flowers with extremely narrow, fringelike petals. Female plants will have small, olive-like blue fruits if a male plant is present. The fringe tree leafs out quite late in spring (late May in Connecticut), producing simple ovate leaves up to 8 inches long that are green in summer and a clear bright yellow in autumn.

Cordyline australis 'Atropurpurea'
TI PLANT

The ti plant is often more familiar as a houseplant, although it is an evergreen, palmlike tree that is surprisingly hardy (to 15°F). It has a carrotlike taproot and is drought tolerant. A young ti plant grows as an erect fountain of 3-foot-long, swordlike leaves, 2 to 5 inches wide. It can grow 20 to 30 feet tall at maturity, with sparse branches high on the main trunk. To provide a more lavish appearance, plant it in groups or prune it hard when young to encourage production of multiple trunks. 'Atropurpurea' has bronze-red foliage and a slower habit of growth.

Cornus florida
FLOWERING DOGWOOD

This is deservedly one of our most popular native understory trees. It is hardy to –10°F and grows 25 to 45 feet tall; it has a spreading crown that is rather open in shade but is more compact if grown in full sun. Recent problems with anthracnose (a leaf disease) and bark borers suggest some caution in planting, especially where this tree is marginally hardy. Its berries are a favorite of many species of birds. It grows best in a slightly to moderately acid soil that is high in oganic matter so it does not dry out; it is important to water in times of drought. Its broad oval leaves are bright green in summer and a brilliant scarlet color in autumn. 'Welchii' is a cultivar with tricolor leaves marked green, creamy white, and pink. It is attractive in light shade; it can burn in full sun, although the coloration is better. Watch for reversion.

Cotinus americanus
AMERICAN SMOKEBUSH

Native to the southeastern United States, this small tree grows to 30 feet in height and has a narrow, rather upright habit. Hardy to –10° F, it can be grown north of its natural range. It is related to the sumac, and, like sumac, is most valuable for its fall color. Given full sun and a well-drained, only moderately fertile soil, the simple leaves turn a brilliant scarlet to orange.

Eriobotrya japonica
LOQUAT

Cultivated for its fruit, the loquat is an evergreen tree that grows 15 to 30 feet tall and is hardy to 20°F. It has big, broad, leathery leaves that are 6 to 12 inches long and 2 to 4 inches wide; they are strongly serrate and a deep, glossy green above, with dense rust-colored, woolly hairs underneath. Loquat requires full sun and rich well-drained soil for best growth. It can be used as a container plant in cold winter areas.

Eucalyptus spp. (See also under "Shrubs," pages 90-91.)
EUCALYPTUS

Native to Australia, eucalyptus has become the most widely planted non-native tree in California and Arizona. It is drought and heat tolerant and adapts well to areas with a Mediterranean climate. Few, if any, insect pests or diseases at-

tack the leaves. Eucalyptus is both fast growing and generally long lived, and it usually has two kinds of foliage, both fragrant: soft juvenile leaves on young plants and shoots arising from cut-back stumps, and tougher foliage on mature trees and shrubs. The attractive foliage of some species is sold by florists.

BLUE BOX *(Eucalyptus baueriana)* is hardy to 10° to 18°F and has broadly oval, gray-green leaves on an attractively rounded young tree that becomes tall and straight with age.

BLUE GUM *(Eucalyptus globulus)* is hardy to 17° to 22°F and reaches 150 to 200 feet in height at maturity. The lower-growing form 'Compacta' (to 65 feet tall) is multibranched and can be kept sheared as low as 10 feet tall. On both, the juvenile foliage is silver in color and oval in shape, while the mature foliage is dark green and sickle shaped, as much as 10 inches long. Both are untidy trees, dropping foliage and branches, and are better grown along the coastal slopes of California.

Eucalyptus caesia is hardy to 22° to 25°F and grows 15 to 20 feet tall. The leaves are small and bluish-gray (hence the name caesia). It is not wind tolerant and needs a light soil. It is best grown as a multitrunked small tree or large shrub.

Eucalyptus cineraria is hardy to 14° to 17°F and grows 25 to 50 feet tall. The juvenile leaves are rounded and light in color (cineraria means ash colored), and the mature foliage is longer and narrower in shape. It is wind and drought tolerant and grows best on sandy, quick-draining soils. Prune to encourage growth of juvenile gray-foliaged branches.

NICHOL'S WILLOW-LEAFED PEPPERMINT GUM *(Eucalyptus nicholii)* is hardy to 12° to 15°F; it has a graceful weeping form and grows quickly to 40 feet tall. The purple-tinged, light green, very narrow leaves have a strong peppermint fragrance when crushed.

ROUND-LEAVED SNOW GUM *(Eucalyptus perriniana)* is hardy to 10° to 15°F, and grows as a loose straggly tree 15 to 30 feet high. The attractive juvenile leaves are silver, growing as a circle around the stem; mature leaves are long and lanceolate. Keep pruned back to shrub form for a more attractive shape and to maintain production of young shoots with juvenile foliage.

SILVER-DOLLAR GUM *(Eucalyptus polyanthemos)* is hardy to 14° to 18°F and grows as a single-trunked or multistemmed tree, quickly reaching 20 to 60 feet in height. The 2- to 3-inch, round or oval juvenile leaves are gray with light reddish margins; mature leaves are lanceolate. The juvenile foliage is drought tolerant; these young leaves are useful for cut flower arrangements.

SILVER-LEAVED MOUNTAIN GUM *(Eucalyptus pulverulenta)* is hardy to 15° to 21°F. It is a straggly small tree that grows 15 to 30 feet tall. The juvenile leaves are silver gray (*pulverulenta* means "powdered as with dust") and grow in a perfoliate fashion, appearing skewered by the stems; mature leaves are long and pointed. Prune to grow as a large shrub for more attractive form and to encourage the more desirable juvenile leaf growth.

SNOW GUM *(Eucalyptus niphophila)* is very hardy (to 0° to 10°F) and is drought and wind tolerant. It grows slowly to a height of 20 feet. The silvery blue, lanceolate leaves may reach as much as 4 inches in length but are often shorter. Its hardiness as well as its silver foliage and crooked trunk, which give it a picturesque appearance, make the snow gum a desirable small tree.

Fagus sylvatica
BEECH

The European beech is a splendid tree with a commanding presence, both noble and graceful in appearance. A single tree makes a superb specimen. Slow growing, these beeches require plenty of room at maturity, for they reach 90 feet tall and have a huge, broad crown. Their fibrous root system makes them easy to move but, coupled with the very dense shade under their low-spreading branches, this root system also makes it very difficult to grow anything underneath them. Beech is hardy to –20°F. Select cultivars include purple beech (*F. sylvatica* 'Atropunicea'), which has purple leaves; copper beech (*F. sylvatica* 'Cuprea'), whose new leaves are reddish bronze and lighter than those of purple beech; weeping purple beech (*F. sylvatica* 'Purpureo-pendula'), which has pendulous branches and purple leaves and is usually smaller than other beeches (40 feet tall at maturity); and 'Rohanii' (*F. sylvatica* 'Rohanii'), with narrow, deeply cut, laciniate, purple leaves.

Ginkgo biloba
GINKGO

One of the most ancient species of trees alive today as evidenced by fossil records, the ginkgo is an excellent specimen tree. It grows to 80 feet or more, although it is somewhat gawky in form while young. It is variable in form with some having a narrow, upright growth habit, and others, broader, more spreading. The fruit of female plants has an extremely unpleasant odor. Plant in deep, loose soil and water thoroughly in times of drought until the tree is well established and beginning to mature. There are few if any problems with insect pests or disease. Although it is related to conifers, the ginkgo is deciduous and has beautiful fan-shaped leaves, which turn a lovely clear yellow in autumn.

Gleditsia tricanthos
HONEY LOCUST

This frequently used tree grows quickly to a height of 70 feet. It is hardy to –15°F and is tolerant of heat, cold, wind, and some drought, as well as compacted soils and road salt, making it good for city use. Honey locust leaves are pinnately or bipinnately compound with numerous oval leaflets, providing very light shade; it is one of the last trees to leaf out in spring and one of the first to shed in autumn. The species itself is rarely planted due to its stiff, 4-inch-long thorns. *G. tricanthos inermis* is thornless, as are its cultivars: 'Moraine', 'Shademaster', and 'Sunburst'. 'Sunburst' has bright golden-yellow leaves when they first appear in spring and is elegant when combined with bronze foliage such as that of *Acer* 'Crimson King'.

Ilex aquifolium
ENGLISH HOLLY

A familiar broad-leaved evergreen, English holly is winter hardy to –5°F. It has very glossy, leathery, oblong leaves, approximately 1 inch long with spiny teeth, and is the holly used at Christmas for decoration. It grows slowly to 40 feet tall, but it can grow higher. For the most compact form, English holly requires a deep, rich, somewhat acid soil that is moist but well drained and a location in full sun. Sexes occur on separate plants, and only the females will have berries. English holly is of value for its winter effect. Cultivars include 'Albomarginata', a name applied to several cultivars with white or creamy-white margins on the leaves; 'Argentea Regina' ('Silver King', 'Silver Queen') has leaves with a mottled gray appearance and white margins; 'Elegantissima' has spiny, creamy-white margins on the leaves; 'Ferox Argentea' has leaves with white spines on the upper surface of the leaf and white margins; 'Aureo-marginata' is a name applied to several female cultivars with gold margins on the leaves; 'Aurea Medio-picta' ('Golden Butterfly') are cultivars with a gold center and green margins on the leaves; 'Aurea Regina' ('Golden King', 'Golden Queen') are cultivars with deep yellow variegation; 'Ferox Aurea' has leaves blotched with gold to chartreuse in the center; and 'Flavescens' has leaves tinged soft yellow all season long, most noticeable in plants grown in sunny sites.

Juniperus spp. and cultivars (See also under "Shrubs," pages 94-96.)
JUNIPERS

This genus provides the gardener with a diverse group of both trees and shrubs. As a general rule, junipers grow in full sun in sandy, well-drained soils and tolerate drought; wet soil can result in root rot. Like yews and hollies, junipers are separately sexed, and only the female plants will bear fruit, which is attractive to birds. Young plants are easy to move, older specimens less so. If planted near native crab apples or shadbush, cedar-apple rust can be a problem. Juniper blight, a disease that causes young shoots to die back, can be controlled with copper sprays such as bordeaux mixture. Junipers are popular despite these two problems because they grow well and tend to be otherwise free of problems in difficult dry areas.

EASTERN RED CEDAR *(Juniperus virginiana)* is native from Canada to Florida, from the Atlantic seaboard westward to the Rocky Mountains, giving a good idea of its adaptability and hardiness. Southern forms tend to be broader in habit with pendulous branches; northern forms (sometimes specified as *J. virginiana crebra)* are more erect, sometimes columnar. Eastern red cedar is the old field cedar of abandoned pastures, one of the first trees to move in and colonize. It needs full sun to grow well. The fragrant red heartwood is prized as a moth repellent, and the rot-resistant wood is useful for fence posts, arbors, and benches. Additionally, forms with especially attractive foliage have been selected for garden use; and more work is currently being done by Dr. J. C. Raulston of the North Carolina State University Arboretum in Raleigh. Some handsome cultivars include 'Burkii', a male clone that grows as a dense pyramid to 20 feet tall or more and has steel blue needles that turn plum purple in winter; 'Cinerascens', with ash gray to silver new growth; 'Glauca', which has silvery blue, very glaucous needles in spring, turning silvery green in summer, and grows as a narrow columnar tree 15 to 20 feet tall; 'Manhattan Blue', which has dark blue-green needles on dense branches that form a compact pyramid 15 feet tall or more; 'Skyrocket', which has blue-gray needles on a narrow, erect spire that grows 10 to 15 feet tall and less than 2 feet wide and is susceptible to snow-load damage in winter; and 'Venusta', which is similar to 'Burkii' except the needles are ash gray rather than steel blue.

WESTERN RED CEDAR or ROCKY MOUNTAIN CEDAR (*Juniperus scopulorum*) is mentioned in *Hortus III* as perhaps only a subspecies of the eastern red cedar to which it is closely allied. Western red cedar grows better in the West, in the Rocky Mountain area and eastward to Illinois. It grows narrowly upright to 35 feet tall. There are several named forms selected for especially glaucous or silvery foliage: 'Argentea' has silvery white needles and a narrow, pyramidal form; 'Blue Moon' has needles of fine texture and a true blue color; 'Gray Gleam' is a male clone with silvery gray foliage that intensifies in color in winter; 'Kansas Silver' has silvery blue needles and a pyra-

midal growth habit; 'Kenyonii' is steely blue, compactly pyramidal in form, and grows slowly to 12 feet tall; 'Moonglow' has intensely blue-silver foliage on a broadly pyramidal form and reaches 20 feet tall; 'Platinum', with brilliant silver needles on a densely pyramidal plant, grows well in the Great Plains and Southwest; 'Wichita Blue' is blue all year around, growing to 20 feet tall in an upright, pyramidal manner.

Leucodendron argenteum
SILVER TREE

Hardy only in frost-free areas, the exquisite silver tree is suitable only for very mild winter areas. The narrow, stiffly erect young trees mature to spreading, irregular specimens that are 40 feet tall. Its superb, silky, silvery white leaves, 3 to 6 inches long, thickly cover the branches, giving a very soft appearance. Silver tree is short-lived (25 to 30 years) and requires sunlight and humidity along with quickly draining soils; it grows well in the coastal California fog belt.

Liquidambar styraciflua
SWEET GUM

This large tree grows 75 to 100 feet tall, spreading to two-thirds that in width. Its deep taproot makes it rather difficult to transplant, and it is often slow to reestablish itself in the new site; small balled-and-burlapped specimens can be moved in early spring. It prefers a moist but well-drained soil. Sweet gum is hardy to −10°F, and south to Florida and Texas. Try to obtain material of southern origin for use in mild winter areas, and the reverse for northern regions. Its maplelike leaves are palmately five- to seven-lobed and finely toothed; they are bright green in summer, turning scarlet red, yellow, or purple in autumn. If particular foliage effects are important, select and tag individual specimens in autumn for spring transplantation. 'Burgundy' has wine-colored autumn foliage that is rather persistent in mild winter areas; 'Festival' has pink, peach, orange, and yellow autumn foliage; 'Palo Alto' has orange-red to bright red autumn coloration; 'Variegata' has leaves that are irregularly marked with yellow during the growing season.

Liriodendron tulipifera
TULIP TREE

Native to the eastern United States, this tree quickly grows 60 to 80 feet tall or more and has a canopy that is one-half the height. Hardy to −10°F in eastern source material, for use in southern California and parts of Florida and Texas, try to select specimens that originated more southerly. Tulip tree grows best in a moist to average soil with good drainage and ample room to grow. It does not transplant readily because its lateral roots are poorly branched; it is best moved in spring. Its simple, palmately lobed leaves grow up to 5 inches long and have a distinctively squared-off end, as though the tip had been trimmed away. The leaves turn a clear lemon yellow in autumn, even in mild winter areas. 'Majestic Beauty' ('Aureo-marginatum') has bright green leaves broadly edged in bright yellow; the coloration varies from leaf to leaf during the growing season.

Magnolia spp.
MAGNOLIA

The magnolia (including bull-bay magnolia and Southern magnolia) is native to the southeastern United States. This outstanding tree has quite showy, large, creamy white flowers. It is hardy only to 0°F but can be grown in slightly colder areas if sheltered by a masonry wall. Winter burn can be a problem in the colder portion of its range. Growing to 75 feet tall or more, magnolia is a superb, single-trunked specimen tree that requires ample room for good development. The lustrous, leathery evergreen leaves vary in shape from tree to tree, but are generally oblong to obovate, often reaching 8 inches in length and having a rusty-brown indumentum beneath. The leaves remain on the tree for two years, creating a full, dense appearance, but they are very resistant to decay after they separate from the tree and must be raked up on a regular basis. Some cultivars selected for foliage effect include 'Cairo', with very glossy, flexible leaves; 'Exmouth', with narrow, more lanceolate leaves; 'Majestic Beauty', with exceptionally long, broad leaves; 'Rotundifolia', with very broad, nearly blunt leaves; 'Samuel Sommer', with large, very dark green, glossy leaves and rust-red indumentum on the underside; 'St. Mary', which has leaves to 10 inches long, lustrous above and rust-red beneath, and is more compact, growing to 20 feet high; and 'Victoria', which has exceptionally broad, dark green, lustrous leaves and is more resistant to cold, withstanding −10°F if protected from wind (parent plant grew in Victoria, British Columbia).

The STAR MAGNOLIA (*Magnolia stellata*) is a delightful small tree with multiple trunks, giving the effect of an outsized shrub. It reaches 20 feet tall and wide and is one of the hardiest of the Asiatic magnolias (to −10°F). Very early in spring it produces white flowers with about twenty straplike petals, which can be damaged by late frosts. Star magnolia is attractive at the edge of woodlands, in dooryard gardens, and in shrub borders. Its thick, rather leathery, dark green leaves are obovate to oblong and 5 inches long; when grown in full sun, the leaves turn a beautiful bronze before they fall.

*B*amboo and blue spruce

Cornus kousa (flowering dogwood), *Acer palmatum* (red Japanese maple)

Cotinus americanus (American smokebush), *Pulmonaria saccharata* (lungwort)

Mahonia japonica

A border with *Malus* sp. (crab apple), dwarf conifers, and perennials in spring

*M*ixed conifer border

*C*otoneaster sp., *Hosta* sp., *Euonymus* sp. in a shady garden

Parthenocissus quinquefolia (Virginia creeper)

Hedera colchica
'Sulphur Heart'
(Persian ivy)

Malus spp. and hybrids
CRAB APPLE

These popular small (to 20 feet tall) trees are generally selected for flower and fruiting effect. Several hybrids have been developed that have good foliage interest as well. Crab apples are quite cold hardy (to –35°F). It is important to remember that native crab apples are susceptible to cedar-apple rust, a disease that alternates between cedar and apple trees. Be sure that these two trees are not planted in close proximity, since cedar-apple rust, as well as apple scab disease, which also affects Oriental crab apples, will spoil the appearance of the foliage.

Malus 'Evelyn' has purplish foliage as it emerges in the spring and bronze-green foliage in summer; it is one of the few crab apples with interesting autumn color and in some years turns orange, red, and purple. 'Radiant' has red-purple leaves in the spring, reddish green in summer.

'Royalty' is notable for its outstanding, red-purple foliage, which has been described as the most intensely colored of any crab apple. The leaves of 'Red Silver' are silvery as they unfold and deep purple for the remainder of the growing season. 'Red Splendor' is an open-pollinated seedling of 'Red Silver'; it, too, has red-purple foliage, and it is more disease resistant than 'Red Silver'.

Musa velutina 'Zebrina' (*M. acuminata*)
BLOOD BANANA

Bananas are included with trees because of their size but are more correctly called herbaceous plants. Heavy feeders, bananas grow best in a rich, moist soil, high in nitrogen and potassium. They are intolerant of frost and easily damaged by wind, which shreds and tatters the large, simple leaves. 'Zebrina' has dark olive green leaves with a wine red midrib; the leaves are also wine red underneath and colored partway in from the edges of the upper surface. It dies down to the roots after flowering, and new shoots form at the crown. Bananas make interesting container plants.

Nyssa sylvatica
BLACK GUM, PEPPERIDGE, SOUR GUM, TUPELO

Hardy to –20°F, this midsized (to 90 feet tall) tree is beautiful as a specimen tree or used in mass plantings. Because it is difficult to transplant, it is best selected as a smaller, balled-and-burlapped or container-grown specimen and planted in early spring. It spreads to two-thirds its height and has a pyramidal growth habit, somewhat similar to that of a pin oak *(Quercus palustris)*. Its glossy, bright to dark green, obovate to oblong leaves grow to 4 inches long; they turn flaming scarlet to orange early in autumn, even in mild winter areas. Native to wet, swampy sites in the eastern United States, it does best in moist but well-drained soil. It will also grow well in drier locations but is intolerant of air pollution; it can withstand occasional drought.

Oxydendrum arboreum
SOURWOOD

This is a 35- to 50-foot-tall understory tree with a narrow crown, often only half as wide as it is high. It is hardy to –10°F. Sourwood is sometimes difficult to transplant because of its deep, coarse, lateral roots and so is best transplanted early in the spring as a balled-and-burlapped small tree; larger sizes are riskier. Although it is shade tolerant, it grows better in full sun and needs a moist but well-drained acid soil; root disturbance should be avoided. In July it produces 8-inch-long, pendulous spikelets of bell-like white flowers (similar in appearance to those of andromeda, *Pieris japonica*). The thick, leathery, glossy, dark green leaves are lanceolate to oblong lanceolate in shape; their color turns to wine red or maroon to purple in the autumn before they drop.

Parrotia persica
PERSIAN PARROTIA

This is a delightful small tree that grows slowly to 30 feet tall but is commonly not much more than 15 feet, at which size it might be considered a large shrub. It is hardy to −5°F. It generally grows with several trunks and has a wide, rather spreading habit as a consequence. The 3- to 4-inch long, dark green leaves are lustrous, oval, and coarsely toothed from the tip to the middle of the leaf. Autumn color is a changing display from golden yellow to orange to rosy pink and finally scarlet.

Phyllostachys spp. See Bamboos, pages 68-70.

Picea pungens 'Glauca'
COLORADO BLUE SPRUCE

This is one of our showiest native conifers. Growing to 100 feet tall, the Colorado blue spruce has a stiff, soldierly growth habit that reflects its hardiness — to −40°F. Densely pyramidal as young trees, they tend to lose their lower branches and become less attractive with age. Their needles are retained for 7 or 8 years, thus giving them a very dense appearance. 'Glauca' refers to their silver-blue appearance; since they are often raised from seed, the degree of blueness varies.

'Hoopsii' is one of the most intense silvery blue forms; it is propagated asexually. 'Koster' is silvery white and has a very stiff and formal habit. 'Moerheimii' is strikingly blue and has a relatively narrow, spirelike growth habit. Dwarf cultivars include 'Globosa', which has a rounded outline and glaucous needles, and grows about 4 feet tall; it has a wider spread after 20 years. *Picea pungens glauca pendula* is a weeping form with silvery blue needles.

Pinus densiflora 'Oculus-draconis'
DRAGON'S-EYE PINE

This selection of the Japanese red pine is interesting for the markings on its needles — two yellow lines on green. When you look at the branches from their tips, you will see concentric green and yellow bands. This pine often has two or more trunks, horizontal branching, and a loose, irregular, somewhat open form; it can grow 100 feet tall but is usually smaller in cultivation. Hardy to −20°F, it will not tolerate windy conditions. It is good for naturalistic, informal plantings.

Pistacia chinensis
PISTACHIO

This is a slow-growing deciduous tree that eventually reaches 60 feet tall; it is hardy to 20°F. With foliage free of insect pests and diseases, pistachio grows best in full sun in deep, well-drained soils. Water deeply and infrequently to reduce danger of verticillium wilt. The beautiful fine-textured leaves of pistachio are similar to sumac, consisting of ten to sixteen paired leaflets that are 2 to 4 inches long by ¾ inch wide. Autumn color is superb — crimson, scarlet, and orange.

Populus tremuloides
QUAKING ASPEN

This is a large understory tree found all across the United States, coast to coast. It is perhaps at its most beautiful in the Rocky Mountains in autumn, when the gold of the turning foliage is displayed against the conifers. Quaking aspen grows 35 to 50 feet tall and is usually rather narrow, one-third to one-half the height. It is intolerant of shade but requires moist to wet soil. Extremely cold tolerant, it will withstand winter temperatures as low as -40°F. It is weak-wooded, susceptible to ice and storm damage, and short-lived, generally doing poorly at lower elevations. This tree can be used for naturalistic effects in small groups interplanted with conifers as a backdrop. Its simple cordate leaves have a deep green upper surface and a whitened lower surface. They flutter in the slightest breeze (hence the common name), creating a sparkling effect. Autumn color is a clear, bright yellow.

Prunus spp. and hybrids
CHERRY

The cherries are beautiful ornamental trees, although they are susceptible to borers, scale, and tent caterpillars. Many have glossy bark, attractive flowers in spring, and fruit that attracts birds.

MYROBALAN PLUM or CHERRY PLUM **(Prunus cerasifera)** is a small tree that grows to 25 feet tall and has a broad crown. It is hardy to −20°F. The type tree itself is rarely grown, but there are several purple-leaved cultivars that are quite popular. If they are grown in even partial shade, the color will fade to a bronzy green, so full sun is required to develop and maintain the best deep purple color. 'Atropurpurea' ('Pissardii') has purple leaves somewhat lighter in color than 'Nigra', which has very dark purple foliage; in addition, 'Atropurpurea' tends to turn somewhat green in summer, primarily in the Midwest. 'Newport' (which may be a hybrid of *P. americana* x *P. cerasifera* 'Atropurpurea') is the most cold-tolerant of the purple-leaved cultivars. 'Thundercloud' has deep purple leaves and holds its color very well; 'Vesuvius' has large leaves, deep purple in color (imagine this displayed against a Colorado blue spruce).

PIN CHERRY **(Prunus pensylvanica)** is short-lived (about 30 years) and is best used grouped at the edge of woodland where the 30-foot-tall trees receive at least a half day of sun and have a reasonably moist, but well-drained, soil. The lanceolate, finely serrate leaves are orange-green in the spring, green in summer, and bright red to orange in autumn.

RUM CHERRY or BLACK CHERRY **(Prunus serotina)** is the best of the native American cherries. Although they can grow to 90 feet tall, it is rare to find one of this size in the wild because the wood has long been highly prized in furniture making. The lanceolate, slightly serrate leaves are shaped like those on a peach tree and are a lustrous, slightly leathery, deep green that turns orange in autumn.

Pseudosasa spp. See Bamboos, pages 68-70.

Pyrus salicifolia
SILVER-LEAVED PEAR

This is a small deciduous tree that grows 25 feet tall. Its willowlike leaves are silvery gray, becoming greener as they grow, and are less than an inch wide, tapering at both ends. They are woolly when they first unfold in the spring but become smooth with maturity. Silver-leaved pear is hardy to −10°F and requires moist but well-drained soil in sunny sites. It can be damaged by fire blight. The cultivar 'Pendula' is a graceful small tree with a weeping form and silvery leaves.

Quercus spp.
OAK

The oaks are outstanding and dependable ornamental trees. Tall, stately, and long-lived, they add tremendous character to the landscape. They provide little competition to other plants growing beneath their canopy because they have deep taproots, although this characteristic also makes them difficult to transplant. Many of these species native to North America and the Orient have good fall color.

BLACK OAK *(Quercus velutina)* is a large, dominant northern oak reaching 100 feet tall with a wide canopy usually three-quarters as wide as the tree is high; it is hardy to –20°F. Unfortunately, this tree is rarely available because it is considered difficult to transplant. It grows best in a moist soil with good drainage but will tolerate drier conditions. The large (to 10 inches long), glossy, dark green leaves are ovate to oblong with seven to nine broad-toothed lobes; they are bright crimson red when they first appear in the spring and in autumn turn golden yellow-brown, red in colder areas.

CALIFORNIA LIVE OAK or COAST LIVE OAK *(Quercus agrifolia)* is a native evergreen species that grows 75 feet tall with spreading branches that form a round-headed crown often wider than the height. It is hardy to 25°F. The hollylike, spiny-toothed leaves are elliptic, to 3 inches long, and are shed almost completely in early spring. In cultivation the young trees grow rapidly, easily reaching 25 feet tall in ten years from a nursery transplant.

PIN OAK *(Quercus palustris)* is the most commonly used species. It has moderate to rapid growth to 70 feet tall and is easy to transplant (it has no taproots), making it popular with landscapers. It is hardy to –20°F. The pin oak has a pyramidal form: the upper branches ascend, the middle branches are horizontal, and the lower branches are drooping and pendulous. If the lower branches are removed, the next branches up the trunk will begin to droop. Plant where this characteristic will not be a problem, since it is possible to walk beneath this tree only when it is mature. The leaves are deeply cut into bristle-tipped lobes and are very glossy; they are yellow-green in spring, turning dark green, then deep scarlet red, and finally russet-brown, and many persist on the tree through the winter. The pin oak needs moist but well-drained soil and adequate room to develop. It is intolerant of alkaline conditions and will quickly develop chlorosis, an iron deficiency revealed during the growing season by yellowed leaves with green veins.

RED OAK *(Quercus rubra, Quercus borealis)* is cold tolerant to –30°F. It is one of the best oaks for use in confined soil volumes, such as along city streets, and is quick growing and easy to transplant because it has insignificant taproots. This is the most shade tolerant of all the oaks. It needs a moist soil that is well drained. Its large leaves are 12 to 20 inches long with broad, bristle-tipped lobes which are a woolly pink when they emerge, becoming pale green as they enlarge. The foliage is a rich lustrous green in summer, changing to bright red in midautumn.

SCARLET OAK *(Quercus coccinea)* is a 75-foot-tall tree at maturity, spreading as wide as it is tall. It is hardy to –10°F. This tree would doubtless be more widely used if its deep taproots did not make it so difficult to transplant; because of this rooting pattern it requires a well-drained soil and is drought tolerant. The 6-inch long, pinnately, deeply lobed, bristle-tipped leaves are a very glossy bright green in summer and turn brilliant scarlet in autumn.

WHITE OAK *(Quercus alba)* is a magnificent sturdy tree that grows over 90 feet tall, frequently spreading even wider, and is hardy to –20°F. It has a short, stocky trunk, but the somewhat open branching pattern still permits adequate light to reach shade-tolerant plants growing beneath it. Its deep taproots and deep laterals reduce competition with other plants for moisture but also make this species difficult to transplant. White oak is one of the monarchs of the forest, commonly surviving for over 300 years. Its large (to 9 inches long) obovate leaves have five to nine entire, rounded lobes. Emerging leaves are bright red to pink with silvery overtones and turn to silver-gray before they become a dull-surfaced, medium green in summer. Autumn color is variable from tree to tree, some turning burgundy and others, brown.

WILLOW OAK *(Quercus phellos)* is an unusual oak that grows 60 feet tall and is two-thirds as wide. It has a form similar to that of the pin oak, with pendulous lower branches. It is hardy to –5°F and has a shallow root system that makes it easy to transplant. The leaves, similiar to those of a willow, are narrow and pointed at both ends and are as much as 5 inches long and scarcely ½ inch wide, providing a fine, somewhat delicate texture for a tree of this size. When they emerge in spring, the leaves are yellow-green, turning green and glossy in summer, and yellow to reddish in autumn. In the Deep South they persist well into winter.

Robinia pseudoacacia
LOCUST, BLACK LOCUST

Black locust is a native North American species,
hardy to –25°F, it grows to 75 feet tall and is able to tolerate the worst sterile, dry, sandy soils that can be imagined, thanks to nitrogen-fixing bacteria present in the root nodules. The several forms available vary in shape from narrow and erect to umbrella-like. Several insects, notably the locust borer and locust twig borer, can be a problem, and the trees are subject to damage by wind and ice which breaks their brittle limbs. Black locust quickly forms a colony because of prolific root-suckering. Its wood is very rot-resistant and is often used for fence posts. The feathery, pinnately compound leaves have seven to nineteen oval leaflets, which cast a very light shade while present; the leaves appear late and drop early. Autumn color is yellow. 'Aurea' has new leaves colored yellow in spring, and 'Frisia' has bright golden yellow foliage and orange branchlets.

Sassafras albidum
SASSAFRAS

This understory tree is considered a pest by some because of its suckering habit. It quickly reaches 20 feet tall and then grows slowly to 35 to 50 feet tall, spreading about two-thirds as wide. It is hardy to –10°F. Used as a specimen tree in the open, it produces a better effect than the narrow, loose, open, and sprawly look it presents growing in groups along the forest edge. It requires a well-drained soil and will tolerate moist to dry conditions. The leaves are 3 to 7 inches long and 3 to 4 inches wide, and are simple, ovate to oblong, and either unlobed or have one or two lobes; this variety of leaves can be all on the same tree. In autumn the leaves turn to fiery tints of yellow, orange, and red. The leaves, bark, and roots are aromatic; the root bark is used for sassafras tea.

Taxus spp.
YEW

The ENGLISH YEW *(Taxus baccata)* is an evergreen conifer hardy to –5°F; it grows slowly to 30 to 60 feet tall. Sexes are separate, and only female plants have the single-seeded red berries attractive to birds. Deer are attracted to this conifer and eat the needles and young branches. The English yew is long-lived, is tolerant of some shade, and can grow in a range of soil pH. It can be sheared to form hedges or topiary. The dark, lustrous evergreen needles turn a very dark, almost blackish green in winter. 'Aurea' has a more compact growth habit, and the new foliage is golden yellow in spring, turning green as it matures; 'Repandens' has a low, spreading branch pattern resulting in a 2-foot-tall ground cover; 'Stricta' (Irish yew), discovered in Ireland in 1780, grows slowly to 20 feet tall and has a densely upright habit of growth with the needles arranged all around the twigs rather than two-ranked in a flat spray.

HYBRID YEWS *(Taxus X media)* include those between the JAPANESE YEW *(T. cuspidata)* and the ENGLISH YEW *(T. baccata)*. They have a central leader rather than the multiple leaders of the English yew. They combine the hardy qualities of the Japanese yew with the ornamental features of the English yew, being somewhat intermediate in color and texture. Like the English yew, these are attractive to deer. Some commonly available cultivars include 'Brownii', a compact, slow-growing form reaching 4 to 8 feet tall, excellent for hedges; 'Hatfieldii', more columnar and taller, reaching 10 feet tall or more, and an excellent dark green color; and 'Hicksii', narrow and upright, reaching 12 feet tall.

$\mathscr{S}$HRUBS

SHRUBS ARE WOODY PLANTS, LIKE TREES. In general they are smaller in size, although there may be overlap in scale between large shrubs and small trees at the 10- to 15-foot range. Shrubs usually have multiple branches or trunks from the ground up, whereas the majority of trees have a single trunk. Shrubs also are deciduous or evergreen. Many large trees, especially conifers, such as pines *(Pinus)*, spruces *(Picea)*, false cypress *(Chamaecyparis)*, arborvitae *(Thuja)*, and others, have slow-growing forms called dwarfs. These are included here because they are the same scale as shrubs.

Acokanthera oppositifolia
BUSHMAN'S-POISON

This slow-growing South African shrub eventually reaches 10 feet high and wide and is hardy only in frost-free areas. It needs full sun, with adequate water supplied in summer, and is wind and salt tolerant. Its lanceolate leaves are a glossy dark green to deep plum-purple; the fruits are highly poisonous.

Amorpha canescens
LEADPLANT

Native to central North America, this deciduous shrub grows to 4 feet tall. Although it is hardy to –30°F, it is often killed back to the ground over much of its range, regenerating from the roots each spring. It needs full sun and a well-drained alkaline soil, and it endures drought and hot summer climates. The leaves are pinnately compound with fifteen to forty-five elliptically oval leaflets that are covered with woolly white hairs on both sides; the leaves are silvery gray in spring, turning gray-green in summer. Leadplant is excellent when combined with other prairie natives such as liatris, milkweed, and grasses.

Aronia spp.
CHOKEBERRY

These are common native shrubs in the eastern United States. Both species have a dense, fibrous root system and transplant well. In addition, they sucker profusely and form dense colonies. They are tolerant of a range of soil conditions, wet to dry, poor to well drained; they prefer an acid pH and will accept some shade. Both are hardy to –15°F.

BLACK CHOKEBERRY *(Aronia melanocarpa)* will grow to 6 feet tall but is generally about half that height, spreading into broad thickets. The simple elliptic to obovate leaves, about 3 inches long and half as wide, are finely toothed along the margins and are reddish green in spring, turning green in summer and crimson in autumn. Black chokeberry is lovely for naturalistic plantings combined with other shrubs for fall foliage effect or with evergreens and grasses along the edge of woodlands.

RED CHOKEBERRY *(Aronia arbutifolia)* grows 6 to 12 feet tall. Its leaves are similar to those of the black chokeberry in shape but are gray with dense, short woolly hairs beneath; the leaves turn a rich, vivid orange to red in autumn and are persistent. Red chokeberry is valuable for use in a shrub border or along the edge of woodlands. Its attractive red fruits are eaten by many species of birds. 'Brilliantissima' has especially bright red berries.

Aucuba japonica
AUCUBA

This evergreen shrub grows 10 to 15 feet tall,

but it can be kept lower by pruning. Although most listings say it is hardy to 5°F, aucuba will often tolerate somewhat colder conditions, especially if sheltered from winter wind; they may, however, die back to ground level. Variegated cultivars in particular require a shady location in order to prevent foliage burn, especially in winter; they also tend to be slower growing. Aucuba prefers a soil that is high in organic matter, moist but well drained; it is drought tolerant once established. Aucuba typically has glossy, dark green leaves up to 8 inches long and 3 inches wide, with toothed margins. A number of selections have been made. Green-leaved cultivars include 'Dentata' and 'Serratifolia', which have leaves that are coarsely toothed along the margins; 'Longifolia' ('Angustifolia', 'Salicifolia'), with narrow, willowlike leaves; 'Macrophylla', which has especially large, broad leaves; and 'Viridis', which is a particularly vigorous selection. Variegated cultivars include 'Crotonifolia', with leaves heavily splashed with white; 'Fructo Albo', which is also white-variegated; 'Goldieana', with mostly yellow foliage; 'Mr. Goldstrike', with leaves heavily splashed with gold; 'Picturata' ('Aureo-maculata'), which has leaves with green edges dotted with yellow around a golden center; 'Sulphur', which has serrated green leaves with broad yellow edges; and 'Variegata', or gold-dust plant, the best-known form, which has gold-spotted, dark green leaves. Yellow-variegated forms are pleasing in a woodland setting with ferns and golden-leaved hosta; white-variegated forms suggest the use of hosta with green or glaucous leaves.

Berberis thunbergii
JAPANESE BARBERRY

This trouble-free and durable landscape plant has densely thorny branches and a tight habit of growth, which make it useful as a barrier hedge. It can be clipped to a more formal shape or allowed to grow in a looser, more billowy outline. It grows 7 feet tall, is hardy to –20°F, is drought tolerant, and adapts to almost any soil; its only drawback is that it is host to a serious black stem wheat rust, which has led to its ban in Canada and major wheat-producing regions of the United States. The small (less than 1 inch long) rhombic oval leaves turn from green to scarlet in autumn before dropping. Several forms and cultivars are available, such as 'Argenteo-marginata', which has white-margined leaves on new shoots; *atropurpurea* and its selected cultivars — 'Cardinal', 'Humber Red', 'Redbird', and 'Sheridan Red', which have deep red-purple leaves throughout the growing season if located in full sun; 'Aurea', which has bright citron yellow leaves if grown in full sun and grows more slowly than other cultivars; 'Crimson Pygmy' ('Atropurpurea Nana'), which is a low-growing dwarf selection less than 4 feet tall; and 'Rose Glow', which has leaves that are mottled green and white with rose and bronze overtones and exceptionally red new growth. 'Crimson Pygmy' is delightful in a mixed border planting of perennials and annuals with orange and chartreuse flowers, or with blue and purple flowers, and is a beautiful foil for silver foliage.

***Calluna*.** See Heaths and Heathers, pages 92-93

Chamaecyparis **spp. and cultivars**
FALSE CYPRESS

This diverse group of evergreens includes dwarf and low, slow-growing forms for use as shrubs. They grow best in soil with adequate moisture but good drainage; they also prefer moist air, so exposure to dry winds often results in winter damage. These garden-worthy trees and shrubs offer a variety of growth habits and foliage colors, and can be used as accent plants. Three species are native to North America (*C. lawsoniana, C. nootkatensis,* and *C. thyoides);* two are Japanese *(C. obtusa* and *C. pisifera).* These are all trees, but over the years numerous dwarf forms have been selected, some so tiny as to be used in a rock garden trough.

HINOKI FALSE CYPRESS **(*Chamaecyparis obtusa)*** has numerous dwarf forms for use in the rock garden or shrub border. Some attractive cultivars include 'Compacta', which is dwarf, broadly pyramidal, and very dense, slowly reaching 7 feet high and wide; 'Coralliformis', which is dwarf and has twisted branchlets that give it a coral-like appearance; 'Crippsii', which has golden yellow foliage; 'Filicoides', which grows 8 to 10 feet tall and less than half as wide and has short and frond-like branchlets, somewhat similar to a fern; 'Lycopodiodes', which is dwarf and has spirally twisted branchlets; 'Nana', which has twisted branchlets and grows slowly to 3 to 4 feet tall; 'Nana Aurea', with golden yellow new growth; 'Pygmaea Aurea', which is a small, low-growing shrub with flat, fan-shaped branchlets that are yellow-bronze in summer turning to copper-bronze in winter; 'Tetragona', which is dwarf and has four-angled branchlets; and 'Tetragona Aurea', which is golden yellow if grown in full sun.

SAWARA FALSE CYPRESS **(*Chamaecyparis pisifera)*** has three groups of cultivars: the "filifera" group, which includes those with threadlike pendant branches and a fine cord-like appearance; those with a feathery appearance; "plumosa," and "squarrosa," those with a soft, mossy appearance because their needles stand away from the stem (more than those in the filifera types). Popular cultivars include 'Boulevard', a squarrosa type that forms a steely blue pyramid, reaching 8 feet high at maturity;

'Filifera', which stays below 10 feet tall for an extended period but matures at ten times this height unless it is kept pruned; 'Filifera Aura', which is bright golden yellow, especially the new growth in full sun; 'Golden Mop', a filifera type with golden yellow foliage that grows less than 4 feet tall; 'Plumosa Compressa', a dwarf with a moundlike growth habit that reaches less than 4 feet tall and 10 feet wide with pale yellow tips to the branchlets. 'Plumosa Nana', which is low growing, dwarf, and flattened, reaching 5 feet tall by 10 feet wide; 'Snow', a squarrosa type that reaches 5 feet high and wide and has gray-green branchlets tipped with white new growth; 'Squarrosa Minima', which includes several compact forms that grow 6 inches high and wide (in five years) to 18 inches high and wider and have gray-green to dark green foliage; and 'White Pygmy', which forms a tight little bun of soft foliage with white tips.

Codiaem variegatum
CROTON

There are literally dozens of named forms of croton. The thick, glossy, somewhat leather-textured leaves may be red, crimson, purple, bronze, pink, or light and deep yellow combined with green, as well as various combinations of several colors. Young leaves are generally green and yellow, and turn red to bronze with maturity. Linear to ovate-lanceolate, the leaves are either entire or lobed; the lobes may be shallow or cut almost to the midrib. Outdoors, crotons grow 6 feet tall, most often as a single-stemmed plant; cultivated as houseplants, they grow 6 to 24 inches tall. They are often used for summer bedding, but they are absolutely frost tender and can be planted out only when the weather is settled and mild, in early June. They need full sun and rich soil.

Comptonia peregrina
SWEETFERN

This is a suckering shrub, closely related to bayberry, that grows in full sun on acid, sandy, well-drained soils that are low in fertility. It grows to 4 feet tall and is hardy to –40°F. Sweetfern would be more widely used if it were easier to propagate and transplant, and thus more available. Pot-grown plants establish most readily, and propagation is best accomplished from the tip growth of the stringy lateral suckers, which should be cut early in the spring and potted in a sand-peat mix. The linear leaves grow to almost 5 inches long and are pinnately lobed, which gives a fernlike appearance; they are aromatic when crushed or bruised. Sweetfern leaves are dark green in summer and turn tan in autumn, with many persisting through the winter. Sweetfern is excellent planted with bayberry, blueberries, juniper, and sumac to develop an attractive naturalistic plant community in harsh, dry situations.

Cornus alba 'Argenteo-marginata'
VARIEGATED SIBERIAN DOGWOOD

This is an elegant foliage form of a shrub that is generally grown for winter bark color. The Siberian dogwood grows to 9 feet tall and produces a thicket of stems with bright red bark on the younger portions. Generally it is pruned severely in the spring to force young growth closer to eye level. It is adaptable to sun or moderate shade and grows in average to moist soil; it is hardy to –35°F. The leaves are up to 5 inches long and are ovate to elliptic. 'Argenteo-marginata' ('Elegantissima') has a clean white margin to the leaves and is very effective in shady situations combined with white impatiens, hosta with white flowers, and Japanese painted fern. Other variegated forms are

'Gouchaulti', which has green leaves variegated with yellow and pink; and 'Spaethii' ('Aurea'), which has leaves broadly margined with yellow.

Corylus spp.
HAZEL, FILBERT

These small trees or large bushes are usually cultivated for their nuts. Their large, pendulous male catkins are attractive in the late-winter/early-spring landscape. The colored-leaved forms can be used as an interesting accent.

EUROPEAN HAZEL (*Corylus avellana*) is a shrub that grows to 25 feet tall; it is hardy to −25°F and tolerates poor, dry soil conditions. The leaves grow to 4 inches long and are somewhat hairy beneath. A few cultivars selected for foliage interest include 'Atropurpurea' ('Fuscorubra'), with brownish red or dull purple leaves; 'Aurea', with bright golden foliage in spring and early summer, later turning dull green; and 'Laciniata', which has pinnately dissected leaves with a fine lacy texture.

FILBERT (*Corylus maxima* 'Purpurea') is a handsome suckering shrub that grows 12 to 15 feet tall; it is hardy to −10°F and tolerates average to moist soil. The leaves are broadly ovate to oblong ovate, doubly toothed along the margins, and grow more than 5 inches long; they are colored deep purple in the cultivar 'Purpurea' when it is grown in full sun, greenish-purple with some shade.

Cotinus coggygria
SMOKEBUSH

This old-fashioned deciduous shrub or small tree is hardy to −10°F and grows to 15 feet tall. It grows best in full sun in a well-drained soil that is low in fertility. If allowed to grow unchecked, it will produce smokelike fruiting panicles in June. Some cultivars have rich purple foliage. The largest leaves, and the best color, are produced by "stooling" — pruning the shrub back to short stubs before growth begins in the spring. New wandlike shoots grow quickly to 6 feet in height. Treated in this manner the shrub will not flower. The elliptical leaves grow to 3 inches long and have excellent autumn color, turning yellow and orange to red. 'Purpureus' has purple leaves that turn greenish purple in summer; 'Notcott's Variety' and 'Royal Purple' have intense purple coloration throughout the growing season. Smokebush is delightful when planted at the back of the border with the redleaf rose combined with red, blue, or violet flowers and silver foliage.

Dodonaea viscosa
PURPLE HOP BUSH

Native from Arizona to South America and the West Indies and Old World tropics, this multistemmed shrub or small tree grows quickly to 15 feet tall and is hardy to about 10°F. The lanceolate leaves are purplish red in the cultivar 'Purpurea' (but variable in plants raised from seed), turning a deeper color in winter. 'Saratoga', produced from cuttings, is uniformly deep purple. Purple hop bush has the best color when grown in full sun; it tolerates drought or ample water, desert heat, and most any kind of soil. It can be pruned as a hedge or left unclipped as an informal screen, or it can be used in a flower bed to contrast with gray foliage and chartreuse or pale yellow flowers.

Erica. See Heaths and Heathers, pages 92-93

Eucalyptus spp.
EUCALYPTUS

These are primarily described under trees, but one that is low enough to be considered as a shrub is Kruse's mallee *(Eucalyptus kruseana)*. It grows only 5 to 8 feet tall and is hardy to 25° to 28°F. The small, round leaves are a beautiful silver-blue. This small, slow-growing shrub is suitable for specimen use.

Euonymus alatus
BURNING BUSH

This deciduous shrub grows 9 feet high by 15 feet wide and is hardy to –25°F. Suitable for hedges or screening, the dense, twiggy growth provides some concealment even when bare, and it is easily pruned to a dense, round-headed specimen or hedge. Its dark green leaves turn a vivid flaming red if grown in full sun, a soft rosy pink in shade. It looks especially good against evergreens such as yews. 'Compacta' is a dwarf variety that grows 4 to 6 feet high and wide.

Fothergilla spp.
FOTHERGILLA, WITCH-ALDER

These are some of our best native North American shrubs for autumn color. Hardy to –10°F, they are little troubled by pest or diseases, and maintenance generally consists of corrective pruning of old specimens. The leaves [similar to those of witch-hazel *(Hamamelis)*] are obovate to oblong obovate, coarsely toothed, and about 4 inches long. Although fothergilla are shade tolerant, they develop their best color in sunny locations, where the leaves turn bright yellow mottled with orange and splashed with red. However, they require mid-day shade during long, hot summers, which are typical in the southeastern United States. Although they adapt to both poorly and well-drained soils they require a moist to average soil if they are to grow well, for they are not drought tolerant. If grown in a moderate to mildly acid soil,

fothergilla makes a suitable deciduous specimen to combine with andromeda, azalea, leucothoe, mountain laurel, and other evergreen shrubs.

ALABAMA FOTHERGILLA *(Fothergilla monticola)* grows to 6 feet tall and has a somewhat suckering growth habit. Its leaves are slightly hairy on the underside.

DWARF FOTHERGILLA *(Fothergilla gardenii)* grows less than 4 feet tall and is useful for foundation plantings or other small-scale situations; it would be appropriate for use in a heath planting. Its leaves are approximately 2 inches long, smaller than other species.

LARGE FOTHERGILLA *(Fothergilla major)* grows 6 to 12 feet tall, making it useful for both specimen treatment or naturalistic plantings along a woodland boundary where it will be seen at some distance.

Griselinia lucida 'Variegata'
GRISELINIA

This New Zealand tree grows to 25 feet tall but is usually seen as a 6 to 8 foot tall shrub in California gardens. It is useful in light shade or as a container plant. The leaves, which are thick, leathery, lustrous, and ovate to oblong, grow 7 inches long; they are marked with white in the form 'Variegata'.

Hamamelis spp. and hybrids
WITCH-HAZEL

These shrubs grow in sun or light shade in moist soil. They are commonly cultivated for their ribbon-petaled flowers that appear in autumn, late winter, or early spring, depending on the species. The leaves are a lovely clear golden yellow color in autumn.

ARNOLD'S PROMISE *(Hamamelis X intermedia* 'Arnold's Promise')* grows to 15 feet tall, and is hardy to –15°F. It flowers in early spring before the appearance of the leaves, which are broadly ovate or obovate and grow to 5 inches long. The autumn color is yellow with a reddish flush. Other hybrids (x *intermedia*) with good autumn color include 'Diane', 'Jelna', and 'Ruby Glow'.

CHINESE WITCH-HAZEL *(Hamamelis mollis)* is hardy to –5°F and grows 30 feet tall in a rounded form which can be kept smaller by pruning. It has very fragrant flowers in early spring. The wavy-toothed leaves are orbicular to obovate and grow 3 to 6 inches long with gray woolly hairs on the underside; autumn color is a clear yellow.

COMMON WITCH-HAZEL *(Hamamelis virginiana)* grows 10 to 15 feet high, and taller, and has an open, vaselike habit; it is hardy to –15°F. The coarsely toothed, obovate leaves grow to 6 inches long and turn yellow to orange in autumn. This shrub flowers in early October.

Heaths and Heathers *(Erica* and *Calluna* spp. and cultivars)

These evergreen shrubs are distinguished, in part, by their foliage: *Erica* spp. have needle-like foliage, *Calluna* spp. have scalelike foliage. A heath, as defined in the dictionary, is "an extensive area of rather level, open uncultivated land, usually with poor, coarse soil, inferior drainage, and a surface rich in peat or peaty humus." This is also a definition of the conditions required by heaths and heathers. They need an acid, peaty, sandy soil that is low in fertility and is moist but well drained. If the soil is too rich or has too much moisture, heaths and heathers are prone to root rot; but drought can also be a problem, and they will grow best with a steady supply of moisture. Heaths and heathers require sunny conditions but are

prone to winter burn in cold winter regions if snow cover is lacking. A winter mulch of pine boughs, applied after the ground is frozen, is the best protection. If their foliage color is poor, apply iron sulphate or a plant food formulated for acid-loving plants in spring. Nurseries that specialize in these shrubs have a wide list of available cultivars. Heathers (and heaths) look good when grown with other low plants that like acid, sandy, peaty conditions. Dwarf blueberries, prostrate junipers, and other low-growing shrubs, as well as herbs (those that tolerate acid soil conditions), low-growing achillea and dianthus (a few can adapt to moderately acid conditions), and dwarf grasses and sedges can all be blended to create a tapestry foliage effect.

SCOTCH HEATHER, LING HEATHER *(Calluna vulgaris)* is an evergreen shrub that is hardy to –10°F or lower, especially with snow cover. The scalelike leaves may be light or dark green, chartreuse, golden yellow, silver, or bronze-purple; and often there will be a change of color in winter. 'Aurea' is golden yellow, turning russet in winter; 'Blazeaway' is golden in summer, rusty red in winter; 'Boskoop' is orange-red in summer, brownish red in winter; 'Christiana' is chartreuse in summer, yellow in winter; 'Crimson Sunset' is yellow in summer, red in winter; 'Cuprea' has golden leaves in summer, turning bronze in winter; 'Fairy' is golden yellow, turning orange in winter; 'Golden Carpet' is golden yellow in summer, bronze in winter; 'Golden Rivulet' is golden yellow, becoming coppery red in winter; 'Gold Haze' is yellow in winter and summer; 'Robert Chapman' is yellow, turning a lively red in winter; and 'Spring Torch' has bright yellow new growth and turns fiery red in winter. Silver-gray foliage is found on some cultivars: 'Anthony Davis' has silvery, somewhat hairy foliage; 'Hirsuta' is gray-tomentose; 'Silver Cloud' has attractive, somewhat hairy, silvery foliage; 'Silver Knight' has silver-gray foliage; and 'Silver Queen' has woolly, silvery foliage. Variegated foliage is less common but can be found on 'Spring Cream', which is bright green with cream-colored new growth in spring; and 'Variegata', which is partially variegated with white.

SPRING HEATH *(Erica carnea)*, a native of central and southern Europe, is hardy to -5°F and grows best with full sun, high humidity, and moderate temperatures, conditions found along the mid-Atlantic coast. Regular pruning immediately after flowering will maintain the best appearance. Hardiest cultivars are 'Springwood White', and 'Springwood Pink', named for their respective flower colors. Both have fine, dark green foliage and grow about a foot high. Some cultivars are noted for their foliage, such as 'Aurea', which has golden yellow foliage, and 'Vivellii', which changes from dark green to bronze-red in winter. The fine texture of spring heaths produces a good effect at the front of a shrub border in combination with other, more coarsely textured shrubs, such as leucothoe, evergreen azaleas, andromeda, and mountain laurel.

Helichrysum petiolatum (Gnaphalium lanatum)
LICORICE PLANT

This shrubby perennial is woody at the base and grows 2 to 4 feet high with trailing stems that reach 4 feet or more. It grows well in full sun and sandy, well-drained soil and is drought tolerant. Hardy to 25°F, it is good for garden use in mild winter areas and container or bedding use in colder regions. Its small, ovate to nearly orbicular leaves, felted with a heavy hairy covering, present a woolly white appearance. 'Limelight', is a cultivar with chartreuse foliage. Either is elegant in combination with purple to bronze foliage or flowers, as a foil to

green foliage, and with white, blue, or lavender flowers.

Hydrangea quercifolia
OAK-LEAF HYDRANGEA

This magnificent native deciduous shrub grows 3 to 6 feet tall and wider, and spreads into broad colonies by means of its stoloniferous root system. Although it is hardy to -5°F, at the colder portion of its range it will occasionally have some top damage; in severe instances it will be killed back to the ground, regenerating from the roots. The handsome leaves are large (8 to 12 inches long) and have three to seven coarsely serrated lobes, resembling those of a red oak. As they emerge in the spring the leaves are covered with woolly white hairs, which they lose and then become dark green in summer, changing to russet red or wine purple in autumn. This is one of the few woody plants to develop good color in shade.

Ilex spp. and cultivars
HOLLY

These evergreen or deciduous trees or shrubs all prefer a garden soil that is rich, moist but well drained, and somewhat acid, in a location that has sun or moderate shade. They have shallow root systems and respond well to the use of mulch, which reduces weed growth and hence the need for cultivation (and thus root disturbance). The two species listed here, both evergreen shrubs, are suitable for hedges or group plantings.

INKBERRY *(Ilex glabra)*, hardy to −15°F grows to 6 to 8 feet tall and has a moundlike habit of growth. It is often found in swampy sites in the wild and is tolerant of similar locations in cultivation. It can be severely pruned to rejuvenate it or to reduce its height. The lustrous oval leaves, 1 to 2 inches long, are dark green in summer and turn yellow-green in winter. Three cultivars are 'Compacta', which is a tight, dwarf form; 'Nigra', which has purple winter leaf color; and 'Viridis', which remains green in winter.

JAPANESE HOLLY, BOX-LEAVED HOLLY (*Ilex crenata*) is a useful evergreen shrub that is hardy to –5°F. It grows rather slowly to 20 feet tall but can be trimmed lower for use as a hedge or screen. It can grow in partial shade in the South, requiring protection from summer sun, or in full sun in the North with protection from winter wind. Mulch can be used to protect the roots from low winter temperatures as well as from drought. Its narrow, glossy leaves are less than an inch long, but the shrub has a very dense form. Japanese holly is a useful substitute where boxwood is not hardy. Selections include 'Compacta', an extremely compact dwarf form that is usually less than 4 feet tall; 'Convexa' ('Bullata'), which has convex leaves highlighted from any direction; 'Helleri', which grows very slowly, forming a compact mound with very small leaves; and 'Microphylla', which has small leaves like 'Helleri' but grows more vigorously.

Juniperus spp. and cultivars (See also under "Trees," pages 74-75.)
JUNIPER

This group provides us with some elegant coniferous shrubs for full sun and well-drained soil. These lower-growing junipers are as useful in the garden as juniper trees are.

CHINESE JUNIPER (*Juniperus chinensis*) is hardy from –25°F southward into mild winter regions, depending on the cultivar. This species offers a diversity of cultivars from tree forms to upright or spreading shrubs to small mounding forms. The needle or scalelike foliage is soft ol-ive-green to green to bluish green with little or no color change in winter. Cultivars include 'Ames', which has a compact, tightly branched pyramidal form that grows slowly to 6 feet tall and is especially well adapted to the Midwest; 'Blaauw', which grows to 4 feet tall in a dense, compact, vaselike pattern form and has blue foliage; 'Blue Point', which grows into a dense, 8-foot-tall, blue pyramid; 'Blue Vase' (Texas star juniper), a dense, blocky 3-foot by 3-foot mound with prickly blue foliage; 'Gold Coast', which grows 4 foot by 4 foot with a full, graceful branching pattern and has an excellent golden color; 'Hetzii', a silvery blue-green, vigorous, wide-spreading form that reaches 15 feet high and wide, with the branches spreading upward and outward like a fountain; 'Mint Julep', which grows into a 6-foot by 6-foot vase-shaped form with mint green foliage; 'Pfitzerana', a spreading form with graceful, arching branches that grow 10 feet high by 20 feet wide and bright to dark green foliage; 'Pfitzerana Aurea', which has bright golden yellow leaves that turn yellowish green later in the season; 'Pfitzerana Compacta', a lower-growing, more compact form that reaches 4 feet tall by 10 feet wide; 'Pfitzerana Glauca', also low-growing and compact, is blue-green in summer changing to purplish blue in winter; and 'San Jose', a very low-growing, dark sage-green form that is less than 2 feet tall but is wide spreading.

COMMON JUNIPER, OLD-FIELD JUNIPER (*Juniperus communis*) is a very cold-hardy (to –35°F), salt-tolerant species, which makes it useful for seashore and roadside situations. There are prostrate cultivars that are useful as ground covers and some with good color, including 'Aurea' and 'Aureospica', with golden yellow new growth that becomes green by the second year; and 'Compressa', which seldom grows over 2 feet tall. Var. *depressa* grows less than 4 feet tall but several times as wide; this is variable in the wild, and selected forms include 'Depressa Aurea', whose new shoots are bright golden yellow changing to dull yellow and then to deep green in the second year; and 'Erecta Glauca', which grows in a fastigiate form to 15 feet tall and has very glaucous foliage. Var. *saxatilis* 'Hornibrookii' has a compact but spreading habit, growing less than 2 feet tall by 4 feet wide; it has an attractive rugged branching pattern and deep green foliage that becomes brownish in winter.

CREEPING JUNIPER (*Juniperus horizontalis*) is extremely hardy (to −45°F) and is tolerant of seashore conditions and road salt. It grows as a procumbent, flat mat, making these junipers ideal as ground covers or for cascading over a wall. There are numerous cultivars available, including 'Bar Harbor', which grows 12 inches high by 10 feet wide and has feathery, blue foliage that turns plum purple in winter; 'Blue Chip', which grows 12 inches tall and has silvery blue foliage; 'Blue Rug' ('Wiltonii'), which grows 4 inches tall by 8 feet wide and has long, trailing branches with dense, short branchlets and an intense silver-blue foliage color; 'Douglasii', which grows 12 inches high by 10 feet wide and has rich green new growth that matures to steel blue and turns silvery purple in winter; 'Emerald Spreader', which grows 6 inches tall and has dense, feathery, bright green foliage; 'Hughes', which reaches 6 inches tall with very dense moundlike growth and has striking, silvery blue foliage; 'Plumosa', which is 18 inches high by 10 feet wide and has upright branchlets on prostrate branches, colored soft green in summer, plum purple in winter; 'Turquoise Spreader', which is 8 inches tall with dense turquoise-green foliage; and 'Yukon Belle', which grows 6 inches tall with bright silver-blue foliage and is extremely tolerant of cold.

EASTERN RED CEDAR (*Juniperus virgin-*

iana) has several shrub forms worthy of cultivation and also one prostrate cultivar that is suitable as a ground cover. The latter is 'Silver Spreader', which is only 18 inches high by 6 to 8 feet wide, with a very feathery, fine texture and silvery green needles that turn dark green on older branches. More shrublike forms include 'Gray Owl' (possibly a hybrid between *J. virginiana* 'Glauca' and *J. chinensis* 'Pfitzerana'), a silvery blue shrub that grows 5 feet high and has a wider spread; 'Kosteri', which is wide spreading but less than 4 feet high and has soft green or blue-green foliage; and 'Tripartita', a dense, spreading, dark green shrub that grows 5 feet high by 10 to 15 feet wide.

ROCKY MOUNTAIN JUNIPER (*Juniperus scopulorum*) has several useful shrub forms, including 'Blue Creeper', which grows 2 feet tall by 6 to 8 feet wide and has blue foliage that intensifies in color in cold weather; 'Silver Star', which is 3 feet high by 6 to 8 feet wide with rich, silvery gray foliage; 'Table Top Blue', a massive, flat-topped, gray shrub that grows 6 feet high by 8 feet wide; 'White's Silver King', which grows 10 inches high by 6 to 8 feet wide and has pale silvery blue foliage; and 'Winter Blue', a spreading, semiprostrate form with silver-blue foliage that retains its blue coloration in winter.

SAVIN JUNIPER (*Juniperus sabina*) is cold hardy (to −35°F) and has some interesting, lower-growing, mounding cultivars, such as 'Broadmoor', which grows to 16 inches tall by 4 feet wide, making a dense mound of bright green foliage with a feathery texture; 'Monard' ('Moor-dense'), a denser, flat-tiered form that hugs the ground and has bright green foliage; 'Tamariscifolia', a very popular cultivar that grows 2 feet tall and has bright green foliage with a feathery texture; 'Tamariscifolia New Blue', which is similar to the previous cultivar but has bluer foliage; and 'Variegata', which has variegated creamy white foliage on its branchlets.

SINGLE-SEED JUNIPER *(Juniperus squamata)* has several shrub forms; the most outstanding one is 'Blue Star', which has steely blue, prickly foliage and is a low, mounding plant that eventually reaches 3 feet high by 5 feet wide.

Kerria japonica
KERRIA

This small shrub reaches 4 to 6 feet high and has a suckering habit of growth. Hardy to –15°F it grows well in moderate shade in a moist but well-drained soil that is rich in organic matter. The oblong to ovate, doubly toothed leaves are about 2 inches long. Some renewal pruning is necessary to thin its dense, twiggy growth. Cultivars for foliage interest include 'Aureo-variegata', with leaves edged in yellow; and 'Picta' ('Argenteo-marginata'), with leaves edged in white. Watch for reversions to more vigorous, completely green leaves and prune out those branchlets. This shrub gives a fine-textured, airy effect in a shady garden and is attractive combined with white impatiens.

Lavandula angustifolia
LAVENDER

A native of the Mediterranean region, lavender has long been used in herb gardens, where it is cultivated for its fragrant flowers and gray foliage. It is hardy to –5°F but does better when protected from winter winds. It prefers a light, sandy, well-drained alkaline soil in full sun. Lavender needs to be pruned right after flowering in early summer to keep it shapely. It grows 2 to 3 feet tall and has linear semievergreen leaves more than 2 inches long but less than ½ inch wide, which are covered with a white,

hairy covering when young, turning gray-green with maturity. 'Hidcote', 'Munstead', and 'Nana' are more compact, and slow-growing.

Leucophyllum frutescens
TEXAS RANGER

This compact shrub is hardy to 15°F and grows to 8 feet tall but usually less, freely branching to form a neat, rounded shrub. Native to New Mexico, Texas, and Mexico, it is tolerant of heat, drought, and wind, as well as alkaline conditions if there is good drainage. Typical of desert plants, the leaves are small, about 1 inch long, and are covered on both sides with small hairs that give a silvery, felt-like appearance. 'Compactum' is a smaller, denser cultivar, growing to about 5 feet tall. Texas ranger is useful as an ornamental hedge, in groups, and as a specimen but is little used outside its natural range.

Leucothoe spp.
LEUCOTHOE

These elegant broad-leaved evergreen shrubs, which have a mounding habit of growth, provide good contrast to more upright shrubs such as mountain laurel and andromeda. They grow best in soils that are acid, moist but well-drained, and high in organic matter, and they are quite tolerant of heavy shade. Leucothoe is useful in foundation plantings or woodland gardens in combination with other evergreen and deciduous shrubs.

DROOPING LEUCOTHOE, LEUCOTHOE *(Leucothoe fontanesiana [catesbaei]),* hardy to –10°F, grows 3 to 6 feet tall and usually wider than high and has stoloniferous stems that aid its spread. Maintenance consists of periodically pruning out old stems at ground level. The 3- to 6-inch-long, lanceolate to oval lanceolate leaves taper to a point, and are a very glossy dark green turning red-green to maroon-purple in sunny locations. 'Rainbow' ('Girard's Rainbow') is a slower-growing cultivar with leaves splashed creamy white, pink, and green, most prominent on new growth in spring. It is easily confused with the coast leucothoe *(Leucothoe axillaris [catesbaei]),* which is hardy only to 0° to –5°F.

JAPANESE LEUCOTHOE *(Leucothoe keiskei)* is lower growing (to 3 feet tall or less) and has smaller leaves to 3 inches long; it is useful where a smaller-scale shrub is desirable, as in a heath setting. It is hardy to –5°F but should be protected from winter wind and exposure in the colder portion of its range.

SWEETBELLS *(Leucothoe racemosa)* is a deciduous shrub that grows 6 to 12 feet tall and is hardy to 0°F. The oblong to ovate leaves are 3 inches long and bright green in summer, turning to red before they separate from the plant. Sweetbells is useful for naturalistic plantings.

Lindera benzoin
SPICEBUSH

This shrub is found in swamps across the eastern United States. It is hardy to –15°F, shade tolerant, prefers soil that is acid, wet (it tolerates poor as well as average drainage), and grows to 15 feet tall and wide. The leaves, which grow to 5 inches long, are obovate, quickly tapering to a pointed tip; they are aromatic when crushed or bruised and turn a beautiful clear lemon yellow in autumn. Spicebush is one of the best choices for wet soil. Female plants have attractive red berries.

Mahonia spp. and cultivars
MAHONIA

These evergreen shrubs are related to barberry and are susceptible to wheat rust, so they should not be grown in grain-producing regions of the Midwest. The pinnately compound, glossy, deep green leaves have oblong ovate leaflets with spiny teeth reminiscent of English holly. Mahonia grow best in moist but well-drained soil high in organic matter with an acid to neutral pH; they are shade tolerant. They have an elegant winter appearance in more southern areas of use and where protected from winter burn in northern regions.

CHINESE MAHONIA *(Mahonia lomariifolia)* has the largest leaves of any mahonia, often to 20 inches long with twelve to twenty pairs of leaflets that are smaller at the base and tip but as much as 3 inches long at midleaf. It grows to 12 feet tall but is hardy only to 20°F and is thus tender over much of the United States. Very dramatic in appearance, it grows with a single stem as a young plant and produces low vertical branches as it matures.

DESERT MAHONIA *(Mahonia fremontii)* is native to southwestern desert areas of Utah and Colorado to Mexico. It is hardy to 5°F, is drought tolerant, growing in full sun or with only light shade, and is an elegant, fine-textured shrub for xeric conditions. It has many stems that grow from 3 to 9 feet tall, sometimes more, with a single pair to four pairs of leaflets, generally two to three. The thick, gray-green leaflets are about 1 inch long and have tough, sharp spines.

LEATHERLEAF MAHONIA *(Mahonia bealei)* is hardy to 0° to –5°F but does best when protected from winter wind and sunscald. It grows 10 feet tall in a similar pattern to Chinese mahonia, with strongly vertical stems and horizontally carried leaves. The 14- to 18-inch long leaves have five to eight pairs of leaflets, which are gray-green above and yellow-green beneath. The terminal leaflet may be as much as 8 inches wide. Leatherleaf mahonia is best grown in shade, except along the coastal California fog belt, where it will tolerate a sunny location. It is superb as an accent plant and in formal settings.

LONGLEAF MAHONIA, OREGON GRAPE *(Mahonia nervosa)* is native to the Pacific Northwest from British Columbia southward to northern California and Idaho; it is hardy to 0°F. Lower growing (to 2 feet tall), it has numerous underground stems and forms a thick carpet, making it a good ground cover. The 10- to 18-inch-long leaves are clustered at the tips of the stems and have three to ten pairs of thickened leaflets that are nearly 3 inches long and even more numerous teeth. These make nice, low foreground plants for taller woodland shrubs such as rhododendrons.

OREGON GRAPE HOLLY *(Mahonia aquifolium)*, native to the West Coast, is hardy to −10°F but needs protection from winter winds and sunscald in colder regions. It reaches 3 to 6 feet tall and has an erect habit of growth and spreading underground stems. The leaves are 4 to 10 inches long with five to nine pairs of 3-inch-long, lustrous green leaflets that are reddish when they first appear in the spring, turning purplish green in winter. Oregon grape holly is nice as a specimen or in massed plantings in a woodland setting with ferns and bold-textured perennials for contrast.

Myrica spp.
BAYBERRY

Bayberry *(Myrica pensylvanica)* is a very hardy native shrub (to −40°F), usually found in coastal settings. Its natural environment gives a good idea of its preference for sandy, well-drained soils and its tolerance of exposed, windy locations and salt. It grows 6 to 10 feet tall with a suckering growth habit and forms a dense mound of moderately fine texture. The oblance-olate leaves are deciduous to semievergreen, depending on winter conditions. They are aromatic, grow to 4 inches long, and are a glossy dark green, turning bronze-tan in winter or before separating from the tree. The small gray berries, borne by the female plants, are attractive to birds and are the source of bayberry wax for candles. Bayberry is excellent for use in poor soil in exposed locations in combination with junipers, sumac, and grasses.

CALIFORNIA BAYBERRY *(Myrica californica)* is a large, evergreen shrub or small tree that grows as much as 30 feet tall and is hardy to 10°F. It grows with multiple trunks whose branches are densely covered with narrow, glossy, dark green leaves that are 2 to more than 4 inches long and are glaucous beneath. It makes an attractive screen year-round since it is evergreen and can be kept pruned to a lower size. Its berries are attractive to birds.

Nandina domestica
SACRED BAMBOO

This species drops its leaves at 10°F and dies back to the ground at 5°F but will regenerate rapidly from the roots; it has been known to survive in coastal Connecticut, with occasional subzero winter temperatures. It is widely used in the Southeast and on the West Coast.

Sacred bamboo has moderate to slow growth, reaching 6 to 8 feet tall, but it can be kept pruned to half that height. The leaves are elaborately divided into numerous pointed, oval, pinnate leaflets. They go through several color changes — pinky bronze-red when first unfolding, soft light green at maturity, fiery crimson red in autumn if grown in sun and exposed to some frost, otherwise purple and bronze tints. Leaf color is better with a sunny location but sacred bamboo will grow in light shade. It is good as a hedge, in containers, and is often grown as a houseplant in cold winter areas.

Numerous cultivars are available, including 'Compacta', which grows 4 to 5 feet tall and has narrower, more numerous leaflets; and 'Moyers Red', which has a brilliant winter color. 'Nana Compacta' is also sold as 'Nana Purpurea', but the two different cultivars both grow about 12 inches tall. One has coarse, somewhat cupped, broad leaflets, purplish green in summer, reddish purple in winter, and spreads slowly; the other is green in summer, bright red in winter, and spreads quickly. 'Umpqua Chief' is a vigorous, fast-growing cultivar that is a little shorter than the type. Early in autumn, red spots develop in the leaves, enlarging and merging to a uniform bright red in winter.

Pieris japonica
JAPANESE ANDROMEDA

This elegant, evergreen shrub is useful in foundation plantings, woodland settings, or as a specimen. Native to Japan, it is more widely used than our native mountain andromeda *(Pieris floribunda)*, especially in the Northeast. It is hardy to −10°F and grows 9 feet tall, requiring the same conditions as azaleas: a soil that is high in organic matter, moist but well-drained, in a location with dappled light and protection from winter sun and drying winds. Andromeda is often attacked by lace bugs, which cause a tarnished appearance of the leaves.

A good number of cultivars have been named, some selected on the basis of flowers. The cultivars chosen for foliage effect include 'Bert Chandler', which has new growth that is salmon pink fading to cream, then white, before turning pale green in summer; 'Forest Flame' (actually a hybrid of *P. forrestii* 'Wake-

hurst' and *P. japonica)*, which has new foliage that is bright red in spring and then changes to green; 'Mountain Fire', with bright red new growth in spring; and 'Variegata', which has leaves that exhibit a narrow, creamy-white edge tinged pink in spring and a slower, more compact growth habit.

Pittosporum tobira
PITTOSPORUM

This broad, dense evergreen shrub or small tree is hardy to 15°F and grows 10 to 18 feet tall. It has leathery, lustrous, dark green leaves that are 2 to 5 inches long and blunt and rounded at the tips. 'Variegata' is a lower-growing (generally to about 5 feet high and wide) cultivar with gray-green leaves edged with white. Pittosporum is useful for seaside plantings and can be carefully pruned as a twisted-stem tree for containers; it is often used indoors in cold winter areas in office lobbies, malls, or as a houseplant.

Platycladus [Thuja] orientalis
ORIENTAL ARBORVITAE

Oriental arborvitae is hardy to 0°F and has several dwarf forms that can be used as shrubs. Most notable are 'Aureus Nana', which grows to 5 feet tall and has yellow-green foliage that turns brown in winter; 'Elegantissima', which is compact and narrowly pyramidal to 12 feet tall and has new growth that is golden in spring, turning greenish gold in summer and reddish brown in winter; 'Golden Biota', a slow-growing upright globe with gold-tipped branches in the summer, turning bright rusty-orange in late autumn; 'Minima Glauca', which grows 3 to 4 feet high and wide and has blue-green foliage; and 'Westmont', which is a slow-growing compact globe that has dark green foliage tipped with bright yellow in spring through fall.

Prunus x cistena
PURPLE-LEAVED SAND CHERRY

This is a hybrid between the sand cherry (*Prunus pumila*) and the myrobalan plum (*Prunus cerasifera* 'Atropurpurea'). In its appearance it presents the best of both parents, growing as a multistemmed shrub 6 to 10 feet tall with deep purple foliage. It is winter hardy to –35°F but often has some winter dieback in the colder portions of its range. The leaves are lanceolate, 1 to 2 inches long, and red-purple when they emerge in the spring, turning dark purple in summer.

Rhododendron spp. and hybrids (See also *Rhododendron [Azalea]* spp. and hybrids, pages 101-2.)
RHODODENDRON

For most gardeners, the difference between azaleas and rhododendrons is that rhododendrons are mostly large, leathery-leaved evergreen shrubs with larger flowers. *Rhododendron* includes everything from epiphytic Malaysian tree-dwelling species to the dwarf Lapland rhododendron (*Rhododendron lapponicum*), which is hardy to –45°F, to the rosebay rhododendron (*Rhododendron maximum*), which grows 15 to 30 feet tall and has 10-inch-long leaves, and everything in between. Rhododendrons grow best in acid, moist but well-drained soils high in organic matter, protected from drying winds and sunscald. Because of their fibrous root systems, even large specimens can be readily transplanted. However, root disturbance through cultivation should be avoided; they are best maintained with an organic mulch which will also help reduce fluctuations of soil moisture. Breeding and selection has almost entirely been based on flower form and color. In cold weather, many will curl their leaves to reduce transpiration losses; these "cigars" are not particularly appealing, making the viewer also feel chilly. Nonetheless, some rhododendrons are quite useful for foliage effect.

CAROLINA RHODODENDRON (*Rhododendron carolinianum*) grows 3 to 6 feet tall as a broad, moundlike shrub and is hardy to –5°F. The elliptic, 3-inch-long leaves are medium green above and have rusty scales on the underside. It grows best in moderate shade, protecting it from sunscald in summer, but flowering is reduced in heavy shade.

CATAWBA RHODODENDRON (*Rhododendron catawbiense*) is a cold-tolerant (to –25°F), spreading, evergreen shrub that grows 6 to 12 feet tall or more. The glossy, dark green, elliptic to obovate leaves grow up to 6 inches long and make a good screen, especially when the shrub is young; it may become more open as it matures, unless it is pruned. This species is the parent of a number of cultivars and hybrids.

Rhododendron impeditum, which has no common name, is hardy to –10°F. This shrub grows 18 inches tall as a dwarf, twiggy cushion. It has gray-blue-green, elliptic to ovate leaves that are less than an inch long and are densely covered with small, thin, dry ("scurfy") scales on both sides. It has a beautiful, fine texture and is useful in rock gardens or in a heath situation, but it needs good drainage to avoid root rot. *Rhododendron fastigiatum*, which is similar but has even smaller leaves, is a parent [with the Carolina rhododendron (*Rhododendron carolinianum*) of two excellent hybrids: 'Purple Gem' and 'Ramapo', which grow to less than 3 feet tall and have neat, small leaves and a compact, moundlike habit of growth.

ROSEBAY RHODODENDRON (*Rhododendron maximum*) grows 15 to 30 feet tall and has oblong leaves that are 10 inches long by 2 inches wide and are glossy dark green above with a light coating of rusty hairs on the underside. This is a good background or screening shrub.

SMIRNOW RHODODENDRON *(Rhododendron smirnowii),* is hardy to –10°F and grows to 10 feet tall. It grows and flowers best with moderate summer shade and protection from winter burn; and it tolerates full shade but will have reduced flowering. The 6-inch-long leaves are covered with white felty hairs as they emerge in the spring, and, with maturity, become smooth, glossy, dark green above and densely rusty brown and woolly beneath. This species is attractive as a specimen plant or combined with small conifers and deciduous shrubs.

WILSON RHODODENDRON *(Rhododendron* X *laetevirens)* is a hybrid between the Carolina rhododendron *(Rhododendron carolinianum)* and the alpine rose *(Rhododendron ferrugineum).* This shrub is a 4-foot-tall, hardy (to –15°F), compact, dense mound of bright green, evergreen leaves that are over 3 inches long. It is useful in a foundation planting, rock garden, or heath situation.

YAKU-SHIMA RHODODENDRON *(Rhododendron yakusimanum)* is hardy to –5°F and in ten years grows as a compact shrub less than 4 feet tall, forming a broad mound. The lustrous, dark green leaves are covered with buff-tan hairs when they emerge in the spring and then mature to 3 inches long with very heavy, buff-colored, feltlike covering on the underside.

Rhododendron [Azalea] **spp. and hybrids** (See also *Rhododendron* spp. and hybrids, pages 100-101.)
AZALEA

This group includes an incredible range of ev-ergreen and deciduous shrubs. Azaleas are woodland plants with a fibrous, shallow root system. They require a moist soil that is high in organic matter so it does not dry out. Provide a mulch year-round to reduce water loss and to lessen root disturbance by cultivation and weeding. Azaleas require an acid soil; they become chlorotic under alkaline conditions. As woodland plants, they grow best with high dappled shade, like that found under oaks. The following are some deciduous species that display attractive fall color:

ALBRECHT AZALEA *(Rhododendron Albrechtii)* is a Japanese species that grows to 5 feet tall and is hardy to –10°F. Its obovate to oblong leaves are nearly 5 inches long and grow in clusters of five toward the ends of the branches; the leaves turn yellow in autumn. The flowers are a clear rose pink.

PINK-SHELL AZALEA *(Rhododendron vaseyi)* is a delightful native azalea that grows to 15 feet tall and is hardy to –10°F. It has elliptic to oblong leaves up to 5 inches long that turn light crimson red to purple in autumn. This species tolerates moist soils along a pond or stream bank. The flower color is variable from medium to light pink or white.

ROYAL AZALEA *(Rhododendron schlippenbachii)*, a beautiful large azalea from Japan, Korea, and Manchuria, grows up to 10 feet tall and wide and is hardy to –10°F. It has rather large (to 5 inches long) obovate to rhombic leaves in whorls of five at the ends of the branches; the leaves turn yellow to orange-red to crimson in autumn. The flowers are large and pale to rose pink lightly marked with reddish brown spots.

SWAMP AZALEA *(Rhododendron viscosum)* is an attractive species that grows 9 to 12 feet tall and is hardy to –20°F. It has narrow, obovate to oblong ovate leaves that are less than 3 inches long and turn yellowish orange to maroon purple in autumn. It is very tolerant of wet soils, as might be expected from the common name. The flowers are white, sometimes flushed with pink, and are very fragrant; they appear in early to midsummer.

SWEET AZALEA *(Rhododendron arborescens),* a counterpart of the swamp azalea, grows in the mountains of Appalachia — from Pennsylvania to northern Alabama. It grows 9 feet tall or more and is wide-spreading; it is hardy to −15°F. The elliptic to obovate leaves are 3 inches long and turn dark glossy red to purple in autumn. The white flowers are very fragrant (heliotrope scented) and bloom in early summer.

Rhus spp.
SUMAC

This group is excellent for dry, poor soil locations in full sun. Even though poison ivy *(Rhus radicans)* and poison oak *(Rhus toxicodendron)* cause a contact dermatitis in sensitive individuals, the other sumacs do not trigger the same allergic reaction. Sumacs are valuable for their delicate, pinnately compound foliage and exceptionally good scarlet to red autumn color. They are best used in a naturalistic planting with other drought-tolerant plants such as junipers, bayberry, yucca, and grasses.

AFRICAN SUMAC *(Rhus lancea)* is an evergreen sumac that is hardy to 12°F and grows to 25 feet tall with an open, airy, spreading habit of growth. It can be grown as a multistemmed large shrub or can be trained to a single trunk for a more treelike appearance. It has three willowlike leaflets that grow to 5 inches long. It is tolerant of heat and drought.

FRAGRANT SUMAC *(Rhus aromatica)* is a quick-growing shrub that is 3 to 6 feet tall and forms a wide-spreading colony by means of suckers. It is hardy to −30°F. The aromatic foliage has three coarsely toothed, ovate leaflets that grow to 3 inches long. 'Laciniata' has narrower, deeply lobed leaflets; 'Low Grow' matures at 2 feet tall.

SHINING SUMAC *(Rhus copallina)* is hardy to −15°F and grows to 20 feet tall, generally less. The pinnately compound leaves have nine to twenty-one shiny leaflets that grow up to 4 inches long and have a distinctive winged rachis between the segments. Autumn color is a brilliant scarlet to wine purple.

SMOOTH SUMAC *(Rhus glabra)* is a large shrub or small tree that grows 10 to 20 feet tall and is hardy to −40°F. The leaves have eleven to twenty-five toothed, oblong leaflets that grow up to 5 inches long and are green above and whitish beneath, turning a brilliant red in autumn. Smooth sumac is tolerant of heat and drought. 'Flavescens' has yellow foliage, rather than red, in autumn; and 'Laciniata' has slashed, deeply cut leaflets that give a fernlike appearance.

STAGHORN SUMAC *(Rhus typhina),* a large shrub or small tree that grows 15 to 30 feet tall, is hardy to −35°F. The common name refers to the velvety hairs on new growth, reminiscent of the velvet on a stag's antlers. The leaves have eleven to thirty-one toothed leaflets that grow to 5 inches long, are deep green above and pale on the underside, and turn orange to scarlet in autumn. 'Dissecta' has leaflets that are deeply divided into numerous slender segments; 'Laciniata' is densely pubescent, with leaflets that are slashed into narrow, pointed lobes. Staghorn sumac is excellent planted with evergreens, which accentuate its fall color.

Ribes spp.
CURRANT

These shrubs were once commonly cultivated for their fruit. As an alternate host for white pine blister rust, they have been banned from areas where white pine is an important timber crop. If there are no five-needled pines growing within 500 feet of the property, and if there are no restrictions on their use, then currants are attractive shrubs to plant; in addition, some species have fragrant flowers.

CLOVE CURRANT, BUFFALO CURRANT **(Ribes odoratum)**, native from South Dakota and Minnesota southward to Texas and Arkansas, is quite cold tolerant (to −30°F) and grows to 6 feet tall. Its simple leaves have three to five deeply palmate lobes and in autumn change to scarlet red and then to deep purple before they fall. It has fragrant yellow flowers and fruit that is attractive to birds. The golden currant, *Ribes aureum,* is very similar.

WINTER CURRANT **(Ribes sanguineum)** is native to the West Coast, from British Columbia to California. Hardy to 0°F it grows 6 to 12 feet tall and has maplelike leaves that are 2 to 4 inches wide. It grows best in sun to light shade in an average soil that does not dry out. One cultivar, 'Brocklebankii', is listed as having yellow foliage; most selections, however, are based on flower effect rather than on foliage.

Rosa spp.
ROSE

These shrubs, like rhododendrons, are cultivated largely for their flowers, but a few also have lovely medium-textured pinnate foliage. Shrub roses are less prone to pests and diseases, and they are far more natural looking than highly pruned hybrid tea roses. These characteristics enable shrub roses to be integrated with other shrubs or with perennials in the mixed border. Grow them in full sun.

PRAIRIE ROSE **(Rosa setigera)**, hardy to −15°F, is a vigorous species that grows to 6 feet tall or occasionally grows like a vine up to 20 feet tall, using a tree for support. This species is late flowering (midsummer); the foliage is deep green in summer and turns yellow, orange, and scarlet red to purple in autumn. Prairie rose needs plenty of room to spread out its canes.

REDLEAF ROSE **(Rosa rubrifolia [glauca])** has lovely fine-textured foliage that is a beautiful bluish green flushed with dark red. This species is very cold tolerant (hardy to −40°F) and grows to 6 feet tall or more.

SALT-SPRAY ROSE, SEA TOMATO **(Rosa rugosa)** is a very hardy rose (to −40°F) with a suckering habit of growth; it is salt tolerant and is able to grow in sandy, well-drained soils. Growing to 6 feet tall, it can be clipped to form a dense, thorny hedge. The wrinkled foliage is an attractive dark green, turning orange in late autumn before the leaves separate from the shrub.

SHINING ROSE **(Rosa nitida)** is low-growing (to less than 2 feet tall) and is hardy to −25°F. The glossy, dark green leaves turn red in autumn.

SWEETBRIAR ROSE **(Rosa eglanteria)** is noted for its fragrant foliage: it has an applelike odor that is noticeable when it is bruised or after a rainstorm. It is hardy to −5°F and grows to 6 feet tall but can be pruned lower.

VIRGINIA ROSE **(Rosa virginiana)** is hardy to −25°F and grows 6 feet tall. The leaves are a lustrous dark green, turning orange to scarlet in autumn.

Rubus odoratus
THIMBLEBERRY

This rangy shrub has arching branches 3 to 6 feet long that often sucker to form large colonies as much as 12 feet across; it is hardy to −25°F. The large, maplelike leaves are broad-ovate or cordate, 6 inches across, with three to five palmate lobes; the leaves turn pale yellow before they drop in autumn. Thimbleberry grows best in partial shade and a moist but well-drained soil where summers are not too hot. It is good for informal woodland plantings with viburnum, spicebush, and ferns.

Salix spp.
WILLOW

The name "willow" commonly brings to mind either large trees for pond-side plantings or pussy-willows cut for indoor decoration in spring. A few species have attractive foliage and are low enough in growth to be called shrubs. They need full sun and prefer moist soil.

CREEPING WILLOW *(Salix repens)* is a low shrub with procumbent branches that grows to 3 feet tall and is hardy to –15°F. The ovate-elliptic leaves grow to over 1 inch long and are gray-green above, with silky white hairs on the underside. Var. *argentea* is densely white woolly on both the upper and the lower leaf surfaces. Creeping willow grows best in wet places in regions with cool summers.

NET-LEAVED WILLOW *(Salix reticulata)* is a low-growing, prostrate shrub whose branches root where they come in contact with the ground. It has elliptic to orbicular, finely wrinkled, netted leaves that are dark glossy green above and pale silvery on the underside. Native to Arctic and Antarctic regions, it is hardy to below –50°F, and grows best in regions with cool summers.

WOOLLY WILLOW *(Salix lanata)* is a compact, widely spreading shrub that grows 4 feet tall and is hardy to –30°F. It grows naturally in gravelly stream banks and wet meadows and requires a moist soil in cultivation. The elliptic to oblong-ovate leaves are almost 3 inches long and have an excellent gray color. Both the leaves and branchlets are covered with woolly hairs.

Salvia spp. and cultivars (See also under "Perennials," page 157.)
SAGE

This group covers a broad spectrum of annuals, perennials, and shrubs. Sage grows in open, sunny situations, usually in dry or stony sites. Some are grown for flowering effect, and others as foliage plants.

BLUE SAGE *(Salvia clevelandii)* is an aromatic shrub that grows to 3 feet tall and has gray-green leaves that are over an inch long. It is hardy to 20°F and is native to the San Diego County chaparral community. It should be pruned at the start of the rainy season for more compact growth and better appearance.

COMMON SAGE, GARDEN SAGE *(Salvia officinalis)* is grown in herb gardens for its use in seasoning. It grows to 2 feet tall as a wide bush and has aromatic, narrow, pebbly textured, gray-green leaves that are 1 to 2 inches long. It should be pruned for shapeliness and rejuvenation after flowering, and it needs to be replaced every four to five years. Cultivars include 'Icterina', which has leaves edged chartreuse-yellow with a fresh green center; 'Purpurascens' and 'Purpurea', which have leaves flushed reddish purple; 'Tricolor', which has white-margined leaves tipped with reddish purple. It can be used in herb garden designs or as a small shrub for foliage effect in a sunny flower garden with well-drained, dry soil.

MEXICAN BUSH SAGE *(Salvia leucantha)* grows 2 to 4 feet tall and wide and has woolly white stems and gray crenate leaves that are 2 to 4 inches long. It is hardy to 20°F. Old stems should be pruned out at the base. This shrub is good for xeric landscapes, combined with succulents and other drought-tolerant plants.

PURPLE SAGE *(Salvia leucophylla)* grows to 5 feet tall and has off-white hairs on its stems and oblong gray leaves that are less than an inch to over 2 inches long. It is hardy to 20°F. This is an evergreen shrub, but its leaves may drop in times of drought.

Sambucus spp. and cultivars
ELDERBERRY

These rather loose-growing shrubs are better suited to informal use. Severe pruning, or stooling, will result in denser, more compact growth. They are excellent for moist to wet soils, and all species have berries that are highly attractive to birds. Species with blue-black fruits are edible by humans, but red-fruited species are not.

AMERICAN ELDERBERRY *(Sambucus canadensis)* is hardy to −25°F, grows to 12 feet tall, and is found in the wild growing on pond and stream banks but will tolerate drier sites under cultivation. It has seven or more lanceolate, pinnately arranged leaflets, which give it a somewhat coarse texture. Cultivars selected for foliage effect include 'Aurea', with intensely golden leaves and red fruit; and 'Acutiloba', with leaflets that are deeply divided into many slender segments, giving it a very lacy appearance.

EUROPEAN ELDER *(Sambucus nigra)* grows to 20 feet tall and is hardy to −25°F. It is a rangy plant that requires pruning to keep it more compact. Cultivars selected for foliage effect include 'Albo-variegata', which has leaves splashed with white; 'Argentea', with leaves that are mostly white; 'Aurea', with golden yellow leaves; 'Aureo-marginata', which has leaves that are edged in creamy yellow; and 'Laciniata', with deeply and regularly dissected leaflets.

Santolina chamaecyparissus
LAVENDER-COTTON

This is an aromatic, many-branched evergreen shrub that grows 2 feet tall; it is hardy to −5°F but is frequently winter damaged. It grows best in full sun in a sandy, well-drained soil and can be used as a low-clipped hedge along a walk or in an herb garden. Lavender-cotton should be pruned in early spring to remove winter-burned portions and to shape it into a low hedge. Its fine, pinnately divided, silver-gray leaves give the shrub a coral-like appearance.

Stephanandra incisa
STEPHANANDRA, CUT-LEAF STEPHANANDRA

This deciduous shrub has a dense, twiggy, arching moundlike form and grows 6 to 8 feet tall; the ovate, deeply lobed leaves are about 2 inches long. It is hardy to −10°F and is shade tolerant, but it has a better appearance when it has some direct sunlight. It grows well in moist but well-drained soil and is good as a tall ground cover or for planting on a bank. Branches root at the tips where they touch the ground. Stephanandra has a fine texture and an autumn color of yellow if grown in shade, reddish in sunny locations. 'Crispa' is a low-growing form to 3 feet tall.

Tamarix spp.
TAMARIX

These deciduous shrubs are unequaled in their resistance to drought, wind, and salt levels toxic to many other plants; they are ideal for use in desert areas or coastal situations. They should be transplanted at a relatively small size because their taproots make the more mature specimens difficult to handle. The leaves are very reduced and scalelike, as might be expected as an adaptation to drought. Additionally, they have glands that secrete salt, another valuable adaptation for desert and seacoast. They provide a feathery, very fine texture under harsh conditions, turning from green or blue-green to yellow before they drop in autumn.

KASHGAR TAMARIX *(Tamarix hispida)* is a smaller shrub, usually growing to 4 feet high, but it can be taller; it is hardy to –10°F. The twigs and leaves are covered with minute hairs, presenting a silvery appearance.

ODESSA TAMARIX *(Tamarix ramosissima [odessana, pentandra])* is a shrub or small tree that grows 6 to 15 feet tall and is hardy to –15°F. If it is pruned hard in early spring, it will maintain a denser habit but otherwise becomes bare and open at the base; pruning will also control height. A line of Odessa tamarix can be used as a windbreak or hedge. The very fine, minute leaves give a feathery texture, changing from blue-green in summer to beige in autumn.

SALT CEDAR *(Tamarix chinensis)* is best pruned heavily in early spring to provide thicker growth that is more suitable for a windbreak and to maintain its height at 6 to 12 feet: unpruned, it can reach 20 to 30 feet and will be more open in habit. The branches are wandlike and flexible. It is hardy to –5°F. It can be invasive in the arid Southwest.

Tetrapanax papyriferus
CHINESE RICE-PAPER PLANT

This bold-foliage, evergreen shrub does well in mild climates. Although foliage is badly damaged at temperatures below 25°F, the plant will often recover, sending up new growth from the roots. It is often invasive, growing as a multi-stemmed, suckering clump; disturbance around the roots often stimulates additional sucker formation. This plant will quickly grow 10 to 15 feet tall. It has deeply cut, five- to seven-lobed leaves, 1 to 2 feet wide; the branches and young leaves are covered with a soft, white, felty down, which persists on the underside of the mature gray-green leaves. The pith of this plant is peeled and unrolled to create rice paper. Chinese rice-paper plant does best in shade, especially when young, as immature plants can sunburn; midday shade is necessary in regions with hot summers. As might be expected, the large leaves can be readily damaged by strong winds. Use this for luxuriant, tropical foliage effects in combination with aucuba, bamboos, and rodgersia.

Thuja occidentalis
AMERICAN ARBORVITAE, EASTERN WHITE CEDAR

American arborvitae is an extremely hardy (to –35°F) native evergreen tree that grows to 60 feet tall. There are, however, a number of dwarf and slow-growing forms available that fit more readily into the "shrub" category. These forms, a little more tender than the tree, are hardy to –20° to –25°F. They require a rich, moist soil that does not dry out. Also, they do poorly in areas with hot, dry summers. There are suitable cultivars for specimen use, to be clipped as a hedge or for screening. In the colder portions of their range, winter burn can be a problem in exposed areas, as can snow and ice damage in those cultivars lacking a strong central leader. 'Aurea' is a bushy cultivar with deep golden needles; 'Ellwangerana Aurea' is a dwarf, broadly pyramidal form that has golden foliage when exposed to full sun and turns bronze in winter; 'Ericoides', 'Froebelii', 'Pumila', 'Pygmaea,' and 'Reidii' are all very dwarf and have green foliage; 'Globosa' is a dense, dark green globe that grows slowly to 3 feet high by 4 feet wide; 'Lutea' is a tall, narrowly pyramidal form with bright golden foliage in spring and early summer; 'Ohlendorfii' is a slow-growing form with both juvenile and mature foliage and is very distinctive in appearance; 'Rheingold' ('Improved Ellwangeriana Aurea') is a tightly globe-shaped, slow-growing, small shrub with rich golden yellow needles that turn copper-gold in winter; 'Smaragd' is emerald green, slow-growing, and compact; 'Umbraculifera' is flat-topped at maturity, reaching 4 feet high by 4 feet wide; 'Watnong Gold' has a broad form and bright yellow foliage in summer, later than some of the other golden forms (all the golden forms are enhanced when planted near dark green conifers).

Thuja orientalis. See *Platycladus orientalis,* pages 99-100.

Vaccinium spp.
BLUEBERRY

This group is more commonly cultivated as fruit-producing shrubs than as ornamentals, although unless caged or protected in some manner, birds will benefit more from the harvest than the gardener. Blueberries grow best with full sun in an acid, peaty, sandy, well-drained soil low in fertility; they are subject to chlorosis (iron deficiency) if the soil pH is alkaline. Most are deciduous; a few are evergreen. Some are suitable for naturalistic plantings, and others are diminutive and creeping and can be used as a ground cover.

BOX BLUEBERRY ***(Vaccinium ovatum)*** is an evergreen species that grows to 10 feet tall in shade, more compact in sunny situations; it is hardy to 5°F. The lustrous, dark green leaves are ovate with a serrate margin and grow just over an inch long. This species is most useful on the West Coast and is used for cut greens in the florist industry.

COMMON DEERBERRY ***(Vaccinium stamineum)*** is a deciduous species that grows 7 to 12 feet tall and has a similar spread; it is hardy to –5°F. The oval to oblong obovate leaves are

up to 4 inches long, smooth above, whitened on the underside, and medium green in summer, turning scarlet red to maroon purple in autumn.

HIGHBUSH BLUEBERRY ***(Vaccinium corymbosum)*** is the species that provides the blueberries of commerce. It grows 7 to 12 feet tall with a similar spread and forms a dense twiggy mass, which can be readily shaped by pruning. Taller specimens can be planted in a mass and pruned to reveal the trunks, forming a coppice; shade-tolerant perennials can be planted with them. This species is also shade-tolerant, but fall color will not be as intense. When grown in full sun, its lustrous, dark green, oval lanceolate leaves have good autumn color, turning yellow, orange, and red to maroon-purple. It is hardy to –25°F.

LOWBUSH BLUEBERRY ***(Vaccinium angustifolium)*** is a low-growing shrub (to 2 or 3 feet tall) with simple, elliptic, lustrous dark green leaves that give a fine texture. It is extremely hardy (to –45°F). If growth becomes loose and open, the shrub can be cut back hard in early spring and will regenerate as a denser, more twiggy mass. It is useful as a ground cover and provides excellent contrast with evergreens for autumn display: the leaves turn scarlet red before dropping in mid- to late September.

Viburnum spp.
VIBURNUM

These shrubs or small trees are very popular, due in part to their diversity. They are deciduous or evergreen and are shade tolerant but grow well in sunny locations. Most prefer a moist but well-drained soil, although they are adaptable to soils that dry out occasionally. They often have attractive flowers and fruit, and important for our consideration, most have excellent foliage, forming dense shrubs suitable for screening or specimen use. Some of the deciduous species have excellent autumn coloration.

ARROWWOOD *(Viburnum dentatum)* is a deciduous species that grows to 15 feet tall, with many stems from the base forming a thicket. It is hardy to −40°F and is shade tolerant. The leaves, which grow to 3 inches long, are glossy, orbicular to ovate, coarsely toothed, and have prominent veins. In autumn the leaves turn bright red to maroon-purple before dropping late in the season. Arrowwood is good for naturalistic woodland plantings in sun or shade and moist or dry soil.

BLACK HAW *(Viburnum prunifolium)* grows 15 feet tall and wide and is hardy to −30°F. It can be grown either as a multi-stemmed shrub or trained as a small tree. The finely toothed leaves are ovate or broadly elliptic, up to 3 inches long, and turn scarlet red to purple in autumn before they drop. It grows best with at least part-day sun.

DAVID VIBURNUM *(Viburnum davidii)* is an evergreen shrub that grows 3 to 4 feet tall and is hardy to 5°F. The leaves are up to nearly 6 inches long and are conspicuously deeply creased or pleated along the three main veins from base to tip. This species needs partial shade, where it combines beautifully with azaleas, leucothoe, and ferns.

HOBBLEBUSH *(Viburnum alnifolium)* grows to 6 to 12 feet tall and nearly as wide and has a leggy, open habit; it is hardy to −30°F. The finely toothed, broadly ovate leaves with deep-set veins have woolly hairs beneath, which are rust-colored in spring and then become paler. In autumn the leaves turn orange to claret red and maroon-purple.

Hobblebush is good for moist and moderate to deeply shaded woodland sites. In less dense shade, it can be combined with swamp azalea, elderberry, and other shrubs that are tolerant of moist soil for an attractive naturalistic display.

JAPANESE VIBURNUM *(Viburnum japonicum)* is an evergreen species that grows 6 to 15 feet high in an upright manner and is hardy to 5°F. The ovate leaves are slightly toothed above the middle, leathery in texture with a glossy upper surface, and grow to 6 inches long. It is a suitable shrub for background or screening purposes and grows best with some shade in hot summer areas.

LEATHERLEAF VIBURNUM *(Viburnum rhytidophyllum)* grows in a rather narrow and upright manner to 10 feet tall and is hardy to −5°F if protected from wind damage. In the colder portions of its range it may be semievergreen. The ovate-oblong evergreen leaves grow 4 to 8 inches long and 2 inches wide and are glossy and very wrinkled on the upper surface with heavy feltlike covering on the lower surface. This shrub is semievergreen in colder regions. Leatherleaf virburnum has been bred with two other species to form two hybrids: with *Viburnum buddleifolium* to create V. x *rhytidocarpum,* a deciduous shrub that is gray-woolly on the underside of its leaves; and with *Viburnum lantana* to create *V. rhytidophylloides* 'Willowwood', which has broader, less wrinkled leaves that are more reliably evergreen than the leatherleaf viburnum, and holds its foliage until severe cold arrives in winter.

LINDEN VIBURNUM *(Viburnum dilatatum)* is a broad and compact shrub that grows to 9 feet tall and is hardy to −10°F. The coarsely toothed, ovate or orbicular, gray-green leaves grow 5 inches long and turn russet-red before they drop. Cultivars include 'Catskill', a smaller shrub that grows to 5 feet tall and 8 feet wide and has smaller leaves that turn yellow, orange, and red in autumn; and 'Iroquois', which is similar to the type species in height and spread, growing 8 feet high by 10 feet wide, with larger leaves and good fall color.

MAPLE-LEAF VIBURNUM *(Viburnum aceri-folium)* grows to 6 feet tall and is hardy to –30°F. The simple, palmately three-lobed leaves are similar to those of a maple (hence its common name). The coarsely toothed leaves grow to 5 inches long and turn yellow, pink to crimson red, and then purplish in autumn before they separate from the shrub. This species is good for moderate to heavy shade, growing poorly in sun, and is attractive with spicebush.

NANNYBERRY *(Viburnum lentago)* can grow as much as 30 feet high, and often the branches will arch over and root at the tips. It can be trained to a more treelike form or grown as a bulky shrub. It is hardy to –40°F. The glossy, finely toothed, ovate leaves grow to 4 inches long and have petioles with distinctive wavy margins; the leaves turn purplish red in autumn before they drop. Nannyberry is useful in woodland plantings or in sunny locations.

SIEBOLD'S VIBURNUM *(Viburnum sieboldii)* grows to 15 feet tall and is hardy to –15°F. The coarsely toothed, elliptic to obovate leaves are pale beneath, leathery, glossy, and wrinkled on the upper surface; they grow 3 to 6 inches long and turn red in autumn before they fall.

WAYFARING TREE *(Viburnum lantana)* grows to 15 feet tall and is hardy to –30°F. This is one of the few species that will tolerate a drier site. The gray-green, finely toothed, ovate leaves are somewhat hairy on both sides and have a wrinkled, leathery appearance; they grow to 5 inches long and turn red in autumn before they drop. 'Mohican' is smaller, growing to 6 feet high by 8 feet wide; 'Rugosum' is a cultivar with larger, more wrinkled leaves.

Weigela florida
WEIGELA

This old-fashioned shrub grows to 9 feet tall and is hardy to –10°F. It is rangy and awkward in appearance unless pruned. It grows well in full sun in a moist but well-drained soil. The leaves are elliptic to obovate and grow 4 inches long. Modern hybrids have larger flowers, but there are selections of the species with attractive foliage. 'Foliis-purpureis' is dwarf in stature, growing only 4 feet tall as a dense, round globe; it has purplish foliage in spring and becomes greener in summer. 'Variegata' grows to 4 feet tall and has green leaves with either a pale yellow or creamy white edge; the pink flowers clash with the foliage and so its appearance is better when out of bloom.

Zauschneria cana
CALIFORNIA FUSCHIA

This is more accurately described as subshrub, since it is woody only at the base and grows 1 to 2 feet tall. Hardy to 15°F, it loses its small, narrow, gray leaves in the colder portion of its range but is evergreen in mild winter areas. Tolerant of hot, dry summers, it needs full sun and good drainage to grow well. It has a somewhat invasive growth habit by spreading roots and re-seeding, so its suggested use is in informal, naturalistic plantings.

INES

VINES AS FOLIAGE PLANTS ENHANCE the garden's appearance with their unique style of growth. They can provide summer shade, screen an unwanted view, cover an unsightly fence, enhance a building, clothe a tree or a tree stump, and add autumn color or evergreen winter interest. The pleasurable chore is sorting through the possibilities to make a selection for a specific place and purpose.

Vines are plants that are unable to hold themselves erect, like shrubs or trees, but have trailing stems instead. Many woody climbers, called *lianas*, are found in tropical rain forests. A number of vines grow in temperate regions, but in areas with severe winters vines become less common. Climbers and vines may vary from shrubs with weak stems such as the so-called "climbing" roses, which use a woody support such as a tree or a trellis. The rose has no means of attaching itself to a support, so it scrambles through the tree, using the framework of branches to hold it in place, or in cultivation, it relies on the gardener to tie it into place. True vines tie themselves to their support by one of three methods: They may have modified leaves or stems called tendrils, which twine around the branches of the supporting plant or trellis, as does a clematis; they may have adventitious roots along the stem, which fasten the vine to a tree trunk or masonry wall, like ivy; or the vine may twine itself around the foundation plant or post, as does bittersweet. In the garden our tendency is to use vines on an artificial support such as a fence, arbor, trellis, or wall. Vines are very effective if used in this manner, but they can also look wonderful when grown as they would in nature, climbing through a tree or shrub; be careful, though, that the vine is not so vigorous as to choke its host. Kudzu *(Pueraria lobata)* is facetiously referred to as "the vine that ate the South." Introduced by the United States Department of Agriculture as a forage crop and for erosion control, this vine will not quite overgrow cows at pasture, but its rampant, rapid growth to 60 feet will cover houses. It is, as always, a matter of choosing a plant and selecting its location. Virginia creeper *(Parthenocissus quinquefolia),* can reach 50 feet in length and so festoon an eastern red cedar *(Juniperus virginiana)* as to cause its eventual death. Correctly placed and used on a fence or wall or trailing over an embankment, its flaming autumn color is quite distinguished.

Actinidia kolomikta
KOLOMIKTA ACTINIDIA

This twining vine grows 15 to 20 feet long and is hardy to –15°F. It grows in sun or light shade and needs a sturdy trellis, arbor, or fence for support. The leaves are heart-shaped and grow to 6 inches long. It is wonderfully variegated with a sizable white and pink to rose-red blotch at the end of the leaf, and some leaves are all white. Male plants are especially variegated.

Akebia quinata
FIVE-LEAF AKEBIA

This dainty twining vine grows quickly to 30 feet long and needs some pruning so it does not become a nuisance by virtue of its speedy growth. Once established it can be cut back to the ground and will quickly regenerate. The palmately compound leaves have five leaflets that are 2 to 3 inches long; they are semievergreen, persisting well into winter. Hardy to –25°F, this vine is an excellent choice for covering a chain-link fence, trellis, or other suitable support in sun or light shade.

Aristolochia durior [macrophylla]
DUTCHMAN'S-PIPE

This deciduous woody climber has twining stems and can reach 30 feet long. It is hardy to −15°F and grows in full sun to moderate shade. The simple leaves are kidney-shaped to orbicular, aromatic when crushed, and grow as much as a foot long. The Dutchman's-pipe takes its name from its wonderfully bizarre, pipe-shaped, yellow-green flowers. Dutchman's-pipe was once a popular, quick-growing vine for screening and shading porches in summer because the leaves grow in a dense, overlapping, shingle-like pattern. Perhaps this vine is not used as much now because houses are infrequently built with porches, and we seldom sit out on those that have them.

Euonymus fortunei
WINTER CREEPER

Winter creeper grows either as a clinging vine to 20 feet long by means of aerial rootlets or as a subshrub when, like ivy, it is propagated from mature shoots. It is hardy to −15°F. The leaves are glossy, elliptic or ovate, crenate to serrate, and grow up to 2 inches long, possibly much smaller in some cultivars. It can climb trees and masonry walls or scramble unsupported on the ground in sun or shade. It does have a problem with euonymus scale, an insect pest that can be quite critical in some areas.

Some of the numerous cultivars include 'Argenteo-variegata', with white-margined leaves; 'Coloratus', which has 1-inch long leaves that turn purple in winter; 'Gracilis', which has leaves edged with white or cream, turning pink in winter; 'Kewensis', with leaves that are less than ½ inch long; and 'Minima' with leaves that are less than an inch long.

Hedera spp. and cultivars
IVY

ALGERIAN IVY (*Hedera canariensis*) is a mild-winter, hot-summer evergreen vine that is use-ful in areas where winter freezes are either light or will not occur. The juvenile leaves are ovate, either unlobed or with three to seven shallow lobes, and grow to 6 inches wide. Algerian ivy is far more tender than English ivy and is also far more vigorous in growth, making a dense mat over a foot deep when used as a ground cover. Cultivars include 'Canary Cream', with leaves heavily blotched ivory-white, sometimes nearly completely cream colored; 'Margine-maculata', which has green leaves with green-speckled, creamy white leaf margins; 'Variegata', which has creamy yellow-white edges with less speckling than the preceding cultivar and a gray-green center; and 'Variegata' ('Gloire de Maregngo'), which has white edges shading into silver-gray with an irregular dark green center.

ENGLISH IVY (*Hedera helix*) cultivars are perhaps the most widely planted vines. It is a climbing, evergreen, woody vine when juvenile; the much more rarely seen adult form is erect and shrubby. The 2- to 3-inch-long juvenile leaves are typically simple, with five lobes; they are a very dark, glossy green with white veins. English ivy climbs by means of aerial rootlets that can attach to trees, masonry, and chain-link fences. It can also be used as a ground cover [it is known as one of the "big three" ground covers, along with myrtle (*Vinca minor*) and pachysandra (*Pachysandra terminalis*)], but frequent trimming (two to four times during the growing season) is necessary to control its spread. Hardy to −5°F or lower, the evergreen foliage is often damaged by sunscald and winter burn if not grown in a sheltered location. The vines may reach 90 feet in length. Variant forms are generally smaller, slower growing, and less hardy. There are numerous cultivars, since different foliage forms arise freely from juvenile shoots — they may differ in size, shape, or color from the type plant. They will revert, since many forms are unstable as they age, and so must be propagated from cuttings of the desired form. Cultivars include 'Angularis Aurea', with yellow new growth; 'Argenteo-variegata', with white variegated leaves; 'Aureo-variegata', with creamy yellow variegated leaves; 'Baltica', an exceptionally cold-tolerant variety (as is '238th Street'); 'Cavendishii', which has triangular/pentagonal leaves with a gray-green center and a creamy white margin; 'Glacier', with small silvery-gray leaves; 'Gold Dust', which has leaves with a cream and yellow center and green edges; 'Green Ripple', which has dark green, frilly, irregular lobed leaves; 'Jubilee', which has small leaves variegated light green, gray, and white; 'Minima', with tiny, dense foliage; and 'Purpurea', which has purplish green leaves that turn purple in winter.

PERSIAN IVY **(Hedera colchica)** is hardy in areas where winter temperatures reach 10°F; with protection it may be possible to use it in slightly colder regions. The evergreen leaves are ovate or heart shaped, either entire or slightly lobed, and may reach 10 inches long and 4 to 7 inches wide; they are typically a dark green. Cultivars include 'Dentato-variegata', which is weakly denticulate along the margins and variegated dark green, gray-green, and creamy yellow; and 'Sulphur Heart', with an irregular yellow center shading to pale green and edged with dark green.

Humulus lupulus 'Aureus'
GOLDEN HOP VINE

This rhizomatous perennial has three to five heart-shaped, lobed, coarsely toothed leaves on vertically twining vines that can reach 15 to 25 feet long in a season. Hardy to –5°F, golden hops should be grown in full sun, in rich moist soil with an adequately sized support trellis or tower. It can be cut back in autumn after a black frost, and growth resumes from the roots in spring. 'Aureus', with its golden leaves is more decorative than the green-leaved form cultivated for flavoring beer.

Hydrangea anomala subsp. petiolaris
CLIMBING HYDRANGEA

Unlike any other hydrangea, this is a true vine that climbs by means of small aerial rootlets that hold fast to masonry or tree trunks. The deciduous leaves are a glossy dark green in summer and are ovate, with a regularly serrate margin; they grow to 5 inches long. This vine grows to 75 feet long in partial shade or full sun and is hardy to –15°F. It is wonderful in a woodland garden, climbing up large canopy trees.

Parthenocissus spp. and cultivars
WOODBINE

BOSTON IVY **(Parthenocissus tricuspidata)** has simple, ovate to orbicular, three-lobed, glossy leaves as much as 8 inches across, which somewhat resemble those of a maple. It is useful for covering masonry walls because its tendrils are tipped with adhesive disks and it can climb to 50 feet or more. It is hardy to –15°F, enabling it to grow where true ivy, *Hedera helix,* cannot. It is tolerant of city conditions and can grow in sun or shade. Autumn color is best in sunny locations, where the leaves turn a vivid orange-red before they fall. Cultivars include 'Lowii', which has a much finer texture, with leaves that are less than 2 inches long and purplish in color when they first emerge in the spring; 'Minutifolia', which also has smaller

A shady garden
of hostas and ferns

Arundinaria viridistriata
(dwarf gold-stripe bamboo)

Stachys byzantina (lamb's-ears)

CHARLES MANN

Sedum spathulifolium
'Cape Blanco',
Sempervivum sp.
(hen-and-chicks)

CHARLES MANN

Sedum spathulifolium
'Purpureum'

Yucca
filamentosa
'Golden Sword'
(Adam's-needle)

JUDY GLATTSTEIN

C. COLSTON BURRELL

DARREL APPS

Rheum palmatum 'Atrosanguineum'

Caladium sp., *Plectranthus coleoides marginata*

Foeniculum vulgare sp. (fennel)

Justicia californica (chuparosa), *Opuntia* sp. (prickly pear)

Gunnera manicata

leaves than the species, usually 1 to 2 inches across; and 'Purpurea', with dark purple leaves.

SILVER-VEIN CREEPER *(Parthenocissus henryana)* is more tender than its relatives, as it is hardy only to 15°F. Its beautiful foliage will develop the best color when it is grown in a location with some shade. The palmately compound leaves have five ovate to obovate leaflets more than 2 inches long, toothed toward the tip. They are bright red when they open, and bright red again in autumn before they fall; their summer color is dark green with silvery white markings along the midrib, claret-purple beneath. This species is a weak climber to 20 feet and is excellent grown in a container, where it can be allowed to trail, with the tips clipped back to keep it more dense.

VIRGINIA CREEPER, or WOODBINE *(Parthenocissus quinquefolia)*, a relative of Boston ivy, has deciduous, palmately compound leaves with five elliptic to ovate, coarsely toothed leaflets that grow to 6 inches long. The stems reach 35 feet or more, and it is very hardy (to –35°F). It fastens to a support by means of tendrils tipped with a suckering disk. If grown in sun, the leaves turn color early in autumn, changing from dark green to a vivid crimson or rose-red before they drop. Cultivars include 'Engelmannii', which has a finer texture, denser growth, and a more refined appearance because of its smaller leaflets; 'Hirsuta', which has leaves that are woolly on the underside; 'Saint-Paulii', which has branching aerial tendrils with numerous adhesive disks, enabling it to cling even more firmly to masonry, and smaller leaflets that are hairy beneath.

Vitis coignetiae
JAPANESE CRIMSON GLORY VINE

This vigorous climber has dense foliage; the leaves are cordate to orbicular, entire or shallowly lobed, rusty or gray woolly beneath, and grow to 10 inches across. Hardy to –15°F, this rapidly growing vine can reach 50 feet high, attaching itself to a trellis or fence by means of twining tendrils. The large, coarse leaves turn brilliant red in autumn before they drop. Its rapid growth rate necessitates a large-scale use.

*G*ROUND *C*OVERS

BY SELF-DEFINITION, ANY PLANT THAT GROWS thickly enough to cover the ground might be termed a ground cover. Azaleas that are planted close enough so as to be impenetrable are certainly covering ground. In general, though, we associate the term "ground cover" with low-growing, trailing plants, often those that root and spread with some rapidity or increase through runners above or below ground. Most desirable, of course, are evergreen plants that provide visual interest year-round and do not expose the ground in winter. Ideally, a ground cover should spread but not be invasive. And if it has flowers, they might be considered a bonus, for foliage is of primary importance in the selection of ground covers. Imagine a sweep of lawn — specialized grasses that withstand foot traffic and frequent mowing, or pachysandra — often used in a monoculture reminiscent of the corn fields of Iowa — filling shady sites near office buildings and in public spaces.

Correctly used, a ground cover enhances the appearance of the site; it serves as a neat and unifying carpet against which to display other plants. Suitable ground covers can reduce maintenance. They fill space and allow us to concentrate on more detailed effects in other areas. Ground covers can hold soil on banks and slopes, reducing erosion. They provide a cover for early-dormant spring bulbs, marking their place and reducing inadvertent disturbance of the dormant bulbs. Numerous classes of plants can serve as ground covers. Many perennials can be used as ground covers if planted in sweeps and masses, and there are also many low-growing, trailing, stem-rooting herbs that are suitable for this purpose. Almost any vine can be allowed to scramble unsupported along the ground. Also, various low-growing shrubs are useful as ground covers, such as the well-known creeping juniper (*Juniperus horizontalis*). There are other possibilities than "the big three" of pachysandra, myrtle, and ivy.

Aegopodium podagraria
BISHOP'S WEED, GOUTWEED

This deciduous plant would be a superb ground cover were it not for its tendency to spread aggressively over more than its allotted space. Where it can be kept under control, it is very attractive — its three-parted leaflets, 1 to 3 inches long, make a dense, lacy mass 6 to 12 inches tall. Where it escapes, it can be frustrating to control. When the creeping underground rootstocks spread into and through the root zones of nearby plants it is difficult to disentangle them. It is best grown in an area where you are growing nothing else, in moderate shade to sun. It is hardy to –20°F.

The attractive cultivar, 'Variegatum', with white-edged leaves, is the most frequently seen and is, alas, as wide ranging as the plain green variety.

Ajuga reptans
AJUGA, BUGLEWEED

This evergreen or semievergreen herbaceous plant is readily established and easily maintained. If it is used to carpet an area adjacent to a lawn, some type of edging strip is useful, because ajuga will frequently extend into the grass. Hardy to –35°F, it is low growing (only 3 to 6 inches tall) and spreads by means of surface runners. It is an excellent choice for shade or sun, contributing blue, pink, or white flowers in spring and neat foliage over an extended period. The simple ovate leaves are over 2 inches long and 1 inch wide when grown in shade, smaller and more compact in sun. Cultivars include 'Atropurpurea', with bronze-purple leaves; 'Bronze Beauty', with bronze-red foliage; 'Burgundy Glow', which is variegated burgundy, creamy white, and green; 'Burgundy Lace', which is variegated pink, white, and green; 'Caitlin's Giant', which has very large bronze leaves; and 'Silver Beauty', which has gray-green leaves edged with white.

Arctostaphylos spp.
BEARBERRY, MANZANITA

Bearberry (*Arctostaphylos uva-ursi*) is an evergreen, prostrate to trailing, woody shrub, hardy to –35°F with winter protection in the form of snow cover, or –15°F in exposed situations. Bearberry is valuable because it thrives in open, sunny situations with dry, infertile, sandy soils. It is easier to establish when it is grown as smaller-size, potting material. The leaves are a smooth, glossy, lustrous green, obovate to spatulate, and an inch long on branches 15 feet long. It is lovely in coastal gardens with junipers, mugo pine, heaths, and heathers, which together create a sturdy, reduced-maintenance foliage shrub garden. Cultivars include 'Big

Bear', which has larger leaves; 'Massachusetts', which is very flat growing and small leaved, and is possibly more tolerant of moisture than the species; 'Point Reyes', a West Coast cultivar that is tolerant of heat and drought, and makes a dense ground cover of closely spaced dark green leaves; and 'Wood's Red', a dwarf selection with small, dark green leaves that turn reddish in winter.

LITTLE SUR MANZANITA **(Arctostaphylos edmundsii)**, found in Monterey County, California, is an evergreen shrub, hardy to 25°F. It has nearly prostrate stems that root upon soil contact and elliptic to broadly ovate green leaves just over an inch long. It is excellent for mild winter areas. Several cultivars have been introduced: 'Danville' is variable in height, from 4 to 20 inches tall, and spreads 12 feet wide; 'Carmel Sur' is fast growing, with attractive gray-green foliage; 'Little Sur' is slow growing, with a very flat growth habit and bronze new leaves that mature to green with reddish margins.

VINE-HILL MANZANITA **(Arctostaphylos densiflora)** is a trailing, procumbent shrub with outer stems that root on soil contact. The center of the shrub mounds up to 4 feet or more, and the outer branches are more prostrate; careful pruning of the center can reduce its height, leaving the outer branches to trail. Native to Sonoma County, California, this plant is hardy to 25°F. The glossy, light to dark green leaves are elliptic and just over 1 inch long. It grows best with some protection from intense midday sun, such as on an east- or northeast-facing slope. Cultivars such as 'Harmony' and 'Howard McMinn' grow 5 to 6 feet high and spread 7 feet wide.

Arundinaria spp. See Bamboos, page 120.

Asarum spp.
WILD GINGER

These plants have a gingery aromatic root but are unrelated to the spice of the same name. They are herbaceous perennials with rhizomatous roots. Their leaves, which are sometimes evergreen and sometimes deciduous, are mostly cordate at the base. Wild gingers are excellent for woodland conditions. They grow in a moist but well-drained soil high in organic matter in dappled to heavy shade. These plants are elegant as a ground cover with woodland shrubs and perennials such as ferns, baneberry, astilbe, and liriope. Wild gingers are all hardy to 0°F and probably lower, especially with snow cover in winter.

They are difficult to find in nurseries and thus are more available for use as specimen plants than as ground cover.

AMERICAN WILD GINGER **(Asarum canadense)** is deciduous, with leaves to 6 inches across, grows 12 inches tall, and is hardy to −25°F.

BRITISH COLUMBIA WILD GINGER **(Asarum caudatum)** is an evergreen species that is hardy to −5°F, colder if snow cover is reliable, grows 6 to 8 inches high, and has leaves 4 to 6 inches across.

EUROPEAN GINGER **(Asarum europaeum)**, probably the most well-known species, has glossy green leaves to 3 inches across, grows 6 inches tall, and is hardy to −10°F.

There are various mottle-leafed evergreen species from the southeastern United States: **Asarum arifolium**, which has arrow-shaped evergreen leaves to 5 inches long, spotted with silvery white; **Asarum hartwegii**, with white-mottled leaves that are 5 inches wide; **Asarum shuttleworthii**, with 3-inch-wide leaves that are usually mottled but sometimes not; and **Asarum virginicum**, with evergreen leaves to

3 inches across; the veins form a tracery of silvery white.

Athyrium filix-femina. See page 162.

Bamboos (*Arundinaria* spp., *Sasa* spp.)

For general information about bamboos, see pages 68-69.

DWARF FERN-LEAF BAMBOO *(Arundinaria disticha [Bambusa disticha])* has slender stems that grow 2 to 3 feet tall and delicate, bright green, ferny leaves that grow in pairs bunched toward the tips of the branches. The dainty appearance is camouflage for its rampant spreading habits. It is hardy to 10°F. Dwarf fern-leaf bamboo is attractive when grown in a large container, which will check its spread, or as a vigorous ground cover. Cut it back to the ground if it becomes overgrown and ragged.

DWARF GOLD-STRIPE BAMBOO *(Arundinaria viridistriata)* is a running bamboo that grows to 30 inches tall; it is hardy to 0°F. The leaves are 8 inches long by nearly 2 inches wide, rounded at the base and abruptly pointed at the tip, and very hairy underneath; they are strikingly variegated with bright green stripes on golden yellow. Variegation is stronger on the upper surface than the underside of the leaf and is variable from leaf to leaf; it is frequently more pronounced on one side of the midrib. For best color, grow this bamboo in full sun. The color will be maintained if the canes are cut to the ground in autumn, as new growth has the brightest color. If this is not done, mulch in cold winters.

DWARF WHITE-STRIPE BAMBOO *(Arundinaria variegata [Sasa variegata])* grows 2 to 3 feet tall and is hardy to 0°F. This bamboo is an aggressive spreader and is best grown in containers, confined in some manner, or it can be grown as a vigorous ground cover in sun or light shade. The leaves are narrower and more delicate than those of the dwarf gold-stripe bamboo and are attractively striped pure white on an olive-green ground. Old canes will often die back in cold winter areas.

KUMA BAMBOO GRASS *(Sasa veitchii)* is a running species that grows 2 to 3 feet tall, and is hardy to 0°F. The large, 7-inch by 1-inch leaves turn light brown along the edges in autumn, creating a variegated effect.

Bergenia spp. and cultivars. See page 136.

Caluna spp. See pages 92-93.

Convallaria majalis
LILY-OF-THE-VALLEY

This rhizomatous, herbaceous perennial has been long cherished for its sweetly fragrant, white bell-like flowers in spring. It is equally valuable as a long-lived ground cover, needing little attention once established. Each bud or "pip" along the horizontal rhizome develops into two or three lanceolate-ovate to elliptic leaves up to 8 inches long. Where conditions are suitable, the rich green leaves will make a dense mat that should be thinned and top-dressed with organic matter periodically to keep it in best condition. Hardy to −30°F, it grows best in woodland conditions of partial to full shade, in moist but well-drained soil that is high in organic matter. It can become a problem if the rhizomes extend beyond the desired area.

'Aureo-variegata', also called, 'Striata', has golden yellow vertical striping on a dark green leaf; since it is infrequently available and has a tendency to revert to plain green, it is better used as a specimen than a ground cover.

Cotoneaster spp. and cultivars
COTONEASTER

This group includes a number of low-growing, creeping or sprawling, evergreen or deciduous shrubs, which can be used as ground covers trailing over rocks and at the top of retaining walls to soften their appearance. They prefer a sunny location with average but well-drained soil and are often tolerant of drier conditions once established.

BEARBERRY COTONEASTER *(Cotoneaster dammeri [C. humifusus])* is a prostrate evergreen shrub that grows 10 inches high by 3 to 6 feet wide; its branches will root where in contact with soil. The leathery obovate leaves are nearly an inch long, glossy and dark green above, paler beneath. It is a good ground cover for sun or light shade, tumbling over walls and rocks, and is hardy to –5°F.

CREEPING COTONEASTER *(Cotoneaster adpressus)* is a deciduous, prostrate, slow-growing species that reaches 10 to 12 inches high with a 6-foot spread. The dark green leaves, which are broadly ovate and less than an inch long, provide a fine texture. Creeping cotoneaster is good for covering walls, rocks, and banks or can be used as a ground cover in small- to moderate-scale situations. It is hardy to –15°F.

NECKLACE COTONEASTER *(Cotoneaster conspicuus var. decorus)* is a matlike prostrate form of the taller species. It has short, stiff branches from the main stems and grows as a tight, ground-hugging carpet covered with evergreen, small, oval, dark green leaves ¼ inch long, pale on the underside. It needs protection from wind damage and sunscald in winter and is hardy to 5°F. It is good for use in rock gardens or heath situations.

ROCK COTONEASTER *(Cotoneaster horizontalis)* is semievergreen — bare of foliage for only a brief period. The round, glossy bright green leaves, pale beneath, are less than an inch long and turn orange to red before falling in autumn. It grows 12 to 24 inches high, spreading to 15 feet wide, and has stiffly angled branches; it is hardy to –5°F. Rock cotoneaster is good for large-scale situations. Var. *perpusillus* is lower growing with densely intertwined branches and smaller foliage.

SPREADING WILLOW-LEAF COTONEASTER *(Cotoneaster salicifolius* 'Repens')* has a weeping, trailing habit and is densely branched and low growing, reaching 8 feet wide. The narrow, semievergreen leaves are from 1 to over 3 inches long, wrinkled, and dark green above, grayish green beneath. It is useful as a large-scale ground cover, weeping over a bank or wall.

THYME ROCK-SPRAY COTONEASTER *(Cotoneaster microphyllus forma thymifolius)* is a small, evergreen cotoneaster cultivar with compact growth and tightly spaced branches that hug the ground. The glossy, dark green leaves are spirally arranged along the branches. It is hardy to –5°F but needs winter protection from sun and wind. Planted in light shade, it is excellent for small-scale locations in a rock garden or heath setting.

Dennstaedtia punctilobula. See page 162.

Epimedium spp.
EPIMEDIUM

These rhizomatous perennials have evergreen or semievergreen compound leaves with three primary divisions, which are, in turn, pinnately divided. The 2- to 3-inch-long, leathery, heart-shaped leaflets are finely toothed along the margins and are carried on wiry, stemlike petioles. The leaves are reddish bronze in color when they appear in the spring, turning light green in summer and persisting until severe winter weather.

Hardy to –30°F, this plant is excellent when grown as a ground cover or for specimen use. It grows best in shade in a soil that is high in organic matter and, once established, is tolerant of a range of conditions, from moist to dry. It is lovely combined with any of the deciduous or evergreen woodland shrubs such as azalea, leucothoe, pieris, and mountain laurel, and perennials such as hosta, bloodroot, and ferns. Selections are based on flower color, and many cultivars and even species are very mixed up in the trade.

Erica **spp.** See pages 92-93.

Euonymus **spp.** See page 111.

Galium odoratum [Asperula odorata]
WOODRUFF

This is a vigorous, spreading herbaceous perennial that grows 6 to 12 inches high. The leaves, carried in whorls of six to eight, are over an inch long and are fragrant, especially when dried. Delicate in appearance, this deciduous ground cover quickly overgrows its allotted space, but it will tolerate deep shade and dry soil. With more moisture and a fertile soil, it can become invasive, spreading rampantly.

Heaths and heathers (*Calluna* spp., *Erica* spp.). See pages 92-93.

Hedera **spp.** See pages 111-12.

Hosta **spp.** See pages 145-46.

Juniperus **spp.** See pages 94-96.

Lamiastrum galeobdolon 'Variegatum'
YELLOW ARCHANGEL

This vigorous, rapidly spreading perennial has ovate to orbicular leaves that grow to 3 inches long and are coarsely toothed and spotted, and blotched with silver. Hardy to –10°F, this shade-tolerant ground cover has trailing stems that can root down as it grows, enabling it to become rampant and out of control. It is excellent for a rough woodland area where it can advance unchecked. The yellow flowers differentiate yellow archangel from spotted dead nettle *(Lamium maculatum)*. The cultivar 'Hermann's Pride' has silver-dappled leaves with green veins and a more refined, clumping habit of growth, making it more useful in smaller-scale situations.

Lamium maculatum
SPOTTED DEAD NETTLE

This is a perennial herb with prostrate, trailing stems that are erect at the tips. The basal leaves are cordate, while those along the stem are ovate, all with crenate-dentate margins and a white stripe along the midrib, 1 to 2 inches long. Hardy to –10°F, this herbaceous ground cover is best grown in shade, thus reducing the chance of winter burn and desiccation. It may be evergreen, semievergreen, or deciduous, depending on the severity of the winter. Cultivars include 'Aureum', which has a golden yellow leaf with a central white stripe and is slower growing and more tender than the species; 'Beacon Silver' and 'White Nancy', which have a broad, central silver blotch and a narrow, green leaf margin ('Beacon Silver' has pink flowers and 'White Nancy', white) and both are slower growing than the species; and 'Variegatum', which has a silver, rather than white, central stripe. Spotted dead nettle is lovely in a woodland garden, where its white or silver markings brighten the shade.

Liriope spp. and cultivars
LILYTURF

These useful evergreen herbaceous perennials have clustered grasslike leaves, which make an attractive linear pattern. Some spread by means of underground rhizomes. Lilyturf prefers moist but well-drained soil high in organic matter in woodland settings but is widely adaptable to sun or shade, moist or dry soils, and is even moderately salt tolerant.

Lilyturf is a choice ground cover in the South. Although it may also be used in the north (it can withstand winter temperatures of –5°F), it is often damaged by cold, necessitating trimming of the foliage in spring for better regeneration from the roots; plants in sunny areas will be more noticeably affected. Under milder conditions (winter lows of 10°F), lilyturf will be reliably evergreen. It is useful in mass plantings or in smaller areas as a contrast to hosta, fern, and bloodroot foliage.

BLUE LILYTURF *(Liriope muscari)* grows to 18 inches tall and has a clumping habit of growth. Its arching, straplike leaves are nearly an inch wide. Cultivars include 'Silvery Sunproof', with leaves variegated with gold stripes that fade to white; and 'Variegata', which has new leaves edged with yellow and all-green leaves the second year.

CREEPING LILYTURF *(Liriope spicata)* is a spreading plant with narrow, grasslike leaves that are ¼ inch wide and 18 inches long; arching over, they make an effective carpet 10 inches high. 'Silver Dragon' is striped silvery white and is more tender than the species.

Mahonia spp.
MAHONIA

This group includes a number of shrubs, two of which are small enough for use as a ground cover.

CREEPING MAHONIA *(Mahonia repens)* creeps by means of underground stems, giving it a spreading habit of growth; it reaches 3 feet high. The bluish green, dull-surfaced leaves have four to six ovate leaflets with five to nine spiny teeth. It grows best in sun or light shade in moist but well-drained soil that is rich in humus. Although the plant is hardy to –10°F, it is helpful to protect it from winter sunscald in colder areas.

LONGLEAF MAHONIA *(Mahonia nervosa). See under* "Shrubs," page 98.

Mitchella repens
PARTRIDGE BERRY

This evergreen herbaceous (barely woody) perennial grows 2 inches tall and has trailing stems 12 to 15 inches long that root at the nodes. The nearly orbicular leaves, under an inch long, grow in pairs and are dark green with a central white line. Hardy to –25°F, it needs moderate to deep shade and a moist but well-drained soil high in organic matter. It is perfect for the naturalistic woodland garden, blanketing fallen, rotting logs and mixed with ferns, hosta, epimedium, bloodroot, and astilbe to create a forest floor community.

Ophiopogon spp. and cultivars
MONDO GRASS

Related to lilyturf, these evergreen, sod-forming, herbaceous perennials are valuable as a fine-textured grasslike ground cover. They grow in the same manner as lilyturf, but are reportedly more tender (hardy to 5°F), I have successfully grown these under colder conditions in a sheltered woodland garden. (Microclimates enable the adventurous gardener to explore beyond normal limits.)

BLACK MONDO GRASS *(Ophiopogon planiscapus* **'Arabicus' ['Nigrescens']***)* is one of the few plants with black foliage. It is stoloniferous and grows to 10 inches tall. The ¼-inch-wide leaves grow to 10 inches long and are green when they first emerge, changing to dark purplish black with maturity. Black mondo grass is superb as a specimen plant in combination with gold or silver foliage plants; it is excellent in a container for summer interest.

JABURAN LILYTURF *(Ophiopogon jaburan)* has narrow, linear leaves that are 2 feet long and ½ inch wide. It is often confused in the trade with blue lilyturf *(Liriope muscari)* especially its yellow- or white-striped variegated cultivars such as 'Argenteo-vittatus', 'Aureo-variegatus', 'Javanensis', 'Variegatus', and 'Vittatus', some of which are indistinguishable from one another.

MONDO GRASS *(Ophiopogon japonicus)* has very dark green leaves, ⅛ inch wide and 8 to 15 inches long, standing at an effective height of 12 inches. An even more delightful variety is *O. japonicus* 'Nanus', which is only a few inches tall and more upright in effect.

Pachysandra spp. and cultivars
PACHYSANDRA

PACHYSANDRA *(Pachysandra terminalis)* is another of the "big three" ground covers for shady conditions (the other two are ivy, *Hedera helix,* and myrtle, *Vinca minor).* The lustrous, dark green, evergreen leaves are obovate, toothed along the top half, and wedge-shaped at the base; they grow 2 to 4 inches long in whorls on stems that are 10 inches tall,

although the stems will elongate, reaching twice that length, and scramble up into nearby shrubs. Pachysandra spreads by underground runners but will also grow above the surface where blocked by a hard-surfaced walkway; trimming and edging is important to keep this ground cover within bounds. Hardy to −10°F, once established it makes a very dense carpet that will block weed growth. Few cultivars are offered: 'Green Carpet' has exceptionally dark green, glossy foliage and is lower in growth than the typical form; 'Variegata' has white-variegated leaves; and 'White Edge' has leaves edged in white and is slower growing than the species. 'Laciniata' is a very recent introduction with laciniate foliage.

ALLEGHANY SPURGE *(Pachysandra procumbens)* is the native American counterpart of the ubiquitous Japanese pachysandra, *Pachysandra terminalis.* Found in the southern Appalachian Mountains in woodland areas, it is a useful ground cover for naturalized shady gardens. The broadly ovate to suborbicular leaves, toothed at the tip, are 3 inches long on stems that are 9 inches tall; they are a soft dull green in summer, darker and with faint silver spotting toward autumn, and are evergreen to semievergreen or deciduous, depending on the severity of winter conditions. Allegheny spurge is hardy to −10°F.

Phlox spp.
PHLOX

CREEPING PHLOX *(Phlox stolonifera)* is an herbaceous perennial that grows 6 inches tall and spreads 2 feet wide by means of creeping stems that root upon soil contact. It has oblong to ovate evergreen leaves. Hardy to −20°F, it is an excellent woodland ground cover for moist but well-drained soils high in organic matter, in shady situations. Flowers appear in spring and may be blue, pink, or white depending on the cultivar. One of the prettiest ground covers for woodland gardens, creeping phlox is attractive combined with azaleas, ferns, and hosta.

MOSS PINK *(Phlox subulata)* is an evergreen, creeping, herbaceous perennial, with needlelike foliage reminiscent of a juniper; it reaches 4 to 6 inches high and 2 feet wide. It grows well in full sun and well-drained, moderately fertile soil. Flowering is so profuse that the foliage is completely hidden. It should be cut back hard after flowering to encourage new growth and keep trailing stems full. This is a good choice for rock gardens and as a ground cover over bulbs.

Plumbago larpentiae [Ceratostigma plumbaginoides]
LEADWORT

This herbaceous perennial, woody at the base, grows 12 to 18 inches tall and, once established, spreads somewhat quickly by underground stems. The leaves are ovate, fringed with hairs, and over 3 inches long; they appear late in spring so it is important to avoid inadvertently disturbing them before their growth begins. The leaves turn red in autumn, and although leadwort is evergreen in mild winter areas, it is most suitable handled as a perennial and cut down each spring. Leadwort is hardy to −10°F with winter mulching and protection. It grows best in moderately fertile, moist but well-drained soil, in sun to light shade. It is suitable in a perennial border if kept under control and is even better in a shrub border.

Polystichum acrostichoides. See page 65.

Pulmonaria saccharata. See page 15.

Rhododendron spp. See pages 100-102.

Rhus aromatica. See page 102.

Rosmarinus officinalis 'Prostrata'
ROSEMARY

This prostrate form of the well-known upright shrub is low growing to 2 feet high and 4 to 8 feet wide; it is hardy to 20°F. The aromatic, resinous, dark green, linear foliage has an edge rolled toward the underside, which is gray with densely matted, short, woolly hairs. Native to the Mediterranean and long cultivated in herb gardens, this is an excellent ground cover for sites with full sun, moderate fertility, good drainage, and mild winters. It is widely used in the Southwest and California to cascade over the edge of a raised bed, to trail over a wall, or to cover a slope. Rosemary can be grown with other Mediterranean-climate plants, South African bulbs, gray-leaved herbs, and dryland native plants.

Rubus calycinoides
BRAMBLE

This delightful creeping evergreen shrub has densely packed, glossy, wrinkled, orbicular, 3-lobed leaves that are less than 2 inches across, felted beneath, with a wavy, scalloped edge; the leaves turn coppery bronze in winter. It is best grown in light shade, where it will cover the ground, growing closely over fallen logs and rocks and making a tight ground cover under shrubs. Bramble spreads about 12 inches a year by means of prostrate, thornless branches that root where in contact with the soil. It is hardy to 5°F.

Sarcococca hookerana var. humilis
SWEET BOX

This is a dwarf form of the species and grows less than 2 feet tall, making a dense mass of glossy, leathery, evergreen, lanceolate leaves that are 2 to 4 inches long and broader than in the type species. Hardy to –5°F, it forms a low, densely branched mound as much as 8 feet across, spreading by means of underground runners. It grows best in a moist but well-drained, humus-rich soil in woodland shade. Sweet box is a good choice for a transition plant between low-growing plants and taller evergreen shrubs such as mountain laurel, azalea, and rhododendron.

Sasa spp. See pages 68-70.

Sedum spp. and cultivars
STONECROP

This group covers a diverse collection of succulent perennials and subshrubs. All are tolerant of sun and grow in well-drained soil that is low in fertility, but they can vary widely in hardiness. Sites should be either exposed rock or quite sandy — the key is sharp drainage and full exposure to the sun. Stonecrop are able to reproduce from stem fragments or even a severed leaf, so they can sometimes exceed their allotted space. Some have attractively colored foliage.

GOLDMOSS STONECROP **(Sedum acre)** has bright green foliage, grows 2 to 5 inches tall, and is hardy to –20°F.

Sedum dasyphyllum has small, fine, gray foliage, grows 3 inches tall, and is hardy to 0°F.

Sedum spathulifolium, a West Coast native from British Columbia south through the Coast Range and Sierra Nevada of California, has bluish green leaves tinted reddish purple that are packed into rosettes at the tips of short trailing stems; it is low growing and is hardy to 5°F. Its cultivars include 'Cape Blanco', with beautiful silvery gray leaves, and 'Purpureum', with purple leaves.

SHORT-LEAVED STONECROP **(Sedum brevifolium)** has grayish white leaves, flushed with red, grows 2 to 3 inches tall, and is hardy to –20°F.

STRINGY STONECROP **(Sedum lineare [sarmentosum])** has closely set, linear, light green leaves carried in threes, grows 12 inches high but often trails to half that height, and is hardy to –10°F. The cultivar 'Variegatum' has white-edged leaves.

TWO-ROW STONECROP **(Sedum spurium)** has olive green to deep green or bronze-colored leaves, grows 6 inches tall, and is hardy to –20°F.

WHITE STONECROP **(Sedum album)** has light- to medium-green leaves, sometimes with a red flush, grows 2 to 6 inches tall, and is hardy to –20°F.

Stachys byzantina [S. lanata]
LAMB'S-EARS

This herbaceous perennial herb has woolly, white-haired leaves and stems; the oblong-spatulate leaves reach 4 inches long and grow densely on lax, spreading stems that are 8 to 12 inches tall. It grows best in well-drained soil in full sun but not necessarily xeric conditions. Hardy to –10°F, the leaves will persist through the winter, but there is usually some damage. When this occurs, it should be cut back hard in spring before growth begins. The lovely soft, silver foliage is excellent as an edging ground cover in a perennial border or herb garden, or combined with old shrub roses. It has beautiful white, pink, or deep blue flowers. 'Silver Carpet', is a nonflowering, lower-growing cultivar.

Thymus spp. and cultivars
THYME

These small shrubs or herbaceous perennials

are woody at the base and have small leaves that are aromatic when crushed or bruised. All prefer full sun and good drainage and are hardy in most instances to −20°F. Since they will withstand a moderate amount of foot traffic, these perennials are occasionally used in place of grass or between pavers, releasing their fragrance when trod upon. They are a good ground cover in rock gardens, over small bulbs, and in herb gardens.

CARAWAY THYME *(Thymus herba-barona)*, has a caraway scent and forms a flat, quickly spreading mat of small, dark green leaves.

CREEPING THYME, or MOTHER-OF-THYME *(Thymus praecox [serpyllum])* forms a mat to 4 inches high with creeping stems covered with green leaves.

LEMON THYME *(Thymus X citrodorus)*, a hybrid between *T. pulegiodes* and *T. vulgaris*. A somewhat bushy small shrub that is mostly upright, or occasionally somewhat spreading, it grows 4 to 12 inches tall, and has dainty lemon-scented leaves. Its cultivars include 'Argenteus' and 'Silver Queen', which have white-edged leaves; and 'Aureus', which has golden yellow-edged leaves.

WOOLLY THYME *(Thymus pseudolanuginosus [lanuginosus])* makes a 2- to 3-inch-high mat of gray-woolly leaves; the leaves are intolerant of standing moisture, which leads to mildew and rot.

Tiarella cordifolia
FOAMFLOWER

This is a native rhizomatous (sometimes stoloniferous) herbaceous perennial with ovate-cordate leaves that are dentate on the margins and grow to 4 inches long. Hardy to −10°F, foamflower is semievergreen in the southeastern states and deciduous in colder regions. It

grows best in woodland conditions in moist but well-drained soils high in organic matter. Foamflower dies back if chemical fertilizers contact the foliage. Although it tolerates light to heavy shade, its thickest effect as a ground cover is achieved in light shade. It is attractive as a cover for small woodland bulbs such as snowdrops and spring snowflakes *(Galanthus* spp. and *Leucojum vernum)*, combined with ferns, hosta, and bloodroot.

Tolmiea menziesii
PICK-A-BACK PLANT, YOUTH-ON-AGE

A close relative of foamflower *(Tiarella cordifolia)*, this herbaceous perennial plant needs similar growing conditions. It is often seen as a hanging basket plant in colder areas, but this western North American native is excellent for use outdoors as a ground cover. It has a well-developed rhizome, and cordate, shallowly lobed, hairy leaves that form small new plants at the junction of the leaf blade and leaf stalk. The leaves are up to 4 inches long and 5 inches wide and are a fresh, bright green color. It is hardy to 15°F, often lower with winter protection.

Vaccinium spp.
BLUEBERRY, CRANBERRY, DEERBERRY

MOUNTAIN CRANBERRY (also called lingonberry, cowberry, and foxberry) *(Vaccinium vitis-idaea)* is a creeping evergreen shrub found in dry pine forests (a situation of shade and dry soils), as well as in sphagnum bogs and moors where it is exposed to full sun and very wet soil. In pine forests, sphagnum bogs, and moors, soil fertility and pH are both low. In cultivation, it requires well-drained, sandy-peaty soil; it is hardy to −40°F and is intolerant of hot summers. This shrub grows only 12 inches tall, and its leathery, glossy, dark green leaves are

½ inch to just over an inch long. It is elegant as a fine-textured, small-scale ground cover in a rock garden or heath setting, with heaths and heathers, bearberry and junipers, and is best appreciated if sited where it can be closely observed. Two varieties are offered: Var. *majus* has larger leaves and is less cold hardy (to –15°F). Var. *minus*, the arctic form, is dwarf and low growing, and forms dense mats, with leaves less than an inch long; it is especially intolerant of hot dry summers.

VACCINIUM ANGUSTIFOLIUM (see page 107).

Vinca spp. and cultivars
PERIWINKLE

GREATER PERIWINKLE or VINCA VINE (***Vinca major* 'Variegata'**) is commonly seen trailing from summer window boxes, planted with red geraniums. Vinca's creamy white-edged leaves are decorative when it is used as a container plant or as a ground cover. With long, trailing stems that root at the nodes and 1- to 3-inch-long ovate leaves, this sturdy plant makes a good carpeting plant for shady locations, full sun if given adequate water. Shear occasionally to encourage new growth and to reduce its habit of mounding up as much as 12 inches or more in the center. It is hardy to 15°F: I have had it overwinter in western Connecticut and I have heard that it will do so in Boulder, Colorado.

LESSER PERIWINKLE or MYRTLE (***Vinca minor***) is a sturdy ground cover — one of the "big three," which also includes ivy (*Hedera helix*) and pachysandra (*Pachysandra terminalis*) — and is often persistent in abandoned situations. A trailing evergreen perennial, it grows best in the shade, sending its stems (which root from the nodes upon ground contact) out from the central crown. It will establish as a dense ground cover in a moist but well-drained soil

high in organic matter, but a mulch is needed to protect the soil surface until the plant grows densely enough to cover it. The oblong to ovate lustrous leaves grow to 2 inches long. Myrtle makes an elegant ground cover with shrubs or trees. Cultivars of foliage interest include 'Aureola', with creamy yellow veining in the center of the leaves; 'Sterling Silver' ('Argenteo-variegata'), with leaves edged white; and 'Variegata' ('Aureo-variegata'), with creamy yellow margins on dark green, leathery leaves.

$\mathcal{P}$ERENNIALS

PERENNIALS, IT HAS BEEN SAID, ARE PLANTS that, if they survive, will come back and flower year after year. This mockingly pessimistic viewpoint is matched by a friend's assertion that only if they have problems with pests and diseases, or are difficult to grow, can we call them perennials, otherwise they are weeds. Both statements are true, and both are false. *Herbaceous perennial* is an imprecise term, including as it does any nonwoody plant that survives for more than three seasons. Thus, a peony, growing for fifty years or more, is lumped with shasta daisies, which must be rejuvenated by division every two or three years to prevent their demise. Regional differences influence the duration of a plant's lifespan, with summer heat as much of a problem as winter cold. A perennial in southern California may be treated as an annual in cooler climates. We rarely think of bulbs as perennial but indeed, this is what they are. To a gardener, *perennial* refers to that incredible diversity of nonwoody plants that are not genetically set to self-destruct after one growing season. It is within this group that most of us select plants for our gardens. The diversity that they provide means that whatever the need, a plant exists to fill it. Herbaceous perennials are small, tall, dainty, or coarse; they grow in sun, shade, standing water, or desert drought. Just as woody plants provide the framework, the foliage of herbaceous perennials creates the lush tapestry that decorates the room outdoors.

Acanthus spp. and cultivars
BEAR'S-BREECH

These drought-tolerant plants have strongly architectural foliage that was used as a pattern for ornamentation in classical Grecian columns. The imposing basal foliage makes this a pre-eminent genus for bold foliage effects. The leaves are broadly lobed, sometimes pinnately cut, and grow 2 to 3 feet long. Bear's-breech combines attractively with agaves and grasses, which have more linear foliage.

BEAR'S-BREECH *(Acanthus mollis)* has pinnately cut, dull green leaves up to 2 feet long by 1 foot wide; the lobes may be shallow or deeply cut. The plant overall is 4 to 5 feet high and 2 to 3 feet wide. Despite its height, which would indicate a location at the back of the border, it is elegant if placed where the foliage can be observed unobstructed. Winter wet leads to root rot, so it grows best with full sun (a location that is suitable only where summers are not too hot); it will benefit from light shade, especially at midday. It requires well-drained soil with moderate to adequate fertility (not too rich). Spreading roots make this an invasive plant in milder regions. It is hardy to 0°F, possibly colder with winter mulching. Cultivars include 'Latifolius', which has larger leaves and is reportedly hardy to −10°F; and 'Oak Leaf', which has a broadly lobed leaf.

BEAR'S-BREECH or MOUNTAIN ACANTHUS *(Acanthus montanus)* has leaves that are lustrous dark green above and paler on the underside; they are more or less deeply pinnately cleft and have small spiny teeth. The plant grows to 6 feet tall. It is hardy to 15°F.

SPINY ACANTHUS *(Acanthus spinosissimus [A. spinosus])* has 2- to 3-foot-long leaves that are deeply cut, dark green, leathery, and rigid (similar to those of a thistle); and they have spiny, silvery teeth. It is hardy to 5°F.

Achillea × taygetea 'Moonshine'
YARROW

This is a hybrid of garden origin between *A. clypeolata* and *A. millefolium;* it is easily confused with a Grecian species of the same name *(A. taygeta).* Growing 18 inches high and wide, with twice pinnately dissected gray foliage, this plant is a fine choice to use in the front of a border. It grows well in a sunny area with well-drained soil, and once established, it is drought tolerant. *Achillea clypeolata* grows 18 inches tall and has silvery foliage that is pinnately cut into lanceolate, slightly toothed segments. Two dwarf species — *A. ageratifolia*, which is 8 inches tall and has silvery, hairy, linear, deeply toothed leaves, and *A. clavennae*, which is 4 to 10 inches tall and has once or twice pinnately cut, elliptic leaves that are densely covered with silky white hairs — are often used in rock gardens for their charming little mats of elegant, frosty foliage.

Acorus calamus
SWEET FLAG

This plant has leaves similar to that of Siberian iris in shape; they grow 6 feet tall and 1 inch wide, with a prominent midrib, and are chartreuse in color. Hardy to −5°F, it grows best in full sun in a constantly saturated soil, even shallow standing water. Related to Jack-in-the-pulpit, it has an inconspicuous flower near the base. Cultivars include 'Variegatus', with yellow striped leaves; and var. *angustifolius,* with leaves less than ¼ inch wide. Do not confuse this variety with grassy-leaved sweet flag *(Acorus gramineus)* which is a different species that grows only 18 inches tall and has ¼-inch-wide leaves that are white striped in the cultivar 'Variegatus'.

Actaea pachypoda
DOLL'S-EYES, BANEBERRY, COHOSH

This woodland herbaceous perennial grows 2 feet tall and has thrice-compound, fresh green leaves similar to astilbe and cimicifuga, with each ovate leaflet deeply toothed or cut. It needs moist but well-drained soil rich in humus and dappled to heavy shade. It is good for concealing the yellowing leaves of daffodils and is pleasant in summer combined with hosta, brunnera, Canadian or European ginger, and liriope. It is hardy to –40°F. Red baneberry *(Actaea rubra)* has very similar foliage but red rather than white berries (the berries are poisonous in both species).

Aegopodium podagraria 'Variegatum'.
See page 118.

Aeonium spp. and cultivars
AEONIUM

These are evergreen herbaceous perennials and branching shrubs with leaves that grow in rosettes, somewhat resembling those of hen-and-chicks *(Sempervivum* spp.). They are succulents and are able to withstand drought, infertile sandy soils, and direct sunshine. Excess moisture or fertility generally leads to rot. The majority of aeoniums come from the Canary Islands and are quite tender. They are hardy only in frost-free areas such as the arid Southwest and southern California; elsewhere they can be used as container plants. The leaves are usually obovate or spatulate, often fringed with hairs.

Aeonium arboreum is a popular, branching species that grows to 3 feet tall and has glossy green leaves 2 to 3 inches long. There are several cultivars with strikingly colored foliage, including 'Atropurpureum', with dark purple leaves; 'Foliis Purpurea', with purple leaves; and 'Zwartkop', with glossy purplish black leaves.

Aeonium haworthii is also shrubby but is lower growing, to 2 feet tall, with rosettes of glaucous bluish green leaves edged red.

Agave spp. and cultivars
CENTURY PLANT

These evergreen perennial plants of sculptural stature usually die after flowering. The flower spike is immense, often 8 to 15 or 25 feet tall. The plant flowers infrequently, however, and propagates itself by making offsets, so this characteristic is not as negative as might first appear. Native to the New World, North and South America, agave are best suited to well-drained coarse soils, and their tough, fibrous leaves are an adaptation to drought. Some moisture during the growing season will produce the best appearance; winter wet, however, can kill the plants. The leaves form a basal rosette or grow along a short, stocky stem; each leaf ends in a sharp spine and sometimes has fibrous threads along the margins but is more often toothed. Most agave are immense plants and are used as individual specimens in the landscape. Some smaller western species are suitable, where hardy, for the rock garden. Species and cultivars include the following:

CENTURY PLANT or AMERICAN ALOE *(Agave americana)* has gray-green leaves that grow 5 to 6 feet long and as much as 10 inches across; each leaf has a sharp spine at the tip and hooked spines along the margins. It is hardy to 15°F. Cultivars include Marginata', with yellow to creamy yellow leaf margins; 'Medio-picta', with a wide yellow stripe along the center of the leaf; 'Striata', with leaves striped in yellow or white; and 'Variegata', with dark green-and-yellow twisted leaves.

HEDGEHOG AGAVE *(Agave stricta)* has short stems that become somewhat branched with age and form rounded, congested, globose rosettes of stiff, spreading to erect green leaves; the leaves grow 14 inches long and less than half an inch wide and end in a very sharp, 1-inch-long spine.

MESCAL AGAVE *(Agave parryi)* has erect or spreading, stiff gray leaves with brown marginal teeth tipped with a 1-inch spine; the leaves are broadly oblong, growing to 12 inches long by 4 inches wide, and are arranged in a basal rosette. It is hardy to 10°F.

OCTOPUS AGAVE *(Agave vilmoriniana)* has loose, rather open rosettes, up to 3 feet wide, made up of pale green or chartreuse, curving, twisted leaves that are 36 inches long and 3 to 4 inches wide. It is hardy to 20°F.

QUEEN VICTORIA AGAVE *(Agave victoriae-reginae)* forms a stiff, basal rosette of dark green leaves that are marked with narrow white lines and are 6 inches long and 2 inches wide; they have no terminal spine and no marginal teeth.

KING FERDINAND AGAVE *(Agave fernandi-regis)* is very similar except that the leaves are more strongly tapered, are dark green with a white stripe along the margins, and have a terminal spine less than ½ inch long.

UTAH AGAVE *(Agave utahensis)* has 8-inch-long leaves that are just over an inch wide, with small teeth along the margins; they are ar-ranged in a basal rosette about 18 inches wide and usually form offsets. The leaves end in a terminal spine that may be anywhere from 1 to 8 inches long. Agaves tend to be variable and this species is no exception. Var. *eborispina* has olive-green leaves that end in a 4- to 8-inch-long ivory-colored spine; var. *kaibabensis* is vigorous, with individual rosettes as much as 40 inches across; and var. *nevadensis* has glaucous green leaves and a 1- to 4-inch-long, dark brown terminal spine. These varieties are barely introduced, and it may take some time before they are available. Utah agave is probably hardy to 15°F.

Alchemilla mollis
LADY'S-MANTLE

This plant makes delightful low clumps or sprawling mats of foliage that are useful at the front of a border to spill out and soften the edges of a hard-surfaced path. For the same reason, it can make mowing difficult if used adjacent to a lawn. Growing 12 to 20 inches tall, lady's-mantle has 6-inch-wide green leaves that are palmately cut into seven to eleven lobes with small, serrate teeth along the margins. The leaves have a greyish cast because they are felted with small hairs, which also create an enchanting transitory phenomenon: after a rainfall or in the morning when a heavy dew has fallen, the water droplets that are held on the leaves look like moonstones. Lady's-mantle grows well in full sun in cooler regions, midday shade in hot summer areas, in a moist but well-drained soil; it will also grow in drier, shadier places. It is hardy to –30°F.

Aloe spp. and cultivars
ALOE

These evergreen herbaceous perennials,

shrubs, or trees are native to arid regions, primarily in Africa. As might be expected, they are tender (hardy only to 25°F). Aloes are generally stemless; the leaves are succulent and stiff with sharply pointed tips and are spiny along the margins. They generally grow in tight, compact rosettes. Sometimes aloes are confused with agaves, but unlike aloes, agaves have fibrous leaves and originate in the New World.

Aloes are useful outdoors in southern California and the arid Southwest and as container plants elsewhere. In common with other succulent plants, aloes are drought tolerant and are an excellent choice for xeriscaping. They grow best in well-drained soil with minimal to moderate water and full sun or some light shade in hot summer areas. Some of the species that are useful for in-ground or container cultivation follow:

Aloe brevifolia is a low-growing plant with rosettes of thirty to forty 3-inch-long, smooth, glaucous gray-green leaves armed with horny white teeth along the margins. 'Variegata' is a cultivar with variegated leaves.

CORAL ALOE *(Aloe striata)* has procumbent stems to 3 feet long with twelve to twenty, 20-inch-long, lanceolate gray-green leaves with a pink margin; dead leaves persist and clothe the stems.

GOLDEN-TOOTH ALOE *(Aloe nobilis)*, also called green-and-gold crown aloe, grows to 12 inches tall and has sprawling stems to 6 feet long with dark green, ovate-lanceolate leaves to 8 inches long.

JEWELED ALOE *(Aloe distans)* has stems to 9 feet long that trail along the ground, rooting as they go, and clumps of glaucous green, lanceolate leaves to 6 inches long that are covered with scattered white tubercles and have yellowish white teeth along the margins.

PURPLE-CROWN *(Aloe mitriformis)*, also called purple-and-gold-crown aloe, has sprawl-

ing stems that grow to 6 feet long and have 8-inch-long, lanceolate-ovate leaves with pale, horny spines along the margins.

SPIDER ALOE *(Aloe humilis)*, also known as crocodile-jaws and hedgehog aloe, is low growing with dense clumps of ovate-lanceolate, glaucous leaves that grow 4 inches long and are covered with tubercles (pimplelike rounded bumps) and equipped with numerous sharp white teeth along the margins.

TIGER ALOE *(Aloe variegata)*, also called partridge-breast aloe, is stemless and low growing (9 to 12 inches tall) and spreads by means of stolons into large, triangular rosettes of 4- to 6-inch-long, triangular-lanceolate, white-edged leaves that are attractively marked with irregular transverse bands of white spots.

TORCH PLANT *(Aloe aristata)*, also known as lace aloe, is a dwarf species that grows 8 to 12 inches tall and wide; it has 100 to 150 4-inch-long leaves with crosswise bands of white tubercles on the underside, soft white teeth along the margins, and whiplike threads on the tips.

Artemisia spp. and cultivars
WORMWOOD

This diverse genus includes annuals, biennials, herbaceous perennials, and shrubs, all native of dry areas. They thrive in poor, infertile, sandy, well-drained soils in full sun. Most of them exhibit the silvery, hairy foliage typical of so many dryland plants. Many have aromatic foliage and are tolerant of salt in desert or seacoast conditions.

ABSINTHE *(A. absinthium)* 'Lambrook Silver', preferred to the species, grows 30 inches tall and has numerous branches well clothed with twice to thrice pinnately dissected, pungent leaves that are 2 to 4 inches long; the leaves are less divided as they ascend the stems. The leaves and stems are covered with silky, silvery white hairs and look stunning with purple foliage plants such as smokebush or *Sedum* 'Vera Jameson'. It is hardy to –20°F, but will not tolerate winter wet.

BEACH WORMWOOD or DUSTY-MILLER *(A. stellerana)* 'Silver Brocade' is a superior introduction from the University of British Columbia Botanic Garden. It has pinnately lobed, oblong to ovate leaves that are 4 inches long and are covered with felty white hairs; the foliage is unscented. It grows as a low, prostrate plant as compared to the species, which grows 30 inches tall. It is an excellent seaside plant but must have excellent drainage and poor soil at all times. It looks incredibly handsome with the bright orange flowers of butterfly weed and is superb as a foil to blue, lavender, purple, or mauve flowers and purple or bronze foliage. It is hardy to –20°F.

'POWIS CASTLE', a nonflowering hybrid of absinthe and southernwood, grows 2 to 3 feet tall and has finely dissected silver foliage. Introduced from Powis Castle in England, it is probably hardy to –5°F, but winter wet needs to be avoided.

ROMAN WORMWOOD *(Artemisia pontica)* is an upright shrubby perennial that grows 18 to 36 inches tall and has twice or thrice pinnately dissected, 2-inch-long, hairy, gray-green leaves, which give it a feathery, threadlike appearance. This is combined, however, with a rapidly colonizing root system that makes this species one of the most invasive artemisias. It is excellent for filling bare, poor, sandy soil areas in full sun. It is hardy to –10°F.

SAGEBRUSH *(A. tridentata)* is the sagebrush of Zane Gray's Western classic *Riders of the Purple Sage*. It is a 10-foot-tall evergreen shrub with strongly aromatic, silvery gray, 1-inch-long leaves. Var. *trifida* grows only 30 inches high and is thus more useful; it has aromatic gray leaves that are covered with short, soft, fine hairs. Sagebrush can be used in xeric landscapes with agaves, yucca, eryngium, and drought-tolerant shrubs such as sumac, juniper, and bayberry. It is hardy to –25°F.

SILVER-KING WORMWOOD *(A. ludoviciana albula)*, a perennial, is a native of southern Colorado to southern California, west Texas, and Mexico. It grows 24 to 42 inches tall and has erect stems covered with felted, grayish white, lanceolate, willowlike leaves that are 2 inches long. Near the top of the stems the leaves have no lobes; those near the base have three to five at the leaf tips. The roots are spreading and somewhat invasive. It looks lovely with pink flowers and has a great frosty effect with white asters or *Boltonia*. It is hardy to –10°F.

SILVER-MOUND ARTEMISIA *(A. schmidtiana* 'Silver Mound')* is satisfactory only if grown in nutrient-poor, coarse, sandy, quick-draining soils; otherwise, it is subject to fungal rots in summer which turn the foliage black and slimy. If this happens, it should be cut back hard, and fresh new foliage will emerge from the crown. The plant forms a soft mound of leaves that are nearly 2 inches long and twice palmately divided into linear, threadlike, silvery white segments, very sensuous to stroke. It is superb combined with plum-purple petunias. It is hardy to –20°F.

SILVER-QUEEN WORMWOOD *(A. ludoviciana albula* 'Silver Queen')* is very similar to 'Silver King' but has shorter, less erect stems.

SOUTHERNWOOD *(A. abrotanum)* is a dense, bushy, much-branched subshrub that grows 3 to 6 feet tall. It has aromatic foliage that is once, twice, or thrice pinnately dissected and is a beautiful sage-green color. It is hardy to –5°F.

Arum italicum
LORDS-AND-LADIES

This tuberous perennial is related to our native Jack-in-the-pulpit and is grown in a similar environment — in dappled woodland shade in a soil that is high in organic matter and remains moist at all times. But there the similarities end, for lords-and-ladies is dormant in summer rather than in winter; its leaves come up in early autumn and remain through the winter, until the plant becomes dormant in late spring. If winter conditions are harsh enough to damage the leaves, a second set emerges in the spring in order to supply nutrients to the tuber, which will sustain it through the summer resting phase. The leaves grow to 12 inches long and are oblong to triangular-subhastate, with a petiole that is even longer than the leaf. In the cultivar 'Marmoratum', the leaf blades are marbled along the veins with white; 'Pictum' has creamy white markings. Lords-and-ladies is elegant under a birch with white bark, combined with evergreen Christmas fern and hellebores for an urbane-appearing association of winter foliage. It is hardy to –5°F.

Aruncus dioicus
GOATSBEARD

This tall, fine-textured plant has foliage and flowers similar to that of an astilbe or bugbane. It grows 4 to 7 feet tall on sturdy, self-supporting stems and has large, much-divided, ovate to lanceolate, twice-toothed leaflets. Hardy to –30°F, this herbaceous perennial can provide a shrublike character to moist, rich woodlands but will also grow in drier soils and with direct sun. It is nice combined with large hosta, rodgersias, and Alleghany spurge. Another species, *Aruncus aethusifolius,* is a tight mound of dark green, lacy foliage, 12 inches tall. It is el-

egant in the shady garden in combination with cyclamen, ophiopogon, and small hosta. It is hardy to –10°F, possibly lower.

Asarum spp. and cultivars. See pages 119-20.

Aspidistra elatior
CAST-IRON PLANT

This most forgiving houseplant continues to grow in the darkest corner even if neglected and not watered. The dark green, leathery, lustrous, evergreen, oblong-elliptic, stemless leaves arise from surface rhizomes on a 6- to 8-inch-long leaf stalk; the leaves grow to 30 inches long and 3 to 4 inches wide and have the distinctive monocot parallel arrangement of veins. Cast-iron plant is often used as an ornamental in zoo horticulture, since it is able to tolerate difficult conditions. In the garden (or as a container plant), it grows best with a moist but well-drained, humus-rich soil in dense shade to filtered sun; it is hardy to 0°F, but its appearance suffers below 20°F. 'Variegata' is a cultivar with lengthwise white stripes that disappear if the plant is fertilized heavily. It is elegant with ferns, astilbe, doll's-eyes, and epimedium. *Aspidistra minor* 'Milky Way' (not mentioned in the horticultural reference *Hortus III)* is a smaller plant with lustrous, dark green leaves that are 12 inches long and 2 inches wide and are attractively specked in creamy white.

Astilbe spp. and cultivars
ASTILBE

Although very easy to cultivate, astilbe require fertile soil high in organic matter. They will tolerate fairly heavy shade. If astilbe are grown in the sun, more water is required; moist soil at all times throughout the growing season is best. The leaves are divided into three parts, which are each divided again into three parts. In some astilbes even the secondary divisions are divided into three parts. All astilbes have divided, lacy leaves with a fernlike texture.

Astilbe x arendsii are hybrids developed by George Arends of Germany in the early 1900s. Commonly grown in gardens, they are reliable, sturdy, long-lived plants needing little care. They have attractive flowers and foliage that is twice or thrice compounded, giving it an airy, fernlike appearance. The leaves are glossy green at maturity, but some cultivars, particularly those with red and deep pink flowers, have pleasing mahogany or coppery bronze foliage in spring. They are hardy to −20°F.

Astilbe chinensis has leaves twice to thrice compounded, with doubly serrate, ovate to oblong, fresh green leaflets with a dull surface. The species grows to 2 feet tall, but the lower cultivar 'Pumila' is generally grown in gardens. 'Pumila' is a more dwarf plant (6 to 12 inches tall) with a creeping rootstock, the spreading habit of which makes it useful as a ground cover; it tolerates drier conditions than other astilbe. Other cultivars include 'Finale' and 'Serenade'. It is hardy to −20°F.

Astilbe rivularis is sometimes confused with false goatsbeard, but this is an Asian species. The leaves are twice divided into threes, with 3-inch-long, toothed ovate leaflets. The leaves form a large mass at the base and extend up the stems of the 5- to 6-foot-tall plant. The species *rivularis* has a creeping rhizome and makes an increasing clump. It is hardy to −20°F.

Astilbe simplicifolia is low growing (to 12 inches tall) and has simple leaves that are 3 inches long and deeply lobed or cut. The species itself is rarely grown, but it has been used as a parent to several charming hybrids with compound foliage. Confusingly, the hybrids are offered as though they were cultivars of the species. 'Atrorosea' and 'Sprite' grow 8 to 12 inches tall and have attractive glossy green, compound, lacy foliage; 'Bronze Elegance', 'Dunkelachs', and 'Inshirach Pink' have glossy bronze-green compound leaves; 'William Buchanan' is tiny, growing only 6 inches tall, and has very dense, fine-textured, curly, glossy dark green foliage. They are hardy to −20°F.

Astilbe tacquetii is not listed in the authoritative reference *Hortus III*, but is generally offered as the cultivar 'Superba'. The large, broad, compound leaves have dull-surfaced, dark-tinted green, ovate leaflets that are double toothed along the edge. The plant is erect and grows 3 to 4 feet tall. It is hardy to −20°F.

FALSE GOATSBEARD *(Astilbe biternata)* is a North American species of astilbe (most others are east Asian). This large-scale plant grows up to 6 feet tall and has leaves 2 feet across that are composed of twice-compounded, sharply serrated, ovate leaflets nearly 5 inches long. The imposing bulk of foliage is excellent grown with large hosta, rodgersia, and similar bold, massive plants in moist, lightly shaded woodland settings. It is hardy to −15°F.

Begonia rex
REX BEGONIA

This rhizomatous species has obliquely ovate leaves that are 8 to 12 inches long and 6 to 8 inches wide. The leaves have a wavy margin and a wrinkled, blistered surface. The pure species is metallic green with a broad, silvery gray band on the upper surface of the leaf and is reddish on the underside. The species has largely been supplanted by hybrids (x *rex-cultorum),* which are subtly or boldly spotted, blotched, or marbled in patterns of green, silver-gray, purple, and bronze. They all need shade and a rich, porous soil high in organic matter, moist but not saturated, with moderate to high humidity appreciated. Only in frost-free areas can they be considered for garden use year-round. They are excellent as seasonal bedding plants or for container plantings. Unnamed seedlings are suitable for these purposes and are less expensive than named cultivars, such as 'Helen Teupel', which has silvery green and bronze-red leaves. Cultivars include 'American Beauty', which has serrate-edged, tapered leaves of a deep plum color with maroon centers; 'Autumn Glow', which has mottled rose-and-silver, pointed leaves; 'Elda Haring', with lacy white-and-crimson markings; 'Fireworks', which has silver leaves traced with large, plum-black veins leading to a silver center blotch and raspberry-purple edges; 'Kathlyana', which has heavily silver-specked leaves with long, pointed lobes; 'My Valentine', which has a narrow edging and a large, central blotch, both plum-red, and a greenish silver band between; 'Queen Mother', which has a strongly tapered, rose-red leaf with an irregular, narrow silver band near the edge; and 'Venetian Red', which has new leaves of silver that mature to rich red.

Bergenia spp. and cultivars
BERGENIA

These more-or-less evergreen plants, with their thick, stout rhizomes, grow into large colonies; they have large, thick, leathery, glossy leaves that often turn purplish red in winter. They grow best with some shade but will tolerate full sun, especially in cool summer areas if the soil is moist. Winter burn can be a problem in exposed locations. A moderately fertile soil is needed to maintain best leaf growth and promote flowering. These plants interbreed readily, producing numerous hybrids that have

been selected primarily for flower colors of white, pink, or reddish pink. They are useful as a ground cover in combination with rhododendrons, hellebores, astilbes, and ferns.

Bergenia purpurascens has green leaves sometimes suffused with a purple tinge; in winter they turn beet red on top and mahogany on the underside. The leaves are 8 to 10 inches long, elliptic to ovate-elliptic, and are carried more erect than in other species. It is hardy to –10°F.

HEART-LEAVED BERGENIA *(Bergenia cordifolia)* has leathery, glossy orbicular leaves that are blistered or puckered like a Savoy cabbage leaf; growing to 10 inches long, they are rounded or cordate at the base and have very small, shallow, rounded or sawlike teeth along the margins. The plant grows to 20 inches tall. The cultivar 'Purpurea' turns purplish in winter. Hardy to –20°F, heart-leaved bergenia has a better spring appearance if covered with snow during winter at such low temperatures.

SIBERIAN TEA *(Bergenia crassifolia)* has elliptic to obovate leaves to 8 inches long that are convexly curved like the back of a spoon and have shallow sawlike teeth along the margins. This species turns mahogany-red in winter. It is hardy to –20°F.

WINTER BEGONIA *(Bergenia ciliata)* is exquisite in appearance and has broadly orbicular to obovate-elliptic leaves that are bronze-green when they first emerge, 8 to 14 inches long and wide, denticulate or crenate along the margins, and densely covered with fine hairs on both sides. Although winter begonia is root hardy, the leaves are damaged by frost, so consider this a deciduous species in colder areas. It is hardy to –5°F.

Brunnera macrophylla
SIBERIAN BUGLOSS

This plant has slightly hairy, coarse, heart-shaped (cordate) leaves of a medium to dark green, which remain in good condition until harsh winter conditions arrive. Perfectly scaled to its forget-me-not flowers in spring, the leaves continue to grow, reaching 6 to 8 inches long. Siberian bugloss is excellent for shady woodland gardens, where there is moist but well-drained soil high in organic matter and dappled shade which it prefers, although it will tolerate sunny situations if there is adequate moisture. It is nice in combination with lungwort, epimedium, and Christmas fern under azaleas. Some British cultivars are much more difficult to grow than their reliable parent species and require shade; they include 'Hadspen Cream' and 'Variegata', with creamy white margins; and 'Langtrees', which has leaves that are oval-spotted, silvery aluminum gray toward the margins and is less tempermental. Siberian bugloss is hardy to −30°F.

Caladium x hortulanum
CALADIUM

This tuberous plant is a hybrid of the species that are native to Brazil, Peru, and other regions of tropical America. The leaf blades are translucent, ovate to lanceolate, and cordate or forked where the leaf joins the long petiole, which may be as long or longer than the 10- to 14-inch-long leaf. The leaves are flat or may have an undulating or ruffled surface and are wonderfully variegated with blotches and bands of either a single color or a mixture of red, rose, pink, white, and green. Numerous cultivars are available either as dormant tubers or as potted plants. Often treated as a summer annual in all except the mildest frost-free areas, caladium grows best with a daytime temperature of at least 70°F, and warm nights. The soil, in containers or in the garden, should be a coarse, gritty, quick-draining mixture high in organic

matter and moist at all times. If lifted for winter storage, store the tuber at 55°F. Caladium is an excellent shade-tolerant plant that has been used as a summer bedding plant in sunny areas in the Southeast and in the New York/New Jersey/Connecticut area. (I prefer to use it in the shade.)

Calocephalus brownii
CUSHIONBUSH

This Australian shrub is used as a perennial along coastal areas of California. Cushionbush grows as a dense, silvery, woolly mound of twiggy branches, 3 feet high and wide, and is covered with linear leaves less than ¼ inch long tightly pressed to the branches. It is an excellent seaside plant, growing best in wind-swept shoreline areas, exposed to salt spray. It needs full sun, protection from a surplus of water, and a fast-draining, sandy, gravelly soil. Cushionbush grows well with other drought-tolerant plants such as sedums, aeoniums, and other succulents. It is hardy to 28°F.

Canna x generalis
CANNA

These hybrids are of mixed origin, reflected in their varied heights and leaf colors. They grow best with warm, humid, tropical conditions similar to those in the West Indies, Central and South America, and Florida, where the species originated. Fortunately the rhizomatous roots can be lifted and stored over the winter in colder regions. Canna need a moist but not soggy, fertile soil and full sun for best growth. Their height is variable, with some dwarf cultivars only 18 to 24 inches tall and statuesque cultivars 6 to 9 feet tall. The leaves are like those of a banana — large, broad, and simple, with the base of the leaf clasping the stem; they may be green, bronze, purple, or variegated. 'Bangkok' ('Nirvana') grows 20 inches tall and has creamy yellow-white stripes on fresh green leaves; 'Black Knight' and 'Wyoming' grow 4 feet tall and have bronze foliage; 'King Humbert' reaches 6 feet high or more and has bronze foliage; 'Pretoria' grows 6 feet tall and has green leaves with yellow stripes and a red edge; 'Red Stripe' grows to 6 feet tall and is variegated with red margins and stripes on an olive-green ground. Bold, lush, and tropical in appearance, canna are beautiful near a pond (as long as the soil in which they grow is not saturated) in combination with tall grasses and large ferns. In an annual border, they can be used as background plants with castor beans. In a herbaceous border I have combined bronze-leaved sorts with red-flowered dahlias, liatris, New England asters, and grasses. The Victorians were fond of using canna in carpet bedding schemes — circular beds cut into the lawn with a central group of canna surrounded by a ring of geraniums or bright red salvia.

Cimicifuga spp. and cultivars
BUGBANE

These tall plants have compound leaves that are again divided once or several times, giving a fernlike effect. This pattern is common to false spirea (*Aruncus*), astilbe (*Astilbe*), and doll's-eyes (*Actaea*), all of which have similar foliage; care should be taken to use contrasting foliage shapes to provide diversity with these genera. Bugbane are elegant grown in the back of a shady border or can be used more informally in a naturalistic woodland garden with shrubs and bolder-textured perennials. They require moist but well-drained soil rich in humus and dappled to moderate shade for best growth.

BLACK SNAKEROOT **(*Cimicifuga race-**

mosa), also known as black cohosh, has medium to dark green leaves that grow to 18 inches long and have thrice-divided segments 1 to 4 inches long that are broadly ovate and coarsely toothed along the margins. The plant grows 3 to 8 feet high and has wiry, branched stems. It is hardy to –30°F.

JAPANESE BUGBANE **(*Cimicifuga japonica* var. *acerina*)** has stems about 3 feet tall and low basal foliage with long, palmate lobes, rather maplelike in appearance and very different from other bugbanes. It is hardy to –15°F.

KAMCHATKA BUGBANE **(*Cimicifuga simplex*)** has an unbranched stem that grows 2 to 4 feet high; the 4- to 12-inch leaves are first divided into three parts and then twice pinnately compounded, with the deeply toothed leaflets 2 to 3 inches long. It is late flowering and the buds may be damaged by early autumn frosts. *Cimicifuga simplex ramosa [C. ramosa]*, mentioned in the literature but not in the basic horticultural reference *Hortus III*, has tall (to 7 feet) slender stems with a few branches and large, deeply divided leaves. Most desirable is the cultivar 'Atropurpurea', which has deep purple-black leaves. I have seen it grown (at Hillside Gardens in Norfolk, Connecticut) in combination with a large-leaved, golden yellow hosta and the orange flowers of *Lilium* 'Enchantment'; in July, the result was vibrant. It is hardy to –30°F.

Clivia miniata
CLIVIA

This plant has stiff, fleshy leaves with thickened bases and is thus classified as a bulb. Hardy only to 30°F, this bulb is treated as a container plant by most gardeners in the United States. The thick, glossy evergreen leaves grow to 18 inches long and 2 inches wide and are even more attractive in shady subtropical gardens.

Well-drained soil high in organic matter, moist when the plants are in active growth, and shade to semishade are the most suitable conditions. Clivia can be combined with ferns and other lacy-textured plants. The variegated form is *Clivia miniata* var. *striata*.

Crambe maritima
SEA KALE

In spring this husky perennial sends up purple, knoblike shoots, which quickly expand and grow 3 feet tall; the waxy, glaucous, bluish basal leaves are notched, shallowly lobed, and large, growing 2 feet long or more and nearly as wide to form a low, loose, domed mound of foliage. Sea kale is elegant planted with finer-textured silver foliage plants such as yarrow. The blanched young shoots are eaten like asparagus. It is hardy to –5°F.

Cyclamen spp.
CYCLAMEN

These tuberous plants are native in the Mediterranean region of Greece and Turkey to the Middle East as far as Iran and Israel, and central Europe. The persistent leaves on several species are beautifully marbled or blotched with silver, making them handsome foliage plants for the shady garden. They need well-drained soils high in organic matter and dappled woodland shade for best growth. While resting, usually in summer, moisture can be harmful, but they should not dry out while in active growth. All are under the Conventions on the International Trade of Endangered Species (CITES) regulations as endangered plants since these were formerly collected extensively from wild populations. However, some are easily raised, and commercial propagated stock is available.

Cyclamen coum is a sturdy plant with orbicular, dark green leaves with burgundy red beneath; the leaves, which are almost 3 inches long, appear in early autumn along with the flower buds. The flowers open January to March, and the foliage remains in good condition throughout the winter; the plants do not go dormant until quite late in spring. The leaves are variable and may be plain green or spotted with a silver maple-leaf-shaped zone in the center. This is one of the few plants that does well under maple or beech trees. It is hardy to –5°F.

FLORISTS' CYCLAMEN **(Cyclamen persicum)** hybrids with attractively marbled leaves are popular as container plants and in frost-free areas; the species is rarely offered. Under indoor cultivation, the heart-shaped leaves with light green or silver mottling appear, die down, and are replaced by a second set; the flowers continue with both sets of leaves. These plants are available as 6-inch-tall miniatures and up to 12-inch-tall cultivars, and are hardy to 30°F.

IVY-LEAVED CYCLAMEN **(Cyclamen hederifolium [C. neapolitanum])** has leaves that are shaped like miniature ivy, generally angled to roundish, and attractive from August to the following May. The leaves are marked with silver and are so variable that no two plants seem the same. It is hardy to –5°F, lower with reliable snow cover. This cyclamen flowers in August/September before or just as foliage begins to appear.

Cynara cardunculus
CARDOON

This plant is commonly cultivated as a vegetable but, like rhubarb and globe artichoke (which is another *Cynara*), its foliage justifies finding a place for it in the ornamental landscape as well. The elegantly bold leaves are arching, deeply cleft, pinnate, (thistlelike in appearance), and are gray-green above and white with woolly hairs beneath. The leaves lower on the stem can reach 3 to 4 feet long; they are smaller as they ascend the 6- to 8-foot-high stem. Cardoon is a sizable plant for large-scale gardens with fertile, well-drained soil and adequate moisture with some light shade in frost-free, hot summer areas. In colder areas it should be mulched well in winter or the roots dug and stored indoors like a dahlia. It is hardy to 20°F. Artichoke *(Cynara scolymus)* has similar leaves but no spines and grows only 3 to 5 feet tall.

Dianthus spp. and cultivars
DIANTHUS

These plants are perennial, biennial, or annual, depending on the species. Often known as "pinks," many do indeed have pink flowers, but the common name refers to the ragged edges of the petals, which look as though they have been "pinked" with shears. The narrow, linear leaves grow in pairs and are often united at their base, forming a sheath around the stem. All grow best in alkaline, gritty-sandy, well-drained soil in full sun; in this environment the leaves will make delightful loose mounds of evergreen foliage. Dianthus are excellent at the front of a border spilling over brick or flagstone walks to soften the edges, in a rock garden, and in herb and cottage gardens.

CHEDDAR PINK **(Dianthus gratianopolitanus)** has glaucous blue-gray leaves in a tight mound. It is hardy to –10°F.

CLOVE CARNATION **(Dianthus caryophyllus)** is a vigorous, short-lived perennial that makes rather open mounds of glaucous blue foliage 1 to 3 feet tall. It is hardy to –10°F.

COTTAGE PINK **(Dianthus plumarius)** grows 16 inches tall, forming a wide, open mat

of smooth, glaucous gray leaves. This is one of the parents of *Dianthus* x *allwoodii*, the other being the clove carnation. It is hardy to –20°F.

Dianthus x **allwoodii** is a hybrid with firm, glaucous gray-blue leaves that grow in a 12- to 18-inch-tall, spreading, tufted mound. 'Alpinus' is a strain with variable flower color but consistently produces tidy, dense, 6- to 12-inch-high mounds of linear blue-green leaves. It is hardy to –20°F.

MAIDEN PINK **(Dianthus deltoides)** makes 6-inch-high, loose mats of bright green foliage. It is hardy to –30°F but in severe climates it should be given winter protection in the form of evergreen boughs or salt hay.

Dicentra spp. and cultivars
BLEEDING-HEART

These are useful in light to moderate shade in moist but well-drained soils high in organic matter. A constantly wet soil can be fatal for the many species that have tuberous roots. They grow best in areas with cool summers. The leaves are mostly three-parted or dissected. Bleeding-hearts are attractive in combination with bergenia, hosta, and hellebores.

BLEEDING-HEART **(Dicentra spectabilis)** grows to 30 inches tall and has large, soft, broadly obovate to wedge-shaped green leaf segments that ascend the stems. Typically the plant has pink flowers and goes dormant in early summer. The white-flowered form, usually offered either as 'Alba' or 'Pantaloons', is not so quickly dormant. Bleeding-heart is susceptible to late spring frosts. It is hardy to –30°F.

DUTCHMAN'S-BREECHES **(Dicentra cucullaria),** a woodland plant that blooms in spring and then rapidly withers away, grows from a cluster of small, rice-grainlike tubers. It has glaucous, dissected, 10-inch-high foliage and would be an excellent plant if only it persisted above ground for a longer period. In Connecticut, it is up in March and gone by May. Like other small bulbs, it should be grown with foliage perennials to conceal its dormant state. It is charming in the spring woodland garden with bloodroot, ferns, small hosta, and violets. It is hardy to –30°F.

FRINGED BLEEDING-HEART *(Dicentra eximia)* grows 12 to 18 inches high and has glaucous basal leaves that are finely divided into fernlike segments. 'Bountiful' and 'Luxuriant' are free-blooming cultivars, or possibly hybrids, and are more readily available than the true species. Fringed bleeding-heart has elegant foliage all summer long and will tolerate some direct sun if summers are cool and there is an adequate supply of moisture. It is hardy to –30°F.

GOLDEN-EARDROPS *(Dicentra chrysantha)* is better suited to mild winter areas where the other *Dicentra* species are short lived. It is native to southern California and Baja California's inner Coastal Ranges and the foothills of the Sierra Nevadas. It grows 5 feet tall and has sparse, glaucous, twice-pinnate leaves to 12 inches long. It needs good drainage, low to moderate fertility, and warmth to grow well. It is drought tolerant and is hardy to 20°F.

SQUIRREL CORN *(Dicentra canadensis)* is distinguished from Dutchman's-breeches both by its flowers, which lack the spur of the latter, and by the underground tuber, which is a collection of loosely attached yellow cornlike scales. The foliage of squirrel corn is similar to that of Dutchman's-breeches both in its appearance and brief duration. It is hardy to –30°F.

WESTERN BLEEDING-HEART *(Dicentra formosa)* is similar to fringed bleeding-heart in appearance and can be used in a similar manner. The leaves are usually glaucous beneath but may have a fine whitish or pale blue bloom on the upper surface also.

Echeveria spp. (See also *Sempervivum,* page 158.)
HEN-AND-CHICKS

Like *Sempervivum* spp., these plants usually form rosettes of fleshy, succulent, oblong to obovate leaves (occasionally they have short stems with leaves growing alternately along the length). They are native from Texas to Argentina, with many species found in Mexico, and are far less hardy than *Sempervivum;* they are useful in the garden only in frost-free areas, elsewhere as container plants. The attractive green or gray-green leaves are often flushed with deeper colors such as bronze to purple-lilac to red, or have a pale, mealy, starchlike coating.

Closely related to this genus is *Dudleya,* native to California, Baja California, and Mexico; it also forms drought-tolerant rosettes. Most common in cultivation is *D. brittonii,* from Baja California, which is silvery with heavy, chalky, starchlike coating and has solitary rosettes up to 18 inches across. Hen-and-chicks need shelter from rain and hail, which wear away their distinctive coating.

Echinops ritro
GLOBE THISTLE

This bold plant is good for elegant foliage effects. It grows 2 to 4 feet tall in full sun in a site with well-drained soil. Ascending up the stem, the leaves grow to 8 inches long and are lustrous green above, white woolly beneath, oblong, and pinnately cut into lanceolate segments with spiny teeth along the margins; the leaves are reminiscent of those of thistles. It is hardy to –30°F. Globe thistle is interesting when grown with yuccas (or, in milder areas, agaves) and shrubs such as sumacs, bayberries, and junipers.

Eryngium yuccifolium
RATTLESNAKE-MASTER

This is a wide-ranging plant, found in Connecticut, south to Florida, and west to Minnesota, Kansas, and Texas, indicating its adaptability to extremes of heat and cold. The linear, straplike, evergreen leaves grow more than 3 feet long and have fine bristlelike spines along the margins. It is admirable in the great prairies of the Midwest, growing with the numerous composites and prairie grasses, and is also useful in the garden as a linear foil to broader foliage. It grows well in deep, well-drained soil in full sun; it is drought tolerant once established and is hardy to −30°F. Other eryngiums have equally interesting foliage: *E. amethystinum,* somewhat confused in the trade, grows 2 to 3 feet tall and has a basal rosette of dark green to silver-gray (in the true plant) obovate leaves that are twice pinnate and deeply cut into spiny-edged lobes. *E. bourgatti* grows 18 to 24 inches tall and has stunning orbicular basal leaves, deeply cut into three to five palmate lobes; the crisply curling, prickle-edged foliage is gray-green with broad silvery white veins and spattered with sequinlike spots. It is hardy to −10°F. The larger *E. eburneum* has 2- to 3-foot-long leaves that are very spiny, arching, linear, grassy, and evergreen and grow in rosettes like a bromeliad; it is hardy to 10°F. Other eryngiums are not generally offered and are thus rarely used in gardens, although the increasing interest in drought-tolerant plants may change this.

Filipendula spp. and cultivars
FALSE SPIREA

These plants were once included in the genus *Spiraea* and are somewhat similar in appearance.
QUEEN-OF-THE-MEADOW **(Filipendula ulmaria)** grows 3 to 6 feet tall and has leaves that are usually white woolly beneath; each leaf, with its long petiole, grows 1 to 8 feet long and has two to five pairs of primary ovate leaflets 1 to 3 inches long with sharply double-serrate margins and a terminal three-lobed leaflet. Even more attractive is the cultivar 'Aurea', which has bright golden green leaves that turn creamy yellow in the summer sun. It can be cut down in midsummer to produce a second flush of fresh growth for autumn.

SIBERIAN MEADOWSWEET **(Filipendula palmata)** grows 3 feet tall and has compound pinnate leaves along stems that terminate in a large leaflet (3 to 8 inches across) with seven to nine palmate lobes, white woolly on the underside; often at the side of the terminal leaflet there are two pairs of smaller leaflets, 1 to 3 inches across, incised and lobed. Siberian meadowsweet is easily confused with Japanese meadowsweet (*Filipendula purpurea*), which is often substituted for it. These plants' requirements of full sun and a moist soil suggest a pondside planting with rodgersias and blue flag and yellow flag iris. It is hardy to −25°F, but survives best with a winter mulch, since the roots are near the surface.

Foeniculum vulgare
FENNEL

This 6-foot-tall plant is an herb that is cultivated for use as a seasoning. The very fine, threadlike leaves are pinnately multiple-compounded, providing a dense yet airy texture. It needs full sun and a sandy, well-drained soil. Fennel is elegant as a foil to plants with more substantial foliage, or to "dress" those with sparse foliage of their own, such as lilies. Best for this purpose is *purpurea* or the cultivar 'Bronze', which have mahogany leaves when young and copper-bronze leaves when mature. Although it is a perennial, this plant is often grown as an annual, because the mature plants flower, seed, and "volunteer" in quantity. It is hardy to −20°F.

Geranium sessiliforum var. *nigrum*
BLACK-LEAVED CRANESBILL

This dainty plant occasionally shows up at a sale sponsored by a chapter of The American Rock Garden Society, or in a specialist's catalog. A native of Australia and New Zealand, black-leaved cranesbill produces tufts of congested, basal leaves with scalloped edges, less than an inch across, colored chocolate brown. Because of its diminutive size, it is perhaps better grown in a container. It needs a sunny location and gritty, well-drained soil that does not dry out. It is hardy to 20°F.

Gunnera manicata
GUNNERA

This plant has gargantuan leaves, rough to the touch, that may grow to 9 feet across but are usually two-thirds that size. The orbicular to kidney-shaped leaves have palmate lobes and coarse teeth along the margin as well as fleshy prickles along the veins on the underside of the leaves and all over the 4- to 6-foot-long petioles. To attain this gigantic size each growing season, gunnera needs a rich fertile soil, high in organic matter, and copious moisture, as on a pond bank. It should be fertilized when new leaves appear in the spring and twice during the growing period in order to achieve the greatest dimensions; it grows best in a lightly shaded site protected from drying winds. It is hardy to 10°F, but the football-sized resting bud needs shelter in the form of its old leaves pulled over it, supplemented with additional covering material. The resting bud must be kept dry in winter since soggy conditions around the root crown can lead to rot. An awesome combination might be achieved by planting gunnera with giant hogweed — suitable for a movie thriller!

Helleborus spp.
HELLEBORE

These are elegant plants with mostly basal, palmately divided foliage, evergreen or deciduous. Although hellebores are native to the limestone regions of Europe and Asia, they thrive in more acid soils that are moist but well-drained, high in organic matter, and sheltered by deciduous trees. They flower in winter or earliest spring, and their foliage is elegant for an extended period, dormant only through the worst of winter, or evergreen. Mature plants are difficult to transplant; it is best to plant smaller, container-grown plants in spring so they become established before the stress of winter. Self-sowing colonies develop volunteers that can be moved to new locations around the garden as required or desired.

CHRISTMAS ROSE *(Helleborus niger)* is named for its black roots, but its flowers are white. The evergreen, leathery, stemless leaves have ovate-cuneate leaflets that are somewhat toothed toward the tips. With its ornate, dark green leaves, this species can be planted in combination with Christmas fern and European ginger for elegant foliage effect through the winter. It is hardy to −10°F — lower with reliable snow cover.

CORSICAN HELLEBORE *(Helleborus lividus* ssp. *corsicus [H. argutifolius])* has the most elegant foliage: thick leafy stems of lightly frosted leaves, marbled with pale bluish green, divided into three segments and coarsely toothed along the edges. The stems flower their second year. It is hardy to 0°F but is prone to winter damage from sunscald and windburn.

Helleborus lividus, differentiated by the lack of marginal spines, is even more tender. Some hybrids are available as *H.* x *sternii* and can be tried in a protected location. They are hardy at Wave Hill in Riverdale, New York, but even there the foliage is damaged in hard winters and regenerates from the roots in spring.

LENTEN ROSE *(Helleborus orientalis)* is a stemless species with semievergreen leaves that turn brown late in winter when conditions are harsh. The palmately divided leaves, growing to 16 inches across, have seven to nine sharply serrated, elliptic-oblong segments and are a fresh, bright green as they unfold in spring. Lenten rose is an excellent ground cover around deciduous azaleas or rhododendrons in combination with ferns and spring bulbs in an oak woodland. It is hardy to –20°F.

STINKING HELLEBORE *(Helleborus foetidus)* is an unfortunate name for a laudable plant. This hellebore, which has a stem, is more tender than the preceding, acaulescent (stemless) species. Stinking hellebore grows 18 inches tall and has very dark black-green leaves composed of seven to eleven narrow, lanceolate segments that become broadly ovate, entire bracts near the flower cluster at the top of the stalk. The flower buds are formed late in the summer and remain through the winter, opening in early spring; the whole stalk dies after the seeds mature, and new stalks emerge in summer to continue the cycle. Thus, foliage is always present, but each stem lasts for only a year. It is superb planted with Japanese painted fern, silver forms of dead nettles, daffodils, and snowdrops. It is hardy to –10°F.

Hemerocallis spp. and cultivars
DAYLILIES

These are among the most popular herbaceous perennials in ornamental horticulture. They grow in a graceful, fountainlike clump of green, arching, linear, basal foliage that is grasslike in appearance, and thus they offer more than their flowers to the landscape. They are easy to cultivate and are one of the sturdiest, most trouble-free plants (except that deer treat them as a salad bar) for use in the herbaceous border, as a ground cover, for roadside plantings or edging a driveway, in naturalistic meadow gardens, or in light shade under high-branched trees.

The height of the plant is described in terms of the flower stalk (called a *scape*), instead of the leaves. In daylily breeding, the term *miniature* has in the past referred to the size of the flowers (although it now usually refers to plants with small blooms that are also only 12 to 18 inches tall). *Dwarf* cultivars are those with flower scapes less than 1 foot tall; they are likely to have finer, grassier foliage than that of larger plants. In southern gardens, evergreen daylilies do well and have attractive foliage year-round. This attribute is generally deleterious in colder areas, where repeated winter damage is harmful to plant growth; gardeners in the North should therefore use those cultivars that *are* winter dormant (or possibly semievergreen). In general, daylilies prosper in sun or light shade in moist but well-drained soil of moderate fertility.

The majority of daylilies have solid-colored green leaves, but *Hemerocallis fulva* 'Kwanso', which has double orange flowers marked with a darker V toward the base of the petals, has leaves with attractive white striping; however, there is a marked tendency to revert to all green. Familiar as a naturalized roadside wildflower, the tawny daylily (*Hemerocallis fulva*), has leaves that grow to 24 inches long and almost 1½ inches wide and curve in a graceful manner. *Hemerocallis minor* is a dwarf species with arching leaves that sweep over to touch the ground; its leaves are 20 inches long and ¼ inch wide. Daylilies are useful in combination with bolder-textured perennials, in association with shrubs, or massed on their own. Many are hardy to −20°F.

Heracleum mantegazzianum
GIANT HOGWEED

This massive, coarse-textured perennial grows 8 to 10 feet tall and has thrice-compounded leaves as much as 3 feet across with very large, deeply cut leaflets. This imposing architectural plant grows in sun or light shade in areas with moist soil. Even in a large-scale garden, where bold effect is wanted, one plant is generally adequate. It self-sows freely, but is monocarpic (which means that it dies after fruiting just once). It is hardy to −30°F.

Heuchera spp. and cultivars
ALUMROOT

Native to western North America, these plants consist of clumps of basal leaves, rounded with a cordate base or with five to nine broad lobes, toothed along the margins; the leaves are carried on long petioles above the rhizomatous surface rootstocks, which become woody with age. Evergreen in all but the harshest climates, the leaves are sometimes marbled or flushed with gray and have a fine appearance. Alum root plants grow best with full sun to light shade (in hot summer regions some shade is especially important), in moist but well-drained soil high in organic matter.

CORALBELLS *(Heuchera* x *brizoides)* are hybrids of several species, selected primarily for flower color. In addition, some display the attractive foliage of their *americana, micrantha,* and *sanguinea* parentage. 'Gaiety' has leaves mottled with silver; 'Oakington Jewel' has leaves mottled with bronze. 'Dale's Strain'

has consistently silvery, marbelized leaves.

Heuchera americana have ivylike leaves that are flushed with coppery brown, especially when they open in spring, turning dark green with maturity. This species probably gave rise to *Heuchera* 'Palace Purple', which has large, bronze-purple leaves all year long. Since the cultivar is often produced from seed, the coloration is variable. Shade-grown plants are often bronze-green or olive-green in summer, so color is obviously also dependent on the amount of sunlight available.

Heuchera micrantha is the other possible, although unlikely, parent of *Heuchera* 'Palace Purple' and this cultivar is sometimes listed as *Heuchera micrantha diversiloba* 'Palace Purple'. This species has maplelike leaves that grow 1 to 3 inches long and are marbled with gray. It is hardy to −10°F. An exciting new cultivar from Montrose Nursery in North Carolina is 'Montrose Ruby' (*Heuchera americana* 'Dale's Strain' x *H.* 'Palace Purple'); it has dark purple leaves mottled with silver and maintains a good dark color even in summer, in shade.

Heuchera villosa, grows 2 feet tall and has large, clear green, somewhat hairy, lobed leaves. Bolder in texture than the other *Heuchera* species, it is an attractive plant for light shade or sun. It is hardy to −10°F.

Hosta spp. and cultivars
HOSTA

This genus is one of the first to interest gardeners with the possibilities of using herbaceous perennials as foliage plants. It is difficult to go wrong if hosta are grown in combination with a fern or fernlike astilbe, and grass or grasslike liriope. Most species are native to Japan, with a few found nearby in Korea and China.

The ovate to lanceolate leaves arise in a dense basal clump and have a long petiole and often distinct veins. They range in size from thumbnail small to 30 inches, and they may be dark to medium to apple green, glaucous blue or golden yellow, or variegated white or yellow with marginal bands, central blotches, or softly shaded streaking. It is certain that whatever you need in terms of size and color already exists as a cultivar.

Hostas grow best in moist soils that are high in organic matter. Although they prefer dappled to deep shade, they will grow in full sun if the soil is adequately moist. However, in regions with hot summers, especially, yellow-leafed forms become "crisped" and blue ones turn greener; only the green-leaved forms have been completely satisfactory in my experience. They are hardy to –30°F.

When the plants become crowded and overgrow their site, or when more are wanted, hosta can be readily propagated by division: Dig the clump early in spring before growth begins, or early in autumn as the leaves are yellowing. Hose some soil off the thick, fibrous roots. Cut the crowns of large-growing varieties into smaller pieces with a machete or pry them apart with two spading forks; tease smaller ones apart with the aid of a sturdy hand fork, making sure that three to five buds remain on each division. These divisions will produce plants that are identical, having been produced asexually.

Commercially, hosta are often produced by cloning — tissue-culture propagation in which each plant is created from only a few cells. As might be expected from such a variable genus, the very act of cloning can induce mutation, depending on where on the plant the cells originated; and some are more mutable than others. New cultivars are introduced by the hundreds, and many older cultivars remain popular. The only drawback this plant has is its palatability — deer will devour the leaf blades,

leaving only a tuft of petioles to mark the spot. In suburban areas of the Northeast, whitetail deer have become a major garden pest.

The names of hosta are very confused since some species are variable from seed and there are some hybrids of unknown origin. Only a few of the possibilities are listed here:

GLAUCOUS-LEAVED: *Hh. sieboldiana, sieboldiana* 'Elegans', *tokudama* 'Love Pat', and some *fortunei*, such as 'Big Daddy', 'Big Mama', 'Blue Angel', 'Blue Cadet', 'Blue Skies', 'Bressingham Blue', 'Hadspen Heron', 'Halcyon', 'Krossa Regale', 'Serendipity', 'True Blue', 'Wedgewood Blue'.

GOLDEN-LEAVED: *Hh.* 'August Moon', 'Gold Edger', 'Golden Bullion', 'Golden Medallion', 'Golden Scepter', 'Golden Sunburst', 'Midas Touch', 'Piedmont Gold', 'Sum and Substance', 'Wogan Gold'.

GREEN-LEAVED: *Hh. fortunei, lancifolia, nakaiana, plantaginea, tardiflora, undulata* 'Erromena', *ventricosa, venusta*, 'Green Fountain', 'Saishu Jima'.

WHITE-CENTERED: *Hh. undulata* 'Univittata', 'Celebration', 'Squiggles'.

WHITE-EDGED: *Hh. crispula, decorata* 'Thomas Hogg', *fortunei* 'Albo-marginata', *fortunei* 'Francee', *gracillima* 'Variegated', *sieboldii (albo-marginata), sieboldiana* 'Elegans', 'Northern Halo', *undulata* 'Albo-marginata', 'Fringe Benefit', 'Ginko Craig', and 'North Hills'.

YELLOW-CENTERED: *Hh. fortunei* 'Albo-picta' (turns all green in summer), *tokudama* 'Aureo-nebulosa', 'Gold Standard', 'Kabitan', 'Sea Sprite'.

YELLOW-EDGED: *Hh. fluctuans* 'Variegated', *fortunei* 'Obscura Marginata', *sieboldiana* 'Frances Williams', *tokudama* 'Flavo-circinalis', *ventricosa* 'Aureo-marginata', 'Golden Tiara'.

YELLOW LEAF/WHITE EDGE: 'Lunar Eclipse'.

Iris spp. and cultivars

IRIS

These herbaceous perennials have fibrous, rhizomatous roots or bulbs and elegant linear or swordlike leaves arising in a basal clump. Taxonomically, iris are divided into those with bulbs and those with rhizomes. The latter are in turn divided, based on flower characteristics, into "bearded," which have a furry strip of hairs at the base of the falls; "crested," which have a ridge or crest like a cockscomb; and a third group, with neither beard nor crest. The last, which includes the Japanese and Siberian iris, with relatively long, narrow leaves, is most useful in foliage combinations. Iris grow best in full sun, in neutral to acid pH, with copious moisture during the growing season.

BLUE FLAG *(Iris versicolor)*, a native of eastern North America, has erect, gray-green leaves that are 3 feet long and 1 inch wide. This species will grow with wet feet and is often found in the wild in marshy places and along pond banks. It is hardy to –30°F.

CRESTED IRIS *(Iris cristata)*, native to the southeastern United States, is tolerant of sun or shade and thus is very useful for the transition area between these two conditions. The arching, soft green leaves are 6 to 9 inches long and less than an inch wide and grow in a fan of six or so at the tips of branching surface rhizomes. A running species, this will make a somewhat open ground cover. It grows best in moist but well-drained soils high in organic matter; adequate moisture is especially important in sunny sites. This lovely little woodland plant is elegant with smaller hosta, dwarf astilbe, and shorter ferns. It is hardy to –5°F.

JAPANESE IRIS *(Iris ensata [I. kaempferi])* has elegant, lightly ribbed leaves that grow 2 to 3 feet tall and 1½ to nearly 5 inches wide. Numerous cultivars with showy flowers are available. While in active growth, this iris requires copious moisture, even in shallow standing water, but during the resting season, this same condition will kill it. The closely related *Iris laevigata* can be distinguished by its lack of a prominent midrib on the soft green leaves. Both species are hardy to –10°F.

ORRIS *(Iris pallida)* is a bearded iris that has been cultivated since ancient times for its rhizomes, which when dried and powdered are used as a fixative in perfumes and potpourris. In the garden this species is valued for its glaucous gray foliage and small, lavender-blue flowers. It grows best in full sun with well-drained soil and is hardy to –20°F. There are two variegated cultivars: 'Argenteo-variegata', which has cool, fresh, white-variegated leaves; and 'Aureo-variegata', which has creamy yellow-variegated leaves.

SIBERIAN IRIS *(Iris sibirica)* has 30-inch-long leaves, less than an inch wide, which rustle enchantingly in summer breezes. Many recent cultivars are actually intergeneric crosses involving closely related species. While it grows best with copious moisture, this species does not like standing water around the roots. It is good with peonies and other plants with bold leaf shapes. It is hardy to –20°F.

YELLOW FLAG *(Iris pseudacorus)*, native to western Europe and North Africa, has become naturalized in eastern North America, growing wild in ditches and wet areas. This is a true bog iris and can grow in standing water. The leaves grow to 5 feet long and just over an inch wide; cultivar 'Variegata' has yellow-and-cream variegated leaves in spring, turning all green in summer. Yellow flag iris is excellent for contrast with other moisture-loving species with bold leaves, such as hosta or rodgersia, and lacy leaves, such as ferns or large astilbe, near a pond or other source of water. It will also grow with average moisture. It is hardy to –20°F.

Kirengeshoma palmata
KIRENGESHOMA

This is an herbaceous Japanese woodland plant with the character of a shrub. It grows to 54 inches tall and has large, abutilonlike or maplelike, palmately lobed leaves up to 8 inches long. It adds height and texture to the woodland garden and gives the bonus of yellow, bell-like flowers in late September or October. It grows best in shade in acid soil that is high in organic matter and is moist but not sodden. When you are thinking in terms of textural contrast, Kirengeshoma can be combined with the lacier texture provided by ferns or fernlike plants such as astilbe, goatsbeard, and bugbane. It is hardy to −10°F.

Liriope muscari. See page 123.

Macleaya cordata
PLUME POPPY

This large, impressive plant grows 6 to 8 feet tall but seldom needs staking; its roots are spreading and slightly invasive. The leaves grow from the base, ascending the stem, and are palmately lobed, with small indentations along the margin; they grow as much as 8 to 12 inches long and are light green on the upper surface and densely felted with silvery white hairs. The leaves are very attractive as they twist in a breeze, revealing the green side and then the white side. Hardy to −20°F, plume poppy grows best in moist but well-drained soil, with some midday shade in hot summer areas. Too much shade or excessive fertilization will result in weak stems and will accentuate its invasive tendencies.

Macleaya microcarpa is very similar but has pinkish flowers rather than white and is far more invasive.

Myrrhis odorata
SWEET CICELY

This plant has 12-inch-long leaves that are fernlike and delicate in appearance, so even though it grows 3 to 5 feet tall, it is not coarse. Sweet cicely is related to chervil, parsley, dill, and other fragrant herbs in the Umbelliferae Family. Like them, it has twice to thrice pinnately compound foliage, with toothed or cut lanceolate segments. Sweet cicely's licorice-scented leaves remain until harsh weather sets in. It is suitable for sun or shade but prefers woodland conditions with a moist but well-drained soil high in organic matter. It is delightful interplanted with large, glaucous hosta, for the delicate contrast of the ferny leaves against a strong blue background. It is hardy to −20°F.

Ophiopogon planiscapus 'Arabicus'. See page 120.

Oxalis regnellii
OXALIS

This South American perennial has scaly rhizomes and shamrock leaves of three broadly obtriangular leaflets, each 1 to 3 inches long and purple with a reddish splash in the center; the leaves have 10-inch-long petioles. Oxalis grows well in full sun to light shade in well-drained soil and tolerates dry conditions. It is tender and must be lifted in the winter if not in a mild winter garden.

Paeonia spp. and cultivars
PEONY

These are perennials in the finest sense — they are long lived, easy to cultivate, and have attractive foliage and flowers. They grow best in a deeply prepared, fertile soil that is high in or-

*A*lchemilla mollis (lady's-mantle), *Sempervivum* sp. (hen-and-chicks), ferns

*H*osta sp.,
Adiantum
pedatum
(maidenhair
ferns), and
Athyrium
goeringianum
'Pictum'
(Japanese painted
fern)

Matteuccia pensylvanica (Ostrich fern)

Athyrium goeringianum 'Pictum' (Japanese painted fern)

Shady garden path

DENCY KANE

DENCY KANE

MARGARET HENSEL/POSITIVE IMAGES

Rosa rubifolia (redleaf rose), *Helictotrichon sempervirens* (blue oat grass)

Schizachyrium scoparium (little bluestem)

Miscanthus sinensis (Yakushima dwarf selection), *Imperata cylindrica* 'Red Baron' (Japanese blood grass), *Nandina domestica* (heavenly bamboo, dwarf selection), various perennials, *Calamagrostis* x *Acutiflora* 'Stricta' (reed grass) (counter clockwise from top left)

151

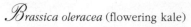

Brassica oleracea (flowering kale)

Coleus blumei Fiji series, *Hosta* 'Piedmont Gold'

Stachys sp., *Pelargonium* 'Mrs. Cox' (geranium)

ganic matter and is moist but well-drained. The rhizomatous, thickened tuberous roots send up red shoots in spring which expand to sturdy stems well clothed with rich green compound leaves; the leaf color may turn to orange in autumn before dormancy. It has white, cream, pink, or red flowers in late spring. Although it prefers full sun, or light shade in hot summer regions, some species of peonies do well as woodland plants. It grows best in areas with cold winters.

COMMON PEONY (*Paeonia lactiflora* and *P. officinalis*) provides the superb flowering plants that are a mainstay in the garden, thriving with little maintenance after the initial thorough preparation of the planting site. *P. lactiflora* has leaves that are twice compounded in threes with elliptic to lanceolate segments, while *P. officinalis* has leaves that are deeply cut into numerous narrow, oblong leaflets. These species are hardy to –40°F; in fact, two specialty growers are located in Minnesota and Michigan.

FERNLEAF PEONY (*Paeonia tenuifolia*) is 18 to 24 inches tall and has leaves that are twice divided in three, with the leaflets dissected into narrow linear segments. This species is usually dormant by late June. Far better are two hybrids, *P.* x *smouthii (P. tenuifolia* x *P. lactifolora)* and 'Early Scout', which remain in excellent condition throughout the summer; both are 2 feet tall and have single red flowers and good cut foliage that is less threadlike than that of the species. Fernleaf peony is hardy to –20°F.

Paeonia obovata alba and *P. japonica* are superb species with soft grayish green, ovate foliage that is flushed with copper in spring, turning green in summer; they are elegant in the woodland garden. *P. mlokosewitschii,* with downy, gray-green leaves, and *P. wittmanniana,* with bold, coarse, blistered and wrinkled, glossy green leaves, are unfortunately rarely seen in the United States; therefore, the enthusiast must raise them from seed, a slow but worthwhile project.

Peltiphyllum peltatum
UMBRELLA PLANT

This plant grows 2 to 4 feet tall and has large, nearly orbicular basal leaves 12 to 24 inches across, with ten to fifteen coarsely serrate lobes; it has a bristly petiole attached to the center of the leaf. The leaves appear after the flowers in spring and are a rich green color in summer, turning bright fiery red in autumn. Hardy to –5°F, this Pacific Northwest native is perfect for wet, marshy soils, where the creeping rhizome will prevent erosion on pond banks or near slow-moving streams. It tolerates sun to shade but must have moisture. The cultivar 'Nanum' grows only 8 to 12 inches high and has proportionally smaller leaves.

Phlox paniculata 'Nora Leigh'
PHLOX

This variegated plant may not appeal to everyone. As with other cultivars of border phlox, this plant's white-edged leaves are prone to mildew, which badly disfigures its appearance. Because a plant must be worthwhile in terms of its resistance to pests and diseases as well as the aspect of its leaf color, this phlox is perhaps best left to the collectors of variegated plants.

Phormium tenax
NEW ZEALAND FLAX

This large New Zealand perennial is popular as a garden plant in the mild winter areas of California and the Southwest, and for container use elsewhere. The tough, leathery, swordlike, evergreen leaves, splitting at the tip, grow in a basal, fanlike clump and can reach 9 feet long and 5 inches wide in the species. Some shorter cultivars are beautifully marked in bronze, red, orange, cream, and yellow. New Zealand flax is able to grow in dry or moist soils, although constantly saturated soils will lead to crown rot. It is salt tolerant and will grow in coastal areas where hardy (to 20°F). Full sun and light shade are equally suitable. Cultivars include 'Jack Spratt', the smallest, which has leaves that are only 18 to 24 inches tall, ½ to 1 inch wide, and are dark maroon with a green blotch at the base; 'Maori Maiden', which has fountain-shaped, 3- to 4-foot-tall fans of leaves with a central light pink band, edged in olive green; 'Maori Queen,' which has 3- to 4-foot-tall leaves with a central olive band, edged in pinky red; 'Maori Sunrise', which has 4- to 5-foot-tall leaves with a deeper pink central band, edged in olive green; 'Purpureum', which has 7-foot-tall, solid red-purple leaves; 'Rainbow Warrior', which has 3- to 4-foot-tall, dark pinky red leaves striped in olive brown; 'Sundowner', which is very heat tolerant and has 5-foot-tall leaves with a dark olive-green central band, edged in pink and white stripes; 'Tom Thumb', which has leaves that are 2 feet tall, ½ to 1 inch wide, and dark green with a narrow purple edge; 'Tricolor', which has 3- to 4-foot-tall leaves striped green and creamy yellow with a thin, purple-striped edging; and 'Yellow Wave', which has 5-foot-tall, bright yellow leaves edged in olive green.

Plantago major
PLANTAIN

This vigorous plant is a pest in lawns. The leaves are coarse lanceolate or elliptic to ovate and grow 4 to 6 inches or more. The question with this species is not how to cultivate it, but rather how to discourage it. However, 'Atro-

purpurea' ('Rubrifolia') is an interesting cultivar worthy of a place in the garden, especially in combination with silver or glaucous blue foliage plants. Hardy to –20°F, it has large, deeply veined leaves that are dark purplish red on the upper surface and bronze-green beneath.

Podophyllum peltatum
MAYAPPLE

This rhizomatous, herbaceous perennial is native from Quebec to Florida and Texas. It is a big, rangy, spreading plant with coarse foliage and is useful in the shady garden as a large-scale ground cover or in informal mixed plantings. The nonflower stems have solitary leaves that grow to 12 inches across and are nearly orbicular with five to nine deeply cut lobes; the petiole attaches near the center. The leaves on flowering stems are palmately lobed and grow in pairs, with the single flower nodding between them. In the spring, the leaves emerge like a partially furled umbrella and often have a coppery olive tint. If adequate moisture is lacking, mayapple will go dormant in mid- to late summer. It can be grown with other coarse, vigorous plants that can successfully compete, such as ostrich fern, rodgersia, and large hosta. It is hardy to –25°F.

Polygonatum spp. and cultivars
SOLOMON'S-SEAL

These deciduous, rhizomatous perennials are found in the woodlands of North America, Europe, and Asia. They require shady conditions and moist but well-drained soil high in organic matter. Where conditions are suitable, the horizontal rhizomes will spread and form extensive patches, and some species will self-sow. They are rather subtle in appearance, with arching stems and ovate leaflets, but are elegant with ferns, astilbe, hosta, Jack-in-the-pulpit, blood-root, epimedium, gingers, and other plants of the forest floor. The bell-like flowers hang in pairs or clusters beneath the stem, distinguishing this genus from false Solomon's-seal (*Smilacina* spp.), which has a fluffy terminal panicle or raceme of flowers; both are also delightful for the woodland garden.

GIANT SOLOMON'S-SEAL *(Polygonatum commutatum)* is sometimes offered in the trade as *P. canaliculatum* (which is an invalid name for *P. biflorum,* just to make things even more confusing). This is a superlative large plant with arching stems 4 to 6 feet tall, and ovate, 7-inch-long leaflets. Giant Solomon's-seal is elegant for adding height and stature in the shady garden. It is hardy to –20°F.

SMALL SOLOMON'S-SEAL *(Polygonatum biflorum),* found wild in the forests of Connecticut to Ontario and Nebraska, south to Florida and Texas, is variable and somewhat daintier than the other species. It has 1- to 3-foot-tall stems and 4-inch-long leaflets. It is hardy to –20°F.

Polygonatum odoratum [japonicum] grows 18 to 24 inches tall and has elliptic to ovate leaflets to 4 inches long. It is hardy to –10°F. Cultivars include var. *thunbergii*, which is more vigorous, growing 40 inches tall, and has 6-inch-long leaflets; and var. *thunbergii* 'Varie-gatum', which has wonderfully pink-flushed shoots in the spring that expand to arching stems of creamy white variegated leaves. This variegated cultivar is superlative grown with Siberian bugloss and is definitely superior to the other variegated form: *P.* x *hybridum* 'Variegatum', a cross between *P. multiflorum* and *P. odoratum.*

Pulmonaria saccharata
LUNGWORT

This herbaceous perennial grows from a creeping rootstock, making an attractive ground cover for the shady garden with a moist soil high in organic matter; it seeds freely but is not a nuisance. Sometimes it is attacked by mildew in hot, humid summer weather. The hairy, bristly elliptic leaves have long petioles and grow to 18 inches in length; their silver spots give the appearance of dappled sunlight coming through the overhead canopy. The leaves are evergreen to semievergreen in harsh winters. Numerous cultivars are selected for both flowers and foliage markings. Some good foliage forms include 'Argentea', which has silver spots run together into a central band; 'Margery Fish', which has consistent silvery markings; 'Mrs. Moon', with large silver blotches; and 'Reginald Kaye', a British introduction, which has large silver spots in the center of the leaf and is edged with a wide margin of smaller spots. Lungwort is good cover for spring bulbs and looks fine planted with azaleas and rhododendrons, as well as with ferns and astilbe (particularly white-flowered cultivars). It is hardy to –25°F. *Pulmonaria rubra* 'David Ward' is a new British introduction from Beth Chatto. Unlike the plain green leaf of the species, this cultivar has a gray-green leaf with a white margin.

Rheum rhabarbarum
RHUBARB

This vegetable garden plant has excellent architectural foliage that provides a bold accent in the ornamental garden. The stems grow to 6 feet and have 18-inch, ovate, wavy-edged leaves. Rhubarb is a greedy feeder so it is nearly impossible to overfertilize it. It is intolerant of hot summers, preferring cool, moist soil. Other species are more often cultivated as ornamentals; these include *R. australe (emodi),* which has broad, more or less cordate leaves with distinctive red veins and grows 7 feet high by 5 feet wide; and *R. palmatum,* which has deeply palmately lobed, almost orbicular leaves and grows 6 feet high and wide. This latter species has several cultivars 'Atrosanguineum' has deep red young leaves that turn dark green above but retain the red coloration on the reverse of the mature leaf until flowering; 'Bowle's Variety' is similar; and *R. palmatum tanguticum* has larger leaves that are less deeply cut but are a rich rosy purple color.

Rodgersia spp. and cultivars
RODGERSIA

These plants make handsome masses of bold architectural foliage that is quite variable from species to species; they may have simple leaves, orbicular with a long petiole attached in the center, or compound leaves, either pinnate or palmate. This allows for the possibility of diverse effects, depending on the species used. Rodgersia prefer a moist, even marshy soil in either sun or shade, but if the shade is too heavy, flowering will be reduced. In dry situations the leaves will scorch along the margins, turning brown and unsightly. Rodgersia are a good choice for use along pond banks, slow-moving streams, or in other permanently moist situations. The thick rhizomes slowly increase to make large clumps. They are attractive in association with other plants that enjoy damp feet, such as Siberian or Japanese iris, astilbes, ferns, and some grasses.

Rodgersia aesculifolia grows 4 to 6 feet tall and has seven oblanceolate, coarsely toothed, crinkled leaflets as much as 10 inches long that are arranged in a palmate fashion like the leaves of a horse chestnut tree; they are flushed bronze-brown. This species is hardy to −20°F.

Rodgersia pinnata 'Superba' grows 3 to 4 feet tall and has five to nine oblanceolate leaflets arranged in a pinnate manner; they are pleated when they first unfurl and then expand to as much as 8 inches long. In this cultivar the new leaflets are colored a rich coppery bronze. It is incomparable when grown with *Hosta* 'Krossa Regale', whose cool grayish leaves make it an elegant companion. It is hardy to −20°F.

Rodgersia podophylla grows 2 feet tall and has five broadly triangular leaflets that are narrower at the base than the much-toothed tip; they grow to 10 inches long and 5 inches wide and are palmately arranged. The leaves are bronze when they first emerge, turning light green in spring and then an attractive metallic bronze-brown in summer. This species is hardy to −20°F.

Rodgersia tabularis grows 3 feet tall and has fresh light green, bold, round leaves that are 2 to 3 feet across and have numerous short, toothlike lobes along the margins; the leaves are peltate — the long petioles are attached to the middle of the leaves like plates balanced on sticks. Bold and coarse in texture, this plant has the substance to contrast with canna, elephant-ear, and massed iris or grasses for a luxuriant, tropical effect. It is hardy to −20°F.

Rohdea japonica
NIPPON LILY

This plant grows in thickets and woods on the Japanese island of Honshu, spreading slowly by means of thickened rhizomes. It prefers woodland shade and a moist but well-drained soil high in organic matter. The dark green, leathery, evergreen leaves are lanceolate to oblanceolate and grow in a basal rosette up to 2 feet long and 3 inches wide. This plant is highly prized in Japan, where it is considered auspicious because it is long lived; there is a plant society that specializes only in this plant and its forms. There are cultivars that have white-edged leaves, and those with white-marbled leaves, as well as those with interestingly pleated or ridged forms; there are dwarf cultivars of all of these. Nippon lily is generally grown in the southeastern states and the Pacific Northwest. However, it may be hardier than previously thought — late-planted specimens that I obtained from the Arnold Arboretum survived the bitter conditions of December 1989 in Connecticut without additional protection.

Ruta graveolens
RUE

This evergreen subshrub is cultivated as a perennial for both ornamental and herbal use. Its glaucous blue-green leaves are twice to thrice pinnately divided into oblong or spatulate segments ½ inch long. If left unpruned, it will grow 3 feet tall, but it is usually cut back in early spring to keep it more compact and shapely. It can cause a contact dermatitis in susceptible individuals, especially if handled on a hot, dry day. It grows best in an alkaline soil in full sun and will tolerate dry conditions. Cultivars include 'Blue Mound', with large, glaucous, deep blue leaves; 'Jackman's Blue', which has deeply divided blue foliage with a somewhat waxy surface and is lower growing (18 to 24 inches tall); and 'Variegata', with foliage splashed with creamy white, especially when young.

Salvia spp. (See also under "Shrubs," pages 104-5.)
SAGE

These herbaceous perennials and shrubs are widely distributed around the world. They often have aromatic foliage and are tolerant of dry, sandy soils low in fertility in full sun. Examples are scarlet salvia, which is used for summer bedding, and garden or common sage, important as a culinary seasoning. Like numerous other plants growing in xeric conditions, many salvia, especially shrubby species, have white, woolly hairs on their leaves to reduce water loss; these species are useful for foliage effect.

COMMON SAGE (*Salvia officinalis*). See page 104.

SILVER SAGE (*Salvia argentea*) is a much-branched perennial that grows 2 to 4 feet tall and has lanceolate to oblong leaves that are 6 to 8 inches long; the leaves are thickly covered with silky, white, woolly hairs when young. This species is most often seen as a juvenile plant with large clumps of broad, irregularly toothed basal foliage. Since it is short lived and often dies after flowering, the flower stalks can be removed to extend the life of the plant. It is commonly treated as an annual for its attractive foliage effect. It is hardy to −15°F.

Sanguinaria canadensis
BLOODROOT

This genus has only one species, named for the reddish sap that oozes from cut or injured tissue. The forking, horizontal, underground tuber produces a single grayish leaf from each growing point, more or less deeply lobed in a palmate pattern. Bloodroot needs shade and a moist but well-drained soil high in organic matter for best growth. It combines nicely with epimedium, ferns, astilbe, and liriope.

Sansevieria trifasciata
MOTHER-IN-LAW'S-TONGUE

Related to agaves, this plant has thick, flat, erect leaves growing in a basal clump. It is a hardy houseplant that is tolerant of dark and drought, performing admirably in frost-free gardens or as a container plant. The patterned leaves are the attractive feature of this plant; they grow 1 to 4 feet tall and 2 to 3 inches wide in rigidly upright rosettes from thick rhizomes. Midday sun will bleach the foliage, so some shade is useful; it prefers heavy but well-drained soil and should be watered thoroughly but infrequently, especially in winter. This plant originated in the arid regions of Africa and southern Asia. Cultivars include 'Craigii', with broad, creamy yellow lengthwise stripes; 'Hahnii', which is lower growing (to 6 inches high) and has broadly triangular, dark green leaves banded with silver; and 'Laurentii', which has creamy yellow marginal striping on dark green leaves with gray-green horizontal banding.

Sedum spp. and cultivars. See page 126.

Sempervivum spp. (See also *Echeveria*, page 141.)
HEN-AND-CHICKS

Native to Europe, Morocco, and western Asia, these plants grow in dense clumps of durable, compact, evergreen basal rosettes made up of somewhat swollen, succulent leaves; the oblong to obovate leaves have little hairs along the margin. The plants spread by means of clustering little rosettes around the original rosette that make a mat. The clustered, starlike flowers are on long stalks; the rosette flowers then dies and is survived by its offsets. Formerly, tender species from the Canary Islands were also included, but now they are classified in a separate genus, *Aeonium*. Sempervivums are cold tolerant and grow best in full sun in a lean, gritty, well-drained soil that is low in fertility but has adequate water, since they are not truly drought tolerant. Numerous named forms are popular with collectors. Many gardeners, however, are content to select plants with varied characteristics: the size of the rosette (from ½ to 3 or even 6 inches across); color (green, green tipped with red, red, red tipped with green);

and the extent of its cobwebbed hairiness (none, downy hairs, completely covered with a web). Hardy to –10°F, they are excellent for the rock garden, growing on a boulder, or planted into crevices of a stone wall or in containers.

Senecio cineraria. See page 179.

Setcreasea pallida 'Purple Heart'
PURPLE-HEART

This old-fashioned houseplant is excellent for summer bedding or garden use in frost-free areas where it is hardy. The cultivars 'Purple Heart' and 'Purple Queen' have intense violet-purple leaves with a silvery overlay and soft hairs along the margins; they are oblong and somewhat trough shaped, 7 inches long and 1 inch wide, and grow 16 inches long on sprawling stems that are erect at the tips. Purple-heart is beautiful early in the morning in the summer when spangled with dew, with droplets of moisture exuding from the plant itself. It is superb with other bronze to purple foliage and contrasted with silver or chartreuse foliage and pink or green flowers. It requires full sun and moist but well-drained soil and is easy to grow from cuttings — a "back door" plant passed from neighbor to neighbor.

Silphium terebinthinaceum
PRAIRIE DOCK

This is a plant of the Great Plains, the sweeping prairies of the Midwest. Like many prairie plants, it has deep taproots and thus needs to be planted as a young specimen. It grows 10 feet tall and has rough, dark green leaves that are mostly basal, growing 2 to 3 feet long; the few sparse leaves ascending the stem are smaller, oblong to elliptic or oblong, cordate at the base, and sharply serrated along the margins. Prairie dock is stupendous with early morning light shining through and illuminating the bold foliage. It requires full sun and deep, well-drained soil and is hardy to –20°F.

Stachys lanata [S. byzantina]. See page 126.

Thalictrum speciosissimum
MEADOW RUE

This plant has mostly basal, columbine-like leaves that are twice or thrice pinnately compounded, with 1½-inch-wide, glaucous blue leaflets that are either entire or three-lobed. The entire effect is one of airiness and grace on a plant that grows 2 to 5 feet tall. It needs a moderately fertile soil that is moist but well drained and high in organic matter; it prefers a lightly shaded site but will tolerate full sun in regions with cool summers. Meadow rue should not need to be staked unless it is grown in windy locations. It is excellent for contrast against bolder foliage of perennials or shrubs. It is hardy to –10°F.

Veratrum viride
FALSE HELLEBORE, WHITE HELLEBORE

This herbaceous plant is native to wet places in North America. It has light green, elliptic to ovate leaves that are 1 foot long and strongly pleated along their length, giving a bold, architectural effect; the stems grow 4 to 7 feet tall. It is best grown in a fertile soil that is constantly moist, and it prefers shade, although in cool summer areas it will tolerate full sun. It is hardy to –25°F. False hellebore is wonderful with goatsbeard, tall astilbes, large ferns, and rodgersias for a splendid textural effect in a damp, shady place.

Viola labradorica
LABRADOR VIOLET

This is a small plant whose dainty appearance belies a rugged constitution. It is low growing (to 3 inches tall) and has ovate leaves that grow to 1½ inches long and are finely scalloped along the edges. The leaves are purple in the spring before the trees leaf out, and later, as the forest canopy closes in, they turn to green with a purple flush. Labrador violet spreads both by underground stems and by seed (seed production is typically extravagant in violets). It is attractive in the shady garden with smaller epimedium, ophiopogon, and small ferns and hosta, together creating a tapestry of foliage shapes and shades of color. It is hardy to –30°F.

Xanthosoma sagittifolium
ELEPHANT-EAR

This is a vegetable that is used as an ornamental for its wonderful, bold, coarse foliage. Related to Jack-in-the-pulpit *(Arisaema triphyllum)*, elephant-ear is cultivated in the tropics for its edible tuber, which is sold in bodegas and in some produce stores as *yautia blanca*. Elephant-ear can be purchased and grown as a summer ornamental in colder areas and then stored indoors over winter or discarded, like a canna; it is a year-round plant only in frost-free areas. The dark green leaves grow to 3 feet long and are broadly ovate to sagittate with broad lobes at the base where the leaf blade joins a 3-foot-long petiole and not as translucent as a caladium. It grows well in a rich, fertile soil that is constantly moist. With age, it develops a stem, which, like the leaves, grows to 3 feet high. Elephant-ear is excellent grown along the banks of a pond or ornamental pool, combined with large cannas, castor bean, and tall grasses for a lush tropical effect. Blue taro or yautia

(*Xanthosoma violaceum*) has oblong-ovate sagittate leaves that are 2 feet long by 18 inches wide and have violet margins; the petioles are 2 feet long or more and are purple with a conspicuous bluish or grayish powdery appearance.

Yucca spp. and cultivars
YUCCA

These plants have similar characteristics to agaves, to which they are related. Yuccas form rosettes of linear, swordlike, evergreen leaves that are sculptural in effect. Since yuccas have a woody stem, they are called shrubs by botanists, but in the horticultural sense yuccas are included with perennials since this is how they are used. Like agave, yuccas require a location in full sun and quick-draining soil, but yuccas are more tolerant of cold and are hardy to –20°F and even lower in some species. This genus of plants is native to the United States, and the various species are adaptable to a wide range of growing conditions. Southwestern yuccas are able to grow in frost-free areas, something that cannot be said about many other cold-hardy plants; and southeastern species will tolerate some degree of frost. In some species, after flowering the individual rosette will die, but continuity is assured by offsets. Yuccas make an excellent case for the practical benefit of using Latin nomenclature, since several different species share common names.

ADAM'S-NEEDLE *(Yucca filamentosa)*, which is nearly stemless, has stiff, narrow leaves 30 inches long and 1 inch wide with loose curly threads along the margins. Some cultivars offered are 'Bright Edge', with leaves margined in creamy white; 'Golden Sword', with leaves centered in soft, rich yellow; and 'Variegata', with leaves variegated in creamy white stripes. It is native to the southwestern United States and is hardy to –25° F.

ADAM'S-NEEDLE or BEAR GRASS *(Yucca smalliana)*, which is stemless, makes a fine-textured dome of foliage with firm, erect, spreading leaves up to 2 feet long, with curly, fibrous threads along the margins. 'Variegata' has variegated leaves. This plant is usually offered as *Yucca filamentosa*. It is native in South Carolina to Florida and Mississippi and is hardy to –20°F.

HARRIMAN'S YUCCA *(Yucca harrimaniae)*, a stemless or short-stemmed species, which is possibly a hybrid between two U.S. southwestern species. The foliage clumps may be single or several clustered together, with yellowish or bluish green leaves that are 4 to 18 inches long and ½ to over 1 inch wide. It is native from Colorado to New Mexico and Oklahoma and is hardy to –5°F.

OUR-LORD'S-CANDLE *(Yucca whipplei)* is stemless or has a very short, condensed stem and rigid, gray-green leaves that are 20 inches long and less than an inch wide. The leaves have a needle-sharp terminal spine and yellow to brown, finely toothed margins. It is native to California and Baja California and is hardy to 20°F.

SMALL SOAPWEED *(Yucca glauca)* has short, prostrate stems with clumps of narrow, linear, pale bluish gray-green leaves that grow to 28 inches long and ½ inch wide and have greenish white or white margins with loose threads. It is native from Montana and South Dakota to Texas and New Mexico and is the most cold tolerant of the yuccas (hardy to –40°F).

SPANISH-BAYONET, DAGGER PLANT *(Yucca aloifolia)* slowly becomes shrublike, growing 6 to 10 feet tall with a branching trunk, sometimes sprawling in an attractive manner. The stems are densely covered with dark green, needle-sharp pointed leaves that grow to 30 inches long and 2 inches wide. Cultivars include 'Marginata', with yellow-edged leaves; 'Tricolor', with leaves that are yellow or white in the center; and 'Variegata', which is variegated in yellow and white. It is native to Mexico, the West Indies, and the southern United States and is hardy to 15°F.

SPANISH-BAYONET, BLUE YUCCA, BANANA YUCCA *(Yucca baccata)* has short, prostrate stems with stiff, swordlike, gray-green, sharp-tipped leaves that are 28 inches long and more than 2 inches wide and have coarse, curly, fibrous threads along the margins. In mild winter areas it grows in clumps with short, leaning trunks up to 3 feet high, and in colder regions as stemless single rosettes. Native to the southwestern United States, it is hardy to –15°F.

SPANISH DAGGER, LORD'S-CANDLESTICK *(Yucca gloriosa)* grows as a multitrunked shrub to 8 feet high in mild winter areas. In cooler areas it is essentially stemless in habit. It has sharply pointed, stiff leaves to 30 inches long and 2 inches wide. 'Variegata' has leaves with yellow stripes. It is native from North Carolina to Florida and is hardy to 5°F.

$\mathcal{F}$ERNS

FERNS ARE A SPLENDID EXAMPLE OF PATTERN and texture of foliage for garden use. They are ancient (growing since the age of dinosaurs), primitive, flowerless plants that reproduce by spores. In fact, ferns were thought to have supernatural power because they could magically procreate without flowers or seeds; and they were thus granted all sorts of sorcerous attributes — they could confer invisibility, reveal hidden treasure, and more. In the garden they have the magical attribute of fine, lacy texture, adding soft, feathery foliage in various shades of green. Ferns are evergreen or deciduous, tall

or small, and grow in clumps or as quick-spreading, invasive ground covers. In the Rocky Mountains there are xeric species that grow in full sun in rocky crevices. The ferns considered here are the more familiar woodland species that prefer a moist soil high in organic matter. Since unrolling fronds are fragile and easily damaged, ferns should be transplanted early in spring before the fragile, new crosiers begin their growth, or late in spring when the fronds have hardened off. Ferns can also be moved in autumn at least six weeks before consistently harsh, cold weather sets in. As for other plants, summer is generally a poor transplanting time because of the stress of heat and lack of rain.

Ferns have simple or compound leaf blades that grow on a petiole from the rhizome. A few ferns, such as the hart's-tongue fern *(Phyllitis scolopendrium)* have a simple, uncut leaf. Christmas fern *(Polystichum acrostichoides)* is once pinnate, with the leaf blade cut into leaflets, divided all the way to the midrib. If these leaflets are in turn divided, the fern is twice pinnate, like the marginal shield fern *(Dryopteris marginalis)*. A very lacy texture is provided when the leaflets are divided yet again (thrice pinnate), as in the spinulose shield fern *(Dryopteris spinulosa)*. Ferns reproduce by spores — small, dust-fine particles; these form on fertile leaves, which may or may not be similar in appearance to the sterile leaves. This *dimorphism* may be slight or glaringly obvious. For example, sensitive fern *(Onoclea sensibilis)* has fertile fronds that look like bead sticks, while the sterile fronds look more like a prototypical "fern." In the interrupted fern *(Osmunda claytoniana)*, the fertile portion of the frond appears as rusty cinnamon leaflets that "interrupt" the green sterile leaflets; both types grow on the same leaf. The Christmas fern *(Polystichum acrostichoides)* has fertile leaflets at the tip of the otherwise sterile frond, noticeable by the narrowing of the segments and brown spores on the reverse.

Adiantum pedatum
MAIDENHAIR FERN

This is one of the most exquisite deciduous ferns. The fronds are nearly orbicular in outline, as much as 18 inches in diameter, and are split into two branches, each having four to twelve once-pinnate, fingerlike projections. The pinnae are rosy red when they first unroll, maturing to a fresh bright green; they are fan shaped (like a ginkgo leaf), and the blade is parallel to the ground, at right angles to the wiry, purple-black petiole. The creeping rhizomes grow in a congested manner, producing a slowly expanding clump. Although this fern looks delicate, it is tough enough to push up through a ground cover of pachysandra year after year once established. It grows best in a loose open soil that is high in organic matter and is moist but well drained. It is hardy to –30°F.

Athyrium spp.

JAPANESE PAINTED FERN (Athyrium goeringianum 'Pictum') is a deciduous fern with broadly lanceolate, once-pinnate fronds that are 18 inches long; the pinnae are soft gray at the base, and the petiole and midrib are reddish purple. These ferns are variable from spores, just as plants raised from seed will differ unless bred for consistency. This is one of the few gray or silver foliage plants for shade, and it has a lacy texture as well. Japanese painted fern is elegant with glaucous blue hosta, white variegated ivy, and bloodroot. It grows well under woodland conditions of dappled to heavy shade and moist but well-drained soil that is high in organic matter. It does not run but will

form increasing clumps that can be lifted and divided in spring. It is hardy to –10°F.

LADY FERN (Athyrium filix-femina) is a deciduous fern with bright green, lanceolate, twice-pinnate fronds that grow 18 to 36 inches long and 15 inches wide. It produces new fronds from early spring into mid- to late summer. Lady fern is a slowly spreading species and grows best with light to moderate shade in a constantly moist but well-drained soil that is high in organic matter and is neutral to somewhat acid. It will tolerate drier conditions, but the fronds will not look as good in late summer. Lady fern is excellent with woodland shrubs or larger herbaceous perennials, and as a disguise for yellowing daffodil foliage. It is hardy to –30°F.

Cyrtomium falcatum
JAPANESE HOLLY FERN

This fern has stiff, erect, once-pinnate, oblong-lanceolate, glossy dark green fronds that are 30 inches long and 6 to 9 inches wide. The fronds resemble the leaf of Oregon grape holly both in shape and in their lustrous dark green color. Japanese holly fern grows best in dappled to medium shade in a loose, open soil that is high in organic matter and is moist but well-drained. It is hardy to 20°F, but this is variable, depending on whether the genetic origin of the plants (or spores) was northern Japan or Hawaii.

Dennstaedtia punctilobula
HAY-SCENTED FERN

This invasive fern has a slender running rhizome that sends up new fronds throughout the growing season; the twice-pinnate fronds are narrowly triangular to lanceolate and 18 to 30 inches long. If this fern's wide-ranging, black-brown rhizomes gain a hold in a stone wall, the wall may need to be disassembled in order to weed them out. This warning aside, it is tolerant of sun, shade, drought, or wet and can be valuable as a ground cover. I remember seeing a power-line right-of-way strewn with granite boulders and carpeted with hay-scented fern, with mountain laurel flowering in profusion — a simple and superbly effective natural landscape. In the sandy soils of Long Island, this fern has been deliberately used as a ground cover in dry, wind-swept woodland gardens. The tough branching rhizomes make a dense network that can reduce erosion in exposed sites. Hay-scented fern sends up new fronds throughout the growing season if moisture is available; the deciduous, fresh green fronds smell of new-mown hay when crushed or cut. It is hardy to −30°F.

Dryopteris spp.

GOLDIE'S FERN or GIANT WOOD FERN *(Dryopteris goldiana)* is an elegant, massive, deciduous fern with once-pinnate fronds that are 4 feet long and 18 inches wide. The crosiers, as they unroll in the spring, are covered with chaffy brown-and-white scales, which give it a pleasing shaggy appearance. The new fronds have a golden flush, maturing to light green. It grows best in a cool, shady site in a moist but well-drained soil high in organic matter, constantly mulched with leaf litter. It is hardy to −30°F.

MARGINAL SHIELD FERN or EVERGREEN SHIELD FERN *(Dryopteris marginalis)* has ovate-lanceolate, twice-pinnate fronds that grow 30 inches long from slowly increasing crowns. In spring the new crosiers are densely covered with coarse, brown, chaffy scales; they are yellow-green when they first unroll, maturing to a glaucous blue-green. These substantial leaves remain green through harsh winter conditions, eventually turning brown; they protect the crown in a self-mulching fashion. This ro-

bust, clump-forming species makes a handsome specimen in stony, humus-rich, moist but well-drained soil in dappled to deep shade. It is often found in the wild on sloping, stony terrain and is excellent for similar locations in the garden. It is hardy to −30°F.

JAPANESE AUTUMN FERN *(Dryopteris erythrosora)* has twice-pinnate, broadly triangular fronds that are 18 inches long and 9 inches wide at the base. In spring the new fronds are an attractive reddish copper color, turning glossy green at maturity.

Matteuccia pensylvanica
OSTRICH FERN

This fern has elliptic-lanceolate, once-pinnate fronds that grow 6 to 9 feet tall; the fronds appear in shuttlecock clusters at intervals along the underground running rhizome. Ostrich fern is strongly dimorphic — the sterile fronds are bronze-brown, and the stiff, woody fertile fronds are half the height of the sterile ones and are persistent through the winter. The sterile fronds come up rather late in spring compared to those of the Christmas, cinnamon, and interrupted ferns, and the fertile fronds do not appear until late June or July. Ostrich fern grows well with other vigorous plants such as mayapple and umbrella leaf in permanently moist sites in light to deep shade; it tolerates full sun if ample moisture is available. It is hardy to −30°F.

Nephrolepis exaltata
SWORD FERN

This fern has stiffly erect, once-pinnate fronds that are 5 feet long and 6 inches wide. This is the "Boston fern" that is grown as a houseplant. The species is native to Florida but is rarely cultivated. There are numerous cultivars with much more cut foliage, as much as four or five times pinnate. Scaly surface runners provide a source of new plants and grow into dense patches in the garden. Sword fern prefers moist but well-drained soil and dappled to deep shade. It is hardy only in frost-free regions.

Onoclea sensibilis
SENSITIVE FERN

This fern has triangular sterile fronds, up to 54 inches long, which are deeply once pinnate; the fronds are scattered along a spreading rhizome. Sensitive fern is strongly dimorphic — the fertile leaves are 30 inches high and twice pinnate but are rolled into beadlike dark brown pieces. It grows well in wet marshy sites, in full sun if moisture is constantly available; it also tolerates average conditions of moist but well-drained sites. The coarse, somewhat tropical-looking foliage is luxuriant and attractive. This rapidly spreading fern can be a problem if the creeping, branching rhizomes, which form a dense mat just below the surface of the soil, are allowed to get out of control. The sterile leaves are sensitive to cold, turning tawny brown at the first frosts. It is hardy to −30°F.

Osmunda spp.
FLOWERING FERN

CINNAMON FERN **(Osmunda cinnamomea)** is a popular clump-forming, deciduous species that usually grows only 2 to 3 feet tall in gardens, taller in constantly moist sites. The plant grows as a vase-shaped clump, with deep, massive, wiry roots — the osmunda fiber used in orchid cultivation. The showy fertile fronds appear first from the center of the crown; they are twice pinnate and covered with cinnamon-brown mature spores. The sterile fronds appear and later in spring are covered with feltlike, creamy beige hairs when they begin to unroll; these medium-green, sterile fronds grow 5 feet long and are once pinnate. They remain green through the summer and then turn an attractive tawny-golden color in autumn before they fall. Cinnamon fern is excellent as a background plant or in combination with large hosta and other herbaceous plants of similar size, and with shrubs tolerant of moist soils such as swamp azalea and spicebush. It grows best in a shady site in an acid soil that is consistently damp. A constantly moist or saturated soil enables it to tolerate full sun. It should not be planted in standing water but rather on a hummock where the roots will reach water but the crown is not saturated. It is hardy to −30°F.

INTERRUPTED FERN **(Osmunda claytoniana)** has once-pinnate fronds that grow to an overall length of 6 feet; the petioles are as much as 2 feet long. The fertile leaflets appear in the middle of the leaf, and after the spores are released, the leaflets wither and drop, leaving a gap, or "interruption," in the middle of the frond. The fronds are densely covered with matted white hairs when they begin to enlarge and unroll, and they are among the first to appear in the spring. Hummingbirds use this chaff to line their nests. Interrupted fern grows in a vaselike clump, slowly enlarging and gradually dying out in the center. It grows best with light shade in a constantly wet or saturated acid soil that is high in organic matter. It will tolerate drier situations than the related cinnamon and royal ferns, although it will be dwarfed if it has less than steady moisture. It is hardy to −30°F.

ROYAL FERN **(Osmunda regalis)** has twice-pinnate fronds that are 6 feet long with a terminal panicle of fertile pinnae. The sterile portion of the fronds is similar to the leaves of a locust tree; and the fertile leaflets are reminiscent of an astilbe flower. New fronds in spring are an attractive coppery red color, maturing to a fresh bright green, then turning yellow and saddle-leather brown in autumn. This is an elegant fern to plant along the banks of a pond, to be reflected in still water; it requires constantly wet soils for best growth. It is luxurious with blue flag and yellow flag iris, large hosta, umbrella leaf, and other bold foliage perennials. Royal fern prefers an acid soil and light shade, although full sunlight is acceptable with constantly saturated soils. It is hardy to –30°F.

Phyllitis scolopendrium
HART'S-TONGUE FERN

This fern has straight, entire (not dissected), leathery, straplike, evergreen fronds that grow 18 inches long and 3 inches wide and sometimes have a wavy margin. In the wild, this fern is found on limestone; in cultivation it grows best in neutral to alkaline soil. Primarily a British fern, this is also found in a few localities in Ontario, Canada; New York; and Tennessee. It prefers a moist but well-drained soil, with some dolomitic limestone added to raise the pH to neutral if the soil is acid. There are a number of named forms with frilled or fringed margins, some with crested tips: *Phyllitis scolopendrium capitatum* has a crest at the end of the frond; *P. s. crispum* has a very frilled and ruffled margin; *P. s. digitatum* has a terminal crest that branches, like fingers; and *P. s. undulatum* has a wavy margin, not as frilly as *P. s. crispum*. All are best grown in protected locations or as container plants. Hart's-tongue fern is hardy to –10°F but grows best with winter protection in colder areas.

Polystichum acrostichoides
CHRISTMAS FERN

This fern has once-pinnate, lanceolate fronds that are 2 to 3 feet long and 5 inches wide. The narrower fertile leaflets appear toward the tips of otherwise sterile fronds. This is one of the first ferns to send up new crosiers in the spring. Covered with scruffy brown scales, they arise from the clump of last year's fronds flattened by winter's snow. The glossy, dark green fronds are more erect in summer, growing in dense, symmetrical clumps. This is one of the best ferns for the woodland garden — it has elegant, evergreen fronds, a neat pattern of growth, and is tolerant of deep shade. It combines well with any woodland shrub and herbaceous perennials, such as hosta, bloodroot, epimedium, hellebores, and liriope. Christmas fern grows best in a fertile, humus-rich soil, moist but well drained, with a constant mulch of leaf litter or other organic matter. If planted relatively thickly, this will serve as an attractive evergreen ground cover. It is hardy to –30°F.

WESTERN SWORD FERN **(*Polystichum munitum*)** has leathery, evergreen, lanceolate, once-pinnate fronds that are 42 inches long and 10 inches wide, somewhat similar to the Christmas fern in appearance. This species is native to Alaska, California, and Montana. It is awesome in the coastal redwood forests, where it makes huge clumps of 75 to 100 glossy, dark green fronds in the deep shade beneath the giant trees. Fern Canyon outside Mendocino, California, is a steep gash with dripping rivulets cascading down and crossing the switchback trails, and it is clothed with western sword ferns in the cathedral gloom, lit with scattered shafts of sunlight. The fern grows well in deep shade to dappled light in humus-rich soil that is moist but well-drained. It is hardy to 0°F, possibly lower for material obtained from northern sources.

Thelypteris hexagonoptera
BROAD BEECH FERN

This deciduous fern has triangular fronds that are 15 inches long and equally wide at the base and are once pinnate, with the segments cut again but not all the way. This is a running fern that spreads by means of branching rhizomes into large colonies, but it is not invasive. New fronds will appear throughout the growing season, especially when there is adequate moisture; at maturity, they are a fresh pea-green color. Hardy to –20°F, broad beech fern grows best with light shade in soil that is high in organic matter.

Woodwardia virginica
CHAIN FERN

This deciduous fern has long, creeping rhizomes with erect, oblong-lanceolate, once-pinnate fronds that are 18 to 24 inches long and 9 inches wide. The new fronds are a bronze-red color when they first uncoil in spring and mature to a glossy, dark green. The rhizome grows as much as 10 feet long and forks and spreads into dense mats; it can become invasive in wet swampy sites but is less of a problem in drier areas. Chain fern is good for a location with partial shade and a constantly moist, acid soil that is high in organic matter. If grown in a constantly wet location, this fern will tolerate full sunlight. It is hardy to –5°F.

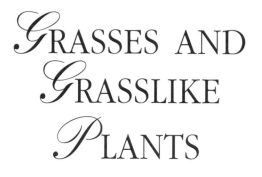

GRASSES AND GRASSLIKE PLANTS

STANDING IN THE PRAIRIE RESTORATION OF THE Shaw Arboretum of the Missouri Botanical Garden at Grey Summit, Missouri, in late August is quite an experience: the wind-hurried rolling swell of 6- and 8-foot-tall grasses is denser than any forest I've ever seen; it is an immensity of landscape that is a vibrant antithesis to the neat, mowed emerald carpet we call lawn. Grasses are members of one of the largest plant families — the Gramineae. They are important for many economic reasons: the seeds of wheat, corn, oats, rice, rye, and millet are basic foodstuffs; the stems of sugarcane and sorghum provide sweeteners. Grass leaves are grown for animal feed, both fresh as pasture grasses and dried for hay. Woody grasses — bamboos — are used as building and craft materials for objects as diverse as fishing poles and baskets, fencing and houses. Sorghum is the source of broom corn; and giant reed provide the "reeds" of clarinets and other woodwind instruments. Sod-forming grasses are used as ornamental ground cover (thus the suburban ritual of "mowing the lawn"), while other grasses with dense, matlike root systems can be used to stabilize soil and prevent erosion.

Grasses may be annual, perennial, evergreen, deciduous, woody, neat clump-formers, or invasive rampant spreaders, and they come in various sizes. They commonly have hollow cylindrical stems with solid joints called nodes, solitary leaves that arise at the nodes and only partially sheath or enclose the stem in most instances, and flat and linear leaf blades with parallel venation. The flowers are inconspicuous, since grasses are wind pollinated and have no need for showy flowers to attract insects, yet grasses have other superlative aesthetic values. Many have handsome seed heads. Some grasses like a moist soil, and others dry, but on the whole grasses require a sunny site. For shady locations a look-alike sedge or rush can be used.

Sedges (*Carex* spp.) differ from grasses in that they usually have solid stems without nodes, are triangular rather than rounded, and often grow in wet, shady places. Rushes (*Juncus* or *Luzula*) usually have solid cylindrical stems without nodes and also grow in wet, shady places. To help keep all of this straight, use the old mnemonic: "Sedges have edges, rushes are rounded, grasses have joints (nodes)."

Grasses and their analogues are easy to care for. They rarely if ever need staking. Deciduous species should be cut back early in spring before new growth begins, but their tawny stems and leaves are attractive in winter as a contrast to evergreen foliage. Evergreen species need a good combing out in early spring to remove dead stems and leaves in order to create a better display. In spring, fertilize them with a blend high in nitrogen, such as 10–6–4, to promote leaf growth; but do not overfeed them because excessive fertilization may result in weak stems. Many grasses can manage without additional fertilization under garden conditions. Grasses and grasslike plants can be thought of as ornamentals with linear texture, so important as a contrast to coarser, bolder, more architectural foliage and lacier, fernlike, more delicate leaves. The simple shape of these plants is enhanced by their colors: glaucous blue, golden yellow, and variegated.

Arrhenatherum elatius spp. *bulbosum* 'Variegatum'
TUBER OAT GRASS

This brightly variegated grass with white-striped leaves is useful as a ground cover, multiplying both by slowly spreading rhizomes and through the formation of bulbs at the base of the stem; the bulbs root where they fall to the ground. The leaves look best from spring into early summer but begin to yellow and look poorly in midsummer, when they should be cut back close to ground level and fertilized to encourage fresh new growth. Tuber oat grass grows 12 inches tall and is adaptable to sun or light shade. It is hardy to –10°F.

Arundo donax
GIANT REED GRASS

This vigorous evergreen grass has tough, somewhat woody stems that resemble a giant corn plant. (In the Midwest, the plain green form of this grass sells poorly for this reason.) The culms reach 9 to 12 feet tall, and the drooping leaf blades are 3 to 4 feet long and 3 inches wide, suiting this grass for bold landscape effects at the edges of the garden, near a pond, or as a quick-growing windbreak. Varieties include 'Macrophylla', with leaves twice as wide as the type plant; and 'Variegata' ('Versicolor') which grows 6 feet tall and has 12-inch-long leaves that are striped with broad white bands at the margins, also more tender than the species (as is common with some other variegated plants). Although this grass is evergreen, it should be thinned early each spring, or in alternate years, to encourage production of vigorous, fresh new growth and maintain its see-through feature. It can be invasive in mild areas but needs a protective mulch in colder regions. It is hardy to 0°F.

Carex spp.
SEDGE

BOWLE'S GOLDEN SEDGE *(Carex stricta [elata]* **'Bowle's Golden')** is an elegant plant for wet soils and dappled light shade. It grows 30 inches tall and has narrow, ¼-inch-wide, golden yellow leaves with a pencil-thin green edge. In cool or foggy regions, such as the San Francisco Bay area of California, it can grow in full sun with constantly moist soil. The dense clump of bright yellow foliage is a showy contrast to *Heuchera* 'Palace Purple', but is a subtle companion for golden hosta and golden feverfew *(Chrysanthemum parthenium* 'Aureum'). If the site has average to dry conditions, sink a 3-gallon plastic nursery pot to its rim, and fill it with soil amended with no more than 15% (by volume) polyacrylamide, such as Terra-sorb or Hydro-gel. Measure the saltlike crystals after they have absorbed water and expanded, not by dry volume. The gels retain water and provide evenly moist conditions, helpful for moisture-loving plants such as Bowle's golden sedge. Plant one to a container, and plan on rejuvenating the plant and refreshing the soil when the roots become crowded in several years.

JAPANESE SEDGE *(Carex morrowii* **'Variegata')** is an elegant, year-round sedge that forms a very dense tuft of leathery, stiffly arching, evergreen leaves that are 12 to 18 inches long by ¼ inch wide; the leaf is dark green with a broad white stripe down the center. This is perhaps the most charming variegated sedge for the shady garden. It grows best in moderately fertile soil that is evenly moist, and is hardy to –10°F.

STRIPED SEDGE *(Carex siderostrica)* is a beautiful sedge with broad green leaves neatly striped with white. It spreads slowly but is not invasive and grows best in woodland shade in moist but well-drained soil high in organic matter. Striped sedge is elegant with glaucous blue hosta and Japanese painted fern *(Athyrium goeringianum* 'Pictum'). It is hardy to –5°F.

WIDE-LEAF SEDGE or PLANTAIN-LEAFED SEDGE *(Carex plantaginea),* an excellent shade-tolerant plant, is useful as a specimen or planted as a ground cover. The evergreen leaves are 6 to 12 inches long and 1 inch wide, and grow in a loose clump. This sedge grows best with dappled to heavy woodland shade in a moist but well-drained soil high in organic matter. It is charming combined with small astilbe (such as *Astilbe simplicifolia* 'Sprite') and small white-variegated hosta. It is hardy to –20°F.

Cortaderia selloana
PAMPAS GRASS

This grass is native to South America and has naturalized in California. I once saw 9-foot-tall plants with great cottony flowering plumes a foot long growing in the scrub along Route 92 near Half Moon Bay, California. The large leaves grow up to 9 feet long and 1 inch wide, and the culms can reach 8 feet tall their first season in the garden, twice that height when mature. It is tolerant of wet or dry sites and of hot, drying winds. Pampas grass is useful massed as a windbreak or grown singly as a specimen plant. Where it grows most vigorously, it can be periodically burned to control growth and remove thatch. Cultivars include 'Albo-lineata', which grows 5 feet tall and has white-edged leaves that become an even cleaner white as they mature; 'Aureo-lineata' ('Gold Band'), which grows 5 feet tall and has leaves with a broad gold edge; 'Bertini', which is dwarf, growing only 3 feet tall; 'Monstrosa', which has long, narrow, graceful leaves (as much as 9 feet long) and 6-foot culms supporting 2-foot flower spikes; and 'Pumila', which is lower growing, 4 to 5 feet tall. Pampas grass grows best in full sun in a fertile, well-drained sandy soil. It should be cut back or burned off in early spring and the dead material from the base of the clump removed. It is hardy to 0°F if the temperature is not low for a sustained period, but does better if the temperature does not go below 20°F. In colder areas the roots can be lifted and stored over winter and replanted each spring, but growth will not be as vigorous.

Elymus arenarius
BLUE LYME GRASS

This true grass is native to coastal sand dunes, where its dense, spreading root system helps to bind the drifting sand. In cultivation it will grow in average garden soil, and there it is also less aggressive. Still, unless it is to be used to stabilize the soil, in light soils it is safest to contain the roots by planting in a dishpan or other container with drainage holes cut in the bottom. Blue Lyme grass grows 2 to 3 feet tall; the leaves are 2 feet long and an inch wide and are a beautiful powdery blue, with the best color developing in full sun and poor soil. It is lovely against a dark background, such as a yew hedge, and with pink flowers such as *Sedum* 'Autumn Joy', and white flowers like Montauk daisy *(Chrysanthemum nipponicum)*. It is deciduous, turning tan in winter, and is hardy to −20°F.

Festuca ovina
SHEEP'S FESCUE

This grass forms a dense tussock of 12- to 16-inch, stiff, erect stems with 9-inch-long, evergreen leaf blades that are colored a beautiful glaucous silvery blue. It grows best with full sun in sandy, well-drained soil. It should be boldly clipped back in early spring and combed to remove old growth, thus encouraging new growth, which has the most intense coloration. It grows so densely that it needs to be lifted, separated, and replanted every two or three years in order to maintain neat symmetrical growth. Sheep's fescue is charming in a heath setting with heathers and small junipers, and with silver foliage plants such as beach wormwood *(Artemisia stellerana* 'Silver Brocade'), and purple foliage plants such as *Sedum* 'Vera Jameson'. *Festuca cinerea* is another tussock-forming blue fescue and has several cultivars that are becoming available on the market. These include 'Azurit', with good blue foliage on a 12-inch-tall tussock; 'Blaufink' ('Blue Finch'), also a 12-inch-tall, compact clump of good blue foliage; 'Blue Fox', which makes a dense 12-inch-tall clump of very fine, silver-blue foliage; 'Daeumling' ('Tom Thumb'), tiny at 4 inches tall; 'Harz', which is 6 inches tall and has foliage with an olive-green cast (like 'Soehrenwald', a little taller at 8 inches); 'Meerblau' ('Blue Sea'), which forms a neat, 6-inch-tall tussock of blue-gray foliage; and 'Seeigel' ('Sea Urchin'), which has a very compact habit, growing 10 inches tall, and blue foliage. Sheep's fescue is hardy to −20°F.

Hakonechloa macra 'Aureola'
JAPANESE WIND-COMBED GRASS

This spectacular grass slowly spreads to form a carpet of arching culms 12 to 15 inches long with leaves 8 inches long by ⅜ inch wide; it is bright golden yellow with narrow, green, pencil-fine stripes. This grass grows best with light to moderate shade in moderately fertile soil that is high in organic matter and is moist but well drained. Unfortunately, it is slow to propagate and therefore is expensive. It is superb in a mass, as a ground cover, or as a container plant. It is hardy to –5°F.

Helictotrichon sempervirens
BLUE OAT GRASS

This true grass grows in a clump as a dense but light-textured 2-foot dome of arching, narrow, brilliant steely blue, evergreen leaves. It needs full sun and a soil high in organic matter with good drainage, and is drought tolerant once established. Blue oat grass is useful as a single specimen or massed in a group planting. It is hardy to –20°F.

Imperata cylindrica 'Red Baron'
JAPANESE BLOOD GRASS

The leaf blades of this grass are green at the base and bright blood red at the tips; it retains this color through the growing season and becomes even more intense in autumn; it is stupendous if sited where sunlight can illuminate it. It slowly spreads by means of rhizomatous roots and grows best with full sun to light shade in a moist but well-drained soil high in organic matter. It is hardy to –10°F.

Luzula sylvatica
GREATER WOOD RUSH

This is a stoloniferous, spreading (but not invasive), shade-tolerant evergreen rush with shiny, dark green leaves that are 12 inches long and ½ inch wide. This accommodating plant grows most luxuriantly in moist, humus-rich soil and is also adjustable to drier situations in moderate to heavy woodland shade, where it forms a dense carpet. *Luzula sylvatica marginata* has an attractive narrow, creamy white band at the margins.

Milium effusum 'Aureum'
BOWLE'S GOLDEN GRASS, GOLDEN WOOD MILLET

This is one of the few true grasses that will grow in light to medium shade. In spring the new leaves are a bright golden yellow, maturing to a fresh light green as the overhead canopy closes in. Growing 15 inches tall, the plant has leaves 12 inches long and ½ inch wide. It is lovely used in a mass planting combined with dark green foliage, smaller blue hosta, golden yellow hosta, and the blue flowers of forget-me-nots (*Myosotis scorpioides*). This grass will re-seed but is not invasive. It is hardy to –10°F.

Miscanthus sinensis
GIANT EULALIA GRASS

This clump-forming deciduous grass has numerous horticultural varieties, some of which are selected for foliage. The stiff, erect culms can grow as much as 12 feet tall in warmer regions of the United States, making this majestic specimen grass a dominant feature in the landscape. The leaves, growing to 3 feet long and 1 inch wide, soften the outline, and the plants rarely if ever need staking. This grass needs full sun; a deep fertile soil high in organic matter; adequate, even levels of moisture; and ample room in which to grow. Too much nitrogen results in soft, weak stems that will need to be staked. Giant eulalia grass is elegant as a specimen in combination with evergreen shrubs. Varieties include 'Gracillimus', with narrow, ¼-inch-wide, somewhat curly leaves that grow 4 to 5 feet tall; 'Morning Light', a 'Gracilimus' type with a narrow white variegation along the margins, delicate and attractive; 'Positano', which grows 6 to 7 feet tall and has good fall color; 'Purpurascens', which is green in spring, turning progressively redder in summer, and grows 4 to 5 feet tall; 'Sarabande', a recent introduction from Germany with lovely silvery foliage; 'Silberspinne', which grows 4 to 5 feet tall and has graceful, narrow leaves; 'Strictus', with a stiff, erect habit of growth to 6 feet tall and horizontal yellow bands across the width of the leaf, looking rather like the quills of an African porcupine; 'Variegatus', which grows 5 to 6 feet tall and has a broad, central creamy white stripe and silver-white narrow stripes toward the edges of the leaf; 'Yaku Jima', which is quite dwarf, only 3 to 4 feet tall, and attractive for winter effect; and 'Zebrinus', which grows 6 to 8 feet tall and has horizontal creamy yellow bands across the width of the arching leaves. Giant eulalia grass is hardy to –10°F.

Pennisetum spp.
FOUNTAIN GRASS

FOUNTAIN GRASS *(Pennisetum alopecuroides)* is deservedly one of the most popular true grasses for ornamental use. Its great, loose, open tuft of foliage fountains out, forming a spray of foliage 16 inches long on stems that are 3 to 4 feet high. It grows best in full sun and fertile soil with adequate moisture. 'Hameln' is a dwarf form that grows 1 to 2 feet tall; and 'Weserbergland' is very similar. Fountain grass is superlative in combination with dwarf red barberry *(Berberis thunbergii atropurpurea nana)*, yuccas, and with black-eyed Susan *(Rudbeckia fulgida* var. *sullivantii* 'Goldsturm'). Its tawny old-gold autumn and winter color adds to the landscape, but it should be cut back in early spring before new growth begins. It is hardy to –20°F.

RED FOUNTAIN GRASS *(Pennisetum setaceum)* is a 42-inch-tall grass with narrow, green leaf blades that are 2 feet long, but it is rarely cultivated in this form. There are a few cultivars with red to purple foliage that are more commonly grown: 'Atrosanguineum', with purple foliage; 'Cupreum', with reddish leaves; and 'Rubrum', with reddish purple foliage. These color forms are elegant combined with purple and lavender flowers, and gray and silver foliage. I have seen red fountain grass growing with rosemary, *(Rosmarinus officinalis)*, agaves, and succulents in a xeric landscape in Borrego Springs, California. It grows well in full sun with average to dry soil and is drought tolerant once established. Hardy to 20°F, it is grown as an annual in colder regions.

Phalaris arundinacea 'Picta'
GARDENER'S-GARTERS GRASS

This is the most common variegated grass, long in cultivation for its white leaves that are narrowly striped with fresh light green; they grow to 14 inches long and ⅔ inch wide. This deciduous to semievergreen grass grows 2 to 3 feet tall, larger in wet areas, and is spreading and invasive; it should be grown in a bottomless container or perforated dishpan to control its spread, unless it is wanted for a ground cover. In drier situations the foliage often looks poor by midsummer; it can then be cut back to the ground, given a liquid fertilizer, and watered thoroughly to encourage fresh new growth to finish the season. It grows best in full sun or light shade in average soil. Other cultivars include 'Feecy's Form', which is finer textured and has pink coloration in spring; and 'Luteo-picta', which is gold variegated but not as crisp and clean in appearance as 'Picta'. Gardener's-garters grass is hardy to –25°F.

Schizachyrium scoparium *[Andropogon scoparius]*
LITTLE BLUESTEM, POVERTY GRASS

This is a clump-forming, deciduous grass that

grows 2 to 3 feet tall and has leaves 20 inches long by ½ inch wide; the leaves are varying shades of blue and green but are most ornamental in autumn and winter when they are a tawny, foxy russet-red. Native to the Midwest and common in eastern meadows, it is useful as forage for grazing animals, from cattle to buffalo. It is attractive massed with any of the daisy-flowered composites such as gaillardia, rudbeckia, coreopsis, and asters, or with butterfly weed (*Asclepias tuberosa*). It grows best in a sunny area with sandy, well-drained, acid soil and is hardy to −20°F.

Sporobolus heterolepis
PRAIRIE DROPSEED

This grass forms an elegant, fine-textured fountain of 15-inch-long, narrow leaf blades, which grow in a dense clump. It prefers full sun and a rather dry site with moderately fertile, well-drained soil. It tends to mound up in the center and so is best maintained by burning early in the year before new growth begins. It is hardy to −25°F.

Zea mays japonica folia-variegata ['Quadricolor', 'Variegata']
VARIEGATED CORN

This coarse, bold annual grass grows 4 to 6 feet tall and has wide, straplike green leaves that are striped with white, yellow, and pink; however, some of the leaves will be plain green. 'Gracillis' is a dwarf corn (3 to 4 feet tall) with bright green, white-striped leaves. When oak trees begin to leaf out and frosts are over, sow several seeds in a small group directly where the plants are to grow. Variegated corn grows best with full sun in fertile soil that is moist but well-drained. Do not remove suckering shoots, but mound earth around the base of the plants as prop roots appear. Variegated corn is an ex-

cellent accent plant, adding height to the back of the border, and is charming with tall pink and white cosmos and cleome for a temporary screening effect. The cobs are reportedly not edible by humans.

ANNUALS

WHEN I BEGAN MY HORTICULTURAL adventures, I grew mostly annuals. Like many other new gardeners, I was too impatient to wait for gratification — I wanted results *now*, this season, right away. As my attention span lengthened, I grew mainly perennials, scorning the quick results that annuals provide. My feelings were that perennials represented gardening sophistication. Now, I have come around to a less dogmatic viewpoint, appreciating and cherishing all sorts of plants for what they have to provide, combining perennials, shrubs, and annuals for the unique effects each can contribute.

Botanically, an annual is a short-lived plant that germinates from seed, matures, and dies within the brief span of one season. Obviously, then, a woody plant is technically not annual, nor is a bulb whose entire mechanism is designed to carry the plant from one year into the next. However, as gardeners we treat some nonannuals as annuals: woody plants such as lantana, bulbs such as caladium, even perennials that need mild winters for survival. Coleus (in all its kaleidoscopic cultivars of *Coleus blumei* and *C.* x *hybridus*), is a tender perennial that is treated as an annual in most of the United States. Plants such as these, whether truly annuals or simply treated as annuals, are a boon to the gardener. They fill in gaps where immature perennials or shrubs have yet to grow. Their annual nature permits facile change from year to year, while their burgeoning growth adds diversity and enlivens the garden display through summer and autumn.

When choosing annuals for your garden, one of your first decisions will be how and where to obtain them. Why make the effort to grow the coleus 'Wizard Velvet' from seed, for instance, when it is available in the neighborhood? The only annuals worth starting yourself are those that cannot be purchased from a reliable local supplier. Unfortunately, all too often the local garden center is more a vendor than a nursery; supplies are purchased from a central wholesaler, and the gardener is provided with little diversity from which to choose. If there is a nursery near you that grows its own plants, cherish and patronize it; such a source will be more likely to have less common plants. If you have a greenhouse, or a grow-light setup, then consider starting uncommon annuals yourself; sunny window ledges, however, lack the space once the tiny seeds begin to grow and need more room. Seed catalogs often offer an intriguing selection of unfamiliar plants. With annuals you are making only a short-term commitment and can usually easily replicate the effects if they please you.

Perennials that are widely grown as annuals in areas where they are not winter hardy are included with the annuals listed here.

Acalypha wilkesiana
COPPERLEAF, BEEFSTEAK PLANT

This very tender shrub grows 15 feet tall in its native South Pacific Islands; it has numerous elliptic or ovate, 5- to 8-inch-long leaves with serrated margins. The leaf color is a bronze-green mottled with copper, red, or purple. Young plants are used for bedding out in mild winter areas of California and Florida, in the Southeast, and even as summer bedding in the Philadelphia area. In protected locations in frost-free regions, it will grow as a shrub to 6 feet tall, but it is unattractive in winter and is susceptible to the lightest frost. It can be propagated in late summer from bedding plants either as softwood cuttings (like coleus) or from heels of older wood from more mature plants. Copperleaf is related to the chenille plant (*Acalypha hispida*), which is grown for its long, drooping, rosy pink, fuzzy flower spike. Cultivars include 'Calcutta', which has narrow trailing foliage, with cream-yellow edges on green leaves; 'Haleakala', which has curled and crested black leaves, a more compact growth habit, and tolerates cooler temperatures better than most other cultivars; 'Macafeeana', which has red leaves marked with crimson and bronze; 'Marginata', which has large bronze-red leaves edged in bright pink and will survive mild frosts if they are not prolonged; and 'Musaica', which has green leaves marked with orange and red.

Amaranthus tricolor
JOSEPH'S COAT

This coarse, bushy annual grows 1 to 4 feet tall and has elliptic to ovate leaves that are 2 to 6 inches long and 2 to 4 inches wide; they are blotched and colored with red, purple, chocolate, orange, or yellow, or a mixture of these colors. They transplant poorly and so should be directly sown in late spring or early summer after the soil has become warm; the seed should be only barely covered, since light aids germination. It grows best with full sun in sandy soil of low fertility and is heat and drought tolerant. Cultivars include 'Early Splendor', which is 3 feet tall and has narrow, deep red leaves at the top of the plant and dark maroon-chocolate leaves lower on the stem; 'Flaming Fountains', which is 3 feet tall and has long willowlike leaves that change from green through bronze to crimson, orange, and red; 'Illumination', which grows 4 feet tall and has broad, luminescent, rose-red leaves tinged with gold on the upper third of the plants; and 'Joseph's Coat', which grows 3 feet tall and has lanceolate upper leaves with distinct bands of bright red, yellow, and green.

Atriplex hortensis
RED ORACH

This annual grows 4 to 6 feet tall and has triangular-ovate or sagittate leaves covered with a crystalline, mealy farina when young; the leaves grow to 5 inches long. It is tolerant of dry soils and alkaline or saline conditions, growing in full sun in desert regions. Early in spring the seeds should be sown where the plants are to grow, since they resent root disturbance; once planted, they will self-sow freely. The plants typically have soft gray-green leaves, except in the following cul-tivars: var. *atrosanguinea* ('Rubra'), with blood-red leaves; cv. 'Cupreatrorosea', with a coppery luster; and 'Rosea', with darker-veined, light red leaves. Red orach looks lovely in the front garden at Wave Hill in Riverdale, New York, planted with purple-leaved smokebush (*Cotinus coggygria*), red-leaved rose (*Rosa rubrifolia*), and an assortment of lavender and mauve flowers.

Brassica oleracea acephala,
Brassica oleracea capitata
ORNAMENTAL KALE,
ORNAMENTAL CABBAGE

These are among the few plants that excel as autumn annuals. They are hardy where winter temperatures do not drop below 25°F, and will lend interest to the garden from fall to spring in milder areas. Since they are biennials, they will flower and then die the second year. In cold winter regions they are raised from seed sown in midsummer and planted out in early autumn, producing small, colorful rosettes of beautiful creamy white, rose-pink, or reddish purple foliage, with a ruff of older blue-green leaves like a collar. Spring-sown seed will produce larger rosettes if the plants do not bolt and flower. Ornamental cabbages have smooth leaves, while the ornamental kales have frilly-edged leaves. They need average soil, moist but well-drained, with full sun and cool temperatures.

Cultivars include 'Cherry Sundae', an F[1] hybrid ornamental cabbage with carmine and cream foliage; 'Color-Up', a hybrid cabbage available in separate colors of white, pink, or red; 'Frizzy Lace', a hybrid kale with laciniate, frilled-edged leaves, available in red, white, or mixed colors; 'Osaka', a hybrid kale available in mixed colors of white, pink, and red; and 'Red and White Peacock', an F[1] hybrid flowering kale with snowflakelike red-and-white foliage. These ornamental vegetables are better in the garden than in the cooking pot, being edible but not very tasty; they are rather tough and lose their attractive colors when cooked.

Other leafy vegetables can be used as edible ornamentals: loose-leaf lettuces such as the frilly, deeply curled, rose-red 'Lollo-rosso' or 'Red Salad Bowl', with deep red color at maturity; crisphead 'Red Grenoble', with shiny, wine red leaves; butterhead/bibb types such as 'Red Riding Hood' or 'Rougette du Midi'; a loose-heading romaine like 'Rouge d'Hiver', which has deep red leaves and is heat tolerant, cos lettuce 'Apache', with reddish bronze outer leaves, or 'Osaka Purple' mustard, with deep purple leaves veined in bright white. Red-leafed spring lettuces look attractive with, for example, blue or white violas; by the time the violas are through flowering, the lettuce is eaten and the space is clear for planting something else. Vegetables need not be relegated only to the vegetables garden — if it is an attractive foliage plant, use it where it looks good, and then enjoy eating it, if it is tasty. Oh yes, Joseph's coat, perilla (called "shi-so" in Japan), and red orach are edible, too.

Caladium x hortulanum. See page 137.

Canna x generalis. See pages 137-38.

Chrysanthemum parthenium 'Aureum' [Matricaria eximia 'Aureum']
GOLDEN-FEATHER, GOLDEN FEVERFEW

This bushy, aromatic, short-lived perennial is often cultivated as an annual. It grows 18 to 36 inches tall and has oblong to broadly ovate, fernlike, pinnatifid, golden yellow leaves that are 3 inches long. Although it is hardy to −10°F, the mature plants are generally discarded and new seedlings are planted each spring. Seed should be sown where plants are to grow as soon as the soil can be cultivated, or cuttings taken in late summer can winter over in a cold frame. It grows best with sun to light shade in moist but well-drained soil with moderate fertility. Golden-feather is lovely with bronze or purple foliage such as *Heuchera* 'Palace Purple', golden-leaved or gold-variegated hosta, gold-variegated plants such as *Liriope muscari* 'Variegata', and blue flowers.

Coleus blumei
COLEUS, FLAME NETTLE

This perennial grows 3 to 6 feet tall and has coarsely toothed, tapering, ovate leaves that are 3 to 8 inches long. The plants in cultivation are more correctly named *Coleus* x *hybridus* since they were developed from other species, such as *C. pumilus* as well as *C. blumei*. Coleus is perennial in frost-free regions but is grown as an annual in most of the United States. It is valued for its colorful foliage in shades of pink, red, bronze, maroon, yellow, chartreuse, and green. Plants are erect or trailing and have ovate leaves 2 to 4 inches long. Certain strains, such as the Fiji series, have a particularly frilled or cut edge. A series has a particular leaf shape and/or margin color and is available in different colors, such as 'Pineapple Wizard', chartreuse-yellow; 'Wizard Sunset', orange-red; and 'Wizard Velvet', deep, soft, dark red. Coleus grows well in a moist but well-drained soil high in organic matter and of moderate fertility; it needs light shade for best foliage color, for some bleaching will occur in full sun. Groups of individual, separate colors have a cleaner, sharper appearance in the garden than mixed, mingled colors, which look muddy together. Deep red coleus is beautiful with Japanese painted fern (*Athyrium goeringianum* 'Pictum'), while golden yellow and chartreuse cultivars are good with glaucous blue hosta. The Dragon series cultivars have a yellow edge to a tapering frilly leaf; coleus in the Fairway series are self-branching from the base of the very compact dwarf plants; Fiji series have deeply cut and fringed leaves with contrasting mixed colors; Poncho series have trailing stems and are most suitable for hanging baskets ('Red Poncho' cultivars have bright red leaves with green speckling, darkening toward the edges, and a narrow yellow-green margin); Sabre series have narrow, sharply tapering leaves in bright colors and grow 8 inches tall; Wizard series grow 10 to 12 inches tall, are freely branching from the base, and have heart-shaped leaves. Cuttings taken from especially pleasing cultivars in late summer can be wintered over indoors.

Euphorbia marginata
SNOW-ON-THE-MOUNTAIN

This annual is native to the Midwest. It grows 2 to 3 feet tall and is somewhat rangy; the ovate to oblong, gray-green leaves grow 1 to 3 inches long and are edged and striped with white on the upper portion of the plant. Snow-on-the-mountain is useful for toning down hot colors — red or orange zinnias, scarlet sage, celosia — and is beautiful with blue flowers or contrasting with bronze foliage. It grows in average conditions in moist but well-drained soil of moderate fertility in full sun, but it grows best in poor, dry soil; it is heat tolerant. The seeds should be sown where the plants are to grow after danger of frost is passed; it will then self-sow where conditions are suitable. When it is cut or bruised, it releases a sticky white sap, which may cause dermatitis in sensitive individuals. Cultivars include 'Summer Icicle', which is lower growing (to 18 inches); and 'White Top', which has mostly white upper leaves.

Hypoestes phyllostachya [sanguinolenta]
POLKA-DOT PLANT

Often cultivated as a houseplant, this tender perennial with a woody base grows 3 feet tall and has ovate, 2½-inch-long, dark green leaves splashed with rose-pink spots. It grows best in dappled to moderate shade in a moist but well-drained soil high in organic matter. The tips can be pinched to control height and keep the plants from getting leggy. Polka-dot plant is easily grown from seed sown indoors two months before the frost-free outdoor planting date. It is attractive in the shady garden with impatiens of appropriate colors. Cultivars include 'Pink Splash', which has larger spots; 'Red Splash', with red blotches; and 'White Splash', with white spots.

Ipomoea batatas 'Blackie'
BLACK-LEAVED SWEET POTATO

This plant is not mentioned in most garden literature but is listed in some houseplant specialty catalogs. It has trailing stems with 6-inch-long, palmately lobed leaves that are green when they first appear, maturing to an intense purplish black, sometimes with faint, lighter blotches. It is superb planted in a container, where it seems to grow more vigorously than in the ground. It needs rich soil, full sun, and adequate moisture for best growth and is easy to start from cuttings of over-wintered plants in spring.

Iresine herbstii
BEEFSTEAK PLANT, BLOODLEAF

This perennial is often grown as a houseplant and can also be used for summer bedding. Growing as a 6-foot-tall, evergreen, shrubby plant in mild winter areas, it can be propagated by late summer cuttings and wintered over under protected conditions (like coleus). Plants grown in this manner usually grow 18 to 24 inches tall and can be kept even smaller by tip-pinching new growth. The broadly ovate leaves are 5 inches long and notched at the tip and are a deep purplish red with lighter veins and midrib. Beefsteak plant grows well with full sun in moist soil, but it is frost sensitive and should not be moved outdoors until the weather is mild and settled. This plant is superb grown with silver foliage plants such as artemisia (*Artemisia ludoviciana albula* 'Silver King') or dusty miller (*Senecio cineraria*). The two cultivars are 'Aureo-reticulata', which has green leaves veined with red and blotched with yellow; and *wallisii*, which grows only 6 to 12 inches tall and has blackish purple leaves.

Kochia scoparia **var.** *trichophylla*
BURNING BUSH

This annual forms a dense, globular mound that is 2 to 3 feet tall and 2 feet wide and has lanceolate or linear leaves that are 3 inches long. The leaves are green in early summer, turning purplish in late summer and then a bright red in autumn. It grows well with full sun in sandy, dry soil of low fertility and is heat tolerant. Seed can be planted directly where plants are to grow after danger of frost is passed or started indoors one month before the frost-free date; the seed should be soaked in tepid water for 24 hours before sowing. The seeds need light to germinate. 'Acapulco Silver' has silvery white leaf tips and is red in autumn.

Ocimum basilicum
BASIL

This is a true annual and is an essential herb in Italian cuisine, as well as Italian romance. One older gentleman of my acquaintance told me that when young men in his village in Italy went courting, they wore a sprig of fragrant basil behind their ear to announce their amorous intentions. Whether for cooking or courting, the purple-leaved cultivars are attractive in the garden or in containers, combined with silver foliage such as dusty miller (*Senecio cineraria*) and flowers in shades of lavender, purple, blue, and yellow. Basil is frost sensitive and should be planted outdoors only after the weather is mild and settled; it grows well in a sunny site with a moderately moist and well-drained soil of average fertility. 'Dark Opal' and 'Fluffy Ruffles' both grow 18 to 24 inches tall and have ovate to elliptic, deep purple leaves that are 3 to 5 inches long; 'Fluffy Ruffles' has a twisted ruffled margin.

Onopordum acanthium
SCOTCH THISTLE

This huge, coarse, architectural, biennial thistle grows 6 to 9 feet tall and has erect branching stems that are covered with woolly white hairs. The spiny, oblong, lobed, silvery gray leaves, covered with cobwebby white hairs, grow as much as 2 feet long and 1 foot wide on the lower portion of the plant; they form a loose, basal rosette the first year before spearing upward in late spring the next year. Scotch thistle grows best in full sun in moist but well-drained rich soil, conditions producing the most imposing, statuesque specimens. It has great presence but needs space to create the best display. It should be deadheaded to control self-sowing, as this plant is overly generous with its progeny.

Pelargonium x *hortorum*
GERANIUM, HORSESHOE GERANIUM, ZONAL GERANIUM

This familiar bedding plant with clustered pink, rose, or red flowers is often combined with vinca vine (*Vinca major* 'Variegata') in summer window boxes and tubs. Actually a shrubby, succulent, evergreen perennial from South Africa, the horseshoe geranium is of complex hybrid origin, primarily based on *P. zonale* and *P. inquinans*. It grows 3 to 5 feet tall in mild winter areas and becomes woody with age; the green leaves are crenate to scalloped, wavy-edged, round to kidney shaped and grow 1 to 5 inches wide. It can have much more interesting, even flamboyant, foliage than the commonplace, dark horseshoe-marked green leaves. Fancy-leaved geranium cultivars have leaves that range from modest, such as a white-margined green leaf, to exotic combinations of yellow, crimson, and brown, to those with up to four-color variegation including maroon, bronze, red, pink, yellow, white, and green. These plants are slower growing, and the flowers are usually smaller and less profuse. They must be propagated from cuttings and do not root quite as easily as the more familiar, showy, flowered cultivars. Cultivars with white-edged green leaves are 'Flower of Spring', 'Foster's Seedling', 'Frank Headley' (dwarf), 'Hills of Snow', 'Jayne Varness', 'Mrs. Parker', 'Mountain of Snow', 'Petals', 'Santa Maria', and 'Silver Ruby'. Green leaves with a central blotch or butterfly marking include 'Happy Thought'. Gold-and-green leaves with a red or bronze to orange zone are represented by 'Contrast', 'Display', 'Dolly Varden', 'Golden Filigree' (dwarf), 'Golden Oriole', 'Lady Cullum', 'Lass O'Gowrie', 'Miss Burdette Coutts', 'Mrs. Strang', 'Skies of Italy', and 'Sophia Dumaresque'. All grow best in a well-drained, sandy soil with moderate fertility and need a very lightly shaded site; the variegated leaves tend to sunburn if grown in full sun. They are most useful in containers, planted outdoors only after all danger of frost has passed.

Perilla frutescens
PERILLA, BEEFSTEAK PLANT

This annual with aromatic foliage grows 3 feet tall and has broadly ovate, toothed, deeply veined leaves that are 5 inches long. Once the plants are established, they will self-sow profusely. Purchased seed, however, will not always germinate as freely, so it is best sown in spring where the plants are to grow. Perilla grows best in full sun to light shade in moderately fertile soil that is moist but well-drained to dry; but it is not drought tolerant. In late summer when the plants begin to flower, the leaves lose their intense coloration and turn greenish purple. Goldfinches eat the seeds, perching on the stalks and scattering the excess seed for

next year's crop. Perilla looks lovely with silver foliage and is also striking with golden foliage; it is a good foil for yellow and orange flowers such as African marigolds and zinnias. Cultivars include 'Atropurpurea', which is a dark purple with metallic blue overtones; and 'Crispa' ('Laciniata'), which is laciniate to dentate with frilled margins, purple or bronze, and is lower growing at 2 to 3 feet.

Ricinus communis
CASTOR BEAN

This big, bold perennial, cultivated as an annual, can grow 15 feet tall in its first season; it needs a long, hot growing season with full sun in a rich, well-drained soil high in organic matter and adequate moisture. The leaves have five to eleven palmate lobes and grow 3 feet long and wide. In most instances, the plants grow 7 to 10 feet tall and have leaves that are 2 feet long and wide. The seed is highly poisonous. Seeds should be planted indoors no more than a month before the weather will be mild and settled, because growth is rapid and seedlings quickly reach an awkward size. Soak the seed in tepid water 24 hours before sowing them individually in quart pots. This lush annual tropical plant is incomparable as an accent plant or for quick screening. In frost-free areas it can self-sow, and individual plants may persist for several years, reaching 20 feet tall, with smaller leaves than on juvenile plants. The cultivar 'Carmencita' grows "only" 5 to 6 feet tall in three months from seed and has wonderful, deep plum–colored leaves and bronze-red stems; it is excellent with purple-leaved cannas and red-flowered dahlias or celosia, and with tall grasses such as maiden grass (*Miscanthus sinensis* 'Morning Light'). 'Cambodgensis' has purplish black stems and very dark foliage; 'Dwarf Red Spire' grows 6 feet tall and has red leaves; 'Gibsonii' is dwarf at 4 to 5 feet tall and has metallic, dark red foliage and stems; 'Sanguineus' has blood-red stems and leaves; 'Scarlet Queen' has maroon leaves; 'Zanzibarensis' has bright green leaves with white veins; and 'Zanzibarensis Enormis' has very large green leaves.

Senecio cineraria [Centaurea maritima, Cineraria maritima]
DUSTY-MILLER

This almost-hardy perennial is very popular as a bedding plant. Where it is hardy, it grows 30 inches tall and has 2- to 6-inch-long, thickly felted, white-woolly leaves that are pinnately cut into blunt oblong segments. It grows best in dry, infertile, sandy soil in full sun, but it will tolerate light shade; it is also tolerant of windy coastal conditions, even salt spray. Where perennial, dusty-miller must be pruned occasionally to prevent loose, leggy, open growth. It is lovely at dusk or in the evening by moonlight and in combination with white flowers. It is an excellent foil for purple foliage and flowers, to cool down hot orange and red flowers, and to accentuate blue ones. It can be propagated from seeds sown three months before frost-free weather or from cuttings taken in late summer. Cultivars include 'Cirrhus', which is dwarf (18 inches tall) and has more rounded, less dissected foliage; 'Diamond', which has very silver and very dissected foliage; 'Silver Dust', which makes a low mound of silvery foliage like hoarfrost; and 'Silver Queen', which grows only 8 inches tall and has finely dissected, lacy, silver foliage. It is hardy to 20°F.

Silybum marianum
MILK THISTLE, ST. MARY'S THISTLE

This plant is an annual or sometimes a biennial and grows 3 to 4 feet tall. The bold spiny, ovate, lobed leaves grow 30 inches long and 6 to 12 inches wide in a flat, basal rosette and are lustrous dark green, beautifully veined and marbled in white. Seeds should be directly sown in autumn or early spring in a sunny location with well-drained soil. It self-sows freely.

Zea mays japonica folia-variegata. See page 172.

Garden Preparation and Maintenance

It is very important in every garden to begin with proper site preparation. How you plant is more important than *what* you plant. Unless plants are well grown and healthy, they cannot flourish as they are intended to and results will be disappointing. They will not thrive if conditions are poor because of improper site selection, poor planting techniques, or lack of water, fertilization, or maintenance. Do not assume that just because you see beautiful wildflowers growing untended, similar plants will prosper on neglect. What you do not see are those plants that did not survive. When pests chew on the leaves, diseases are present, requirements for sun and shade are incorrect, or soil conditions are poor, and then plants cannot produce a display commensurate with their potential. It is important to analyze your garden before even choosing which plants you want to grow so as to avoid disappointments — like the first marigolds that I planted in the shade.

Is Your Site Sunny or Shady?

First, determine whether the garden is sunny or shady. There are wonderful plants that grow under either condition, but sun-loving plants are not shade tolerant. And although some shade-tolerant plants will grow in the sun if the soil is moist, this is not always the case. Sun is easy to define. If there is direct sunlight on an area for six or more hours a day in the summer, the area is considered sunny. Shade is much more variable. A woodland setting may be sunny in the spring and shady in the summer. However, deciduous woodlands usually have dappled, shifting sunlight that does reach the ground below — and the edge of a wooded area is sunnier than it is further in. Additionally, you can modify shady conditions by removing some of the lower branches of tall trees to raise the canopy, as well as selectively thinning the crown of the tree to allow more light to enter.

If a garden is shaded by a building but open to the sky, that area is often very bright. Although it receives no direct sunlight, the ground is considered to be lightly shaded. Especially if the building is white, thus reflecting more light into the area, a surprising range of plants can be grown. Most difficult are areas shaded by evergreens, for there the shade is constant and dry conditions generally prevail; also, between two buildings the shade is both dense and constant. Areas such as these suffer additionally from poor air circulation, which creates mildew and other disease problems.

Soil Texture

After you determine the quality of light, your next step is to look at the soil. A healthy crop of weeds is a good sign; if *nothing* is growing, that's the time to worry. If plants are already growing on the site, it's a good bet that suitable plants that you select will also do well. The different soil types range from sandy soils that are low in fertility but quick draining, to clay soils that are often rich in nutrients but so poorly drained as to be difficult to dig.

Soil is made up of different particles. The very fine ones are called silt or clay, and the coarser ones are sand. Both are mineral fragments. There is an easy way to check soil composition: Dig a representative shovelful of soil, measure one cup, and put it in a clean, 1-quart, clear-glass, screw-cap jar. Add about 1½ pints of water. Screw on the cap and shake the jar vigorously with an up-and-down motion. Set the jar down and let the soil particles precipitate. The coarse, sandy pieces will quickly settle to the bottom. The silt and clay will take longer. Once everything has settled, you will be able to see different layers, which will give you an idea of the proportion of different materials in that particular sample.

Very important for the healthy growth of most plants is organic matter such as humus, leaf mold, or compost. (Desert and seaside plants need less; prairie and woodland plants need more.) Organic matter is important for soil tilth, or structure. It helps to regulate the supply of moisture and the availability of nutrients. In addition, it contains the microorganisms necessary for healthy soil and plants. Think of organic matter as the roughage in your plants' diet. Compost, leaf mold, dried cow or sheep manure, peat moss — all of these are sources of organic matter. To improve your soil, dig these soil amendments into your garden and incorporate them with the soil that is there. Organic matter continues to break down and should be replaced periodically; it breaks down most quickly in hot climates with high rainfall, more slowly in temperate areas, and very little in cold or dry climates.

Once you've selected the area for your garden, remove existing herbaceous plants and shrubs. Any that you intend to reuse should be potted or boxed, watered, and set aside in a lightly shaded area. The sooner these plants can be replanted, the better. Dig the site over, removing rocks, roots, and rubble that would interfere with the growth of the new plants. Add organic matter — a layer at least 2 inches thick, or twice that, if available. The sandier and more depleted the soil, the more organic matter you should add. Dig the soil and the amendments together until they cannot be distinguished. If you are using inorganic fertilizers in granular form, this is the time to incorporate them into the planting area.

Soil Fertility

Nutrients are those elements that the plants use to make food for their growth. Plants grow best with a complete fertilizer — one that contains nitrogen, phosphorus, and potassium. It is important to understand what each of these supplies in order to select the correct balance.

Commercial fertilizers are labeled with three numbers, indicating the N–P–K ratio (nitrogen, phosphorus, and potassium, respectively). Nitrogen encourages stem and leaf growth. This is often the limiting factor in plant growth, for while great quantities of nitrogen are present in the air, plants cannot use it until it is present in the soil. Some is washed in by rain or snow, but it is usually returned to the soil in the form of organic matter. Cottonseed meal or dried blood are organic sources of nitrogen, while nitrate of soda is an inorganic source manufactured in a factory. Since nitrogen is important for leaf growth, it should be applied in greater amounts in the spring, when

plants are actively growing. If nitrogen is applied in the fall, on the other hand, the plants can be pushed into an artificial growth spurt, which, because the growth is new and tender, will die when cold weather comes. Therefore, fertilizer blends higher in nitrogen, such as 10–6–4, should be applied in the spring. A word of caution: Excessive application of nitrogen will lead to soft, lush growth, which is attractive to pests and susceptible to disease. Additionally, lavish application of nitrogen can cause some variegated plants to revert to an all-green coloration.

Phosphorus is particularly important for flowering, and thus for seed and fruit production, as well as good root growth. It also provides increased resistance to disease. This particular element can become bound up in the soil, especially under acid conditions. Microorganisms change the phosphorus present in the soil into a form the plants can utilize. It is important that phosphorus be mixed with the soil at the bottom of a planting hole, so it will be available to the plant roots. An organic source is rock phosphate; superphosphate, considered an inorganic source, is a chemically treated form of rock phosphate.

Potassium is also essential for plant growth. Soils in the western United States tend to have more potassium; those in the East are sometimes deficient in potassium. Like phosphorus, this element is important for disease resistance, as well as for strong stem growth. Under normal growing conditions, many plants need as much potassium as nitrogen. For this reason it is a good idea to add potassium to the garden every year. Greensand, a mineral that is mined from the ocean bottom, is an organic source; muriate or sulphate of potash are two inorganic sources of potassium.

Inorganic fertilizers are available in particulate, granular form or formulated for liquid application. A granular fertilizer must be acted upon by microorganisms in the soil and dissolved in water before the plants can make use of the nutrients. If fertilizer is in the form of a chemical salt, such as muriate of potash or superphosphate, any particles that accidentally contact the foliage must be quickly washed off, since the chemicals can burn and cause damage, just like road salt. Granular fertilizers are best for a slower, more sustained effect, but they must be applied to the ground, not to the plants. Liquid fertilizers are available as crystals, which must be dissolved in water, and as concentrated solutions, which must be diluted before use. Nutrients in these forms are immediately available to the plants. Some liquid fertilizers can be applied to and absorbed through the leaves; this method of fertilization is known as foliar feeding. Liquid feeding results in little, if any, sustained effect; it is most useful at the time of transplanting, for a quick pick-me-up after heavy rains, or in instances where you suspect the plants need some supplemental nutrition right away. It is most commonly used for container plants and to encourage more rapid growth of immature plants.

Putting in the Plants

Once the area has been thoroughly prepared, allow the soil to settle for a week or so. All the digging has added air to the soil, and if you plant immediately, roots may become exposed as the soil settles or plants themselves may settle to an incorrect depth. Planting in a thoroughly prepared site is a joy. The soil is so light you can plant with your bare hands (although a trowel or shovel is still the best). The planting day should be gray, overcast, and drizzly, if at all possible. Bright sunshine, low humidity, and windy conditions are hard on plants trying to adjust to their new home. If the weather isn't optimal, try to plant in the late afternoon or early evening, so a period of darkness will give some protection against the shock of transplanting. Once you have the plants you need — whether your own propagations, gifts from a friend, or purchased — plant them as soon as possible so they can establish themselves in the new location. Overgrown plants in pots that are too small are subject to stress, since their growth is checked and stunted. This is especially true of annuals, but also of perennials and woody plants.

Set the plants down, still in their containers, where you intend to plant them in the garden. Step back and look at them. Does the design look good from all directions? Do any of the plants need a different spacing? Try a rearrangement. Is it an improvement? Most gardens are never installed *exactly* as they are designed on paper. Gardening is, after all, part science and part art. Science and theory will suggest which plants will grow where and recommend combinations, but it is the artistic facet that is intuitive and possibly suggests last-minute changes that transcend a formal plan.

Once the plants are arranged to your satisfaction, planting can begin. Take the plant out of its pot, damaging it as little as possible. If there is a dense mat of roots encircling the soil ball, make three vertical cuts down the sides from top to bottom and an **X** across the bottom, using a sharp knife, such as a linoleum knife or similar implement. This will enable the plant to send new roots into the fresh soil more readily than if the matted roots are left girdling the root ball as in the pot. Dig a hole generously adequate for the size of the root mass. The most common error novice gardeners make is to dig undersized planting holes. An old folk saying recommends putting "A one-dollar plant in a five-dollar hole." So consider the ratio of five to one (ignoring the exact dollar values of the epigram, given the cost of plants and labor these days). The hole should be large enough to spread the roots out in a natural fashion, not cram them into place with a shoehorn. Because the entire bed is well dug, the roots will have an easy time extending into the freshly prepared soil. Set the plant at the same depth it was growing in the pot. Backfill some of the soil, flood the hole with water, wait until it drains, and finish filling the hole.

After all of the plants are in place, water the entire bed — even if the sky is overcast or the weather forecast predicts rain. A mentor of mine insisted that unless it was actually raining while you were planting, it was vital to water afterward. And he was right.

After you have watered, mulch the garden to reduce water loss, moderate soil temperature, and provide an attractive, uniform appearance. Use a readily available material, so it will be simple to replenish as necessary. Some suitable choices are a fine grade of pine bark mulch, chopped leaves, cocoa hulls, crushed peanut hulls, and rough compost.

When you are adding plants to an existing planting, or taking up overgrown specimens for division and replanting, take advantage of the opportunity to amend the soil, refertilize, and plant with the same care and attention as the first time around.

Garden Maintenance

Routine care and maintenance consist of familiar garden chores — watering when rainfall is inadequate, removing weeds *before* they have any chance to release their seeds and aggravate the problem, watching for pests and diseases so treatment can begin early before the problem is severe. Perennials may need to have top-heavy flower stalks staked and faded flowers removed before they seed.

Most plants in average soil will need approximately an inch of water a week during the growing season to remain healthy. Plants in sandy soil need more water, applied more frequently; those in clay soil, less. To estimate the output of your sprinkler, set a few straight-sided containers, such as cat-food cans, at different points in the spray pattern. Let the water run for a measured time period (an hour, for instance) and then check to see how much water is in each container. Generally, it will take an hour or more to apply an inch of water, depending on your water pressure, and the output will not be consistent throughout the area covered by the sprinkler. Once you have taken such a measurement, you will know how long to water and which areas might need more. It is also helpful to use a rain gauge to verify how much rain actually fell in a given period. In fact, it is helpful to place rain gauges at several points in the garden, since the amount of water that falls in an open area differs from that reaching the ground under trees. Plants need the most water while in active growth and need little while dormant. Excess water during dormancy can actually kill them.

Our first house, purchased in 1967, was on an eighth of an acre in Norwalk, Connecticut. The 50' x 100' lot included a garage at the back of the property and a driveway that ran the length of the north side. Here, I began to learn about gardening. In ten years, however, my increasingly avid commitment to gardening meant that I had planted myself out of house and home. There wasn't any room left for new plants without removing existing ones. I explained to my husband why we had to move — and as an alternative, offered to plow up the gravel driveway and turn it into a rock garden. My search was for more land; his limits were more practical — what we could afford to pay and how far he would commute. Real estate agents had a difficult time with me, trying to show me the kitchen while I waved my trowel asking, "Where's the dirt?" In 1977, we bought our present house, which is sited on one acre of land. Plants that were too precious to leave behind were now boarders in friends' gardens. The first year I did little but observe patterns of sun and shade, locate frost pockets, and decide where the paths would go. Planting really started the second year, and the garden is still not near completion more than a decade later. The most important thing I've learned is that larger gardens are not just bigger than small ones. With more area to care for, there is less time to tend individual plants. This circumstance means that foliage effects are especially useful, because they reduce typical routine maintenance. If plants are grown thickly enough, there is less room for weeds to grow, and leaves don't need the same pinching, staking, and deadheading that flowers require. Foliage plants are not maintenance free, however.

Slugs, in particular, are a problem in the shade or in wet conditions. Some proprietary chemicals can be applied as a poison bait. (Commercial slug baits do not attract birds, squirrels, or other small animals.) A homemade trap that is commonly used is a saucer of beer (inexpensive domestic beer is just as effective as foreign imports), or even water with a tablespoon of sugar and a pinch of yeast that is allowed to ferment; slugs will crawl in and drown. Another method is to place a grapefruit or melon rind in the garden overnight. Slugs will congregate inside to feast, and you can pick the rind up, slugs included, wrap in newspaper and discard in the trash. (If you get slug slime on your hands, salt is far more efficient than soap for cleaning it off.)

Deer and rabbits can be much more of a problem, for both can eat favorite plants quite literally to death. Some repellent sprays are moderately effective, but the only reliable method is adequate fencing to keep the creatures out of the garden. Rabbits can be kept out with a closely woven mesh fence; they are more of a problem in or near open, grassy areas. Deer, on the other hand, can clear a 10-foot-high fence with a single bound. An electric fence, using a New Zealand stock-fence pulse charger will mitigate predation effectively. Because deer have hollow hair, a regular stock-fence charger, designed to work with cattle and horses, is less effective, but the New Zealand type was developed to control sheep, even with their dense fleece.

Rodents such as mice, voles, and chipmunks can decimate bulb plantings, girdle tree trunks, gnaw roots, and generally create havoc. In rural and suburban areas, snakes play an important role in maintaining a balance. Cats, also, are notable allies for the gardener — they are organic pest-control devices, so to speak. Devices that make a periodic, rhythmic thumping noise are considered ineffective, as are the deterrents sold as "gopher" plants, unless enough are planted to completely ring the target plant, and often not even then. Various repellent sprays, too, are of limited effectiveness, and the use of poison baits for rodents in the open garden is too risky. Individual plants or small areas can be protected by lining the planting hole with hardware cloth to prevent tunneling.

Diseases are best controlled by prevention rather than treatment after they appear. Healthy plants are, in general, more resistant to disease, besides being more pleasing to look at. Many diseases are more of a problem in damp, stagnant conditions, so mildew-sensitive cultivars, especially, should be planted where there is good air circulation. Consider discarding any plant that proves to be susceptible to botrytis, mildew, or rust and replacing it with a more resistant cultivar. Do not compost any foliage that is diseased, since this only adds a reservoir of infection to the garden.

Plants must be healthy and growing vigorously if they are to produce the best display. A tree with small, stunted leaves because of drought early in the year cannot possibly look good later. Similarly, a tree that has been attacked by a disease such as anthracnose, or chewed by leaf miners or caterpillars, is unsightly no matter whether its leaves are green or gold or scarlet. If you carefully select the shrubs and trees, plant them where they receive the light they require, cultivate them so that they have the nutrients and moisture they need, and treat them for any pests or diseases that occur, you should have good results. But the best treatment is really the most pleasant: Enjoy the garden. An old Chinese proverb says, "The best fertilizer for the land is its owner's footsteps." If you are walking around the garden, enjoying the plants and seeing how they are growing, then you are more likely to see what needs to be done. If you see slugs chewing on the hosta leaves or mildew on the phlox, you can respond right away, before the plants are harmed and become too unsightly.

APPENDIX II

Sources of Plants and Seeds

When I have the idea that the perfect plant for a specific use is out there, somewhere, I am not sure which is more frustrating: not knowing what that plant is, or, not knowing where to find it. Part II addresses the first quandary; this appendix, the second.

Always begin with local nurseries. You can see the exact plant you intend to purchase, and bring smaller ones home immediately or arrange delivery of large items at a convenient time. It is impossible, however, for any one nursery to satisfy the acquisitive tendencies of eager gardeners. Mail-order suppliers provide an invaluable service for gardeners who do not have local sources. Specialty nurseries that might not survive on local trade can draw from a wider pool of customers by providing plants by mail.

This is a comprehensive list of specialty sources, rather than an ultimate list of mail-order sources of more familiar or ordinary plants. I know there are numerous other nurseries of which I am not aware. This is simply a list of suggested sources; any warranty or guarantee is between vendor and purchaser.

Addresses and prices are those in place in 1991 and may, of course, change at any time. A complete list of the Mailorder Association of Nurseries members is available for $1.00 postage and handling from Mailorder Association of Nurseries, Dept. SCI, 8683 Doves Fly Way, Laurel, MD 20723.

ANNUALS

The Country Garden
P.O. Box 3539
Oakland, CA 94609
(415) 658-8777

Catalog $2.00

Primarily lists plants grown for their flowering effect, but includes some desirable foliage plants, such as annual grasses and ornamental leafed corn.

BAMBOOS

Steve Ray's Bamboo Gardens
909 79th Place South
Birmingham, AL 35206
(205) 833-3052

An impressive array of bamboos, including cultural information; retail only.

Tradewinds Bamboo Nursery
P.O. Box 70
Calbella, CA 95418
(707) 485-0835

Excellent selection of seventeen different bamboos, with several available in different sizes.

BEGONIAS

Logee's Greenhouses
141 North Street
Danielson, CT 06239
(203) 774-8038

Color catalog $3.00

Incredible diversity of begonias and rex begonias, including brilliant-leaved, spiral-leaved, dwarf, and predominantly silver-leaved categories. Also ferns, mosses, cacti, and succulents, as well as some fancy-leaved geraniums.

CALADIUMS

Caladium World
P.O. Drawer 629
Sebring, Florida 33871
(813) 385-7661

Minimum order of 25 tubers per variety; information on planting and care is given.

Spaulding Bulb Farm
1811 Howey Road
Sebring, FL 33872
(813) 385-0318

Color brochure $.75

Minimum order of 50 tubers, minimum 10 per variety; strap- and lance-leaf, as well as very new and very old varieties; information on planting and care in the garden and in containers.

COLEUS

Color Farm
2710 Thornhill Road
Auburndale, FL 33823
(813) 967-9895

Lists by leaf color: black, dark purple, red, orange, and yellow; bordered and variegated; old-fashioned varieties and introductions of their own selection; custom-grown plants are shipped as rooted cuttings.

FERNS

Fancy Fronds
1911 4th Avenue West
Seattle, WA 98119
(206) 284-5332

Catalog $1.00, refundable with first order

Thorough descriptions of differences between various offerings, which include crested and variant forms. All ferns raised from spore or by vegetative division and grown to 4-inch pot size for shipping.

Foliage Gardens
2003 128th Avenue S.E.
Bellevue, WA 98005
(206) 747-2998

Remarkable listing of ferns and their cultivars with enticing descriptions.

GERANIUMS

Shady Hill Gardens
821 Walnut Street
Batavia, IL 60510
(708) 879-5665

Color catalog $2.00

Large selection includes fancy-leaved cultivars; custom propagation.

GRASSES

Greenlee Nursery
301 E. Franklin Avenue
Pomona, CA 91766
(714) 629-9045

Catalog $5.00

Inclusive list of ornamental grasses, sedges, and rushes; wholesale and retail.

Kurt Bluemel Inc.
2740 Greene Lane
Baldwin, MD 21013
(301) 557-7229

Ornamental grasses, rushes, and sedges, as well as some bamboo, ferns, ground covers, perennials, and aquatic plants; brief descriptions of all plants, some of which are introductions by this nursery; wholesale and retail.

HERBS

Companion Plants
7247 N. Coolville Ridge Road
Athens, OH 45701
(614) 592-4643

This pleasant catalog offers plants and seeds; nice selection of artemisia, for example.

Goodwin Creek Gardens
P.O. Box 83
Williams, OR 97544
(503) 846-7357

Catalog $1.00

A nice catalog of perennial herb plants and seeds.

Rasland Farm
N.C. 82 at U.S. 13
Godwin, NC 28344
(919) 567-2705

Plants are shipped in 3-inch pot ; diverse collection includes annuals, biennials, and perennials.

Sandy Mush Herb Nursery
Rt. 2, Surrett Cove Road
Leicester, NC 28748
(704) 683-2014

This notable nursery has a free list/order form that is astounding in its diversity — 16 different rosemaries, for example, and 37 different thymes; seeds are also available.

Sunnybrook Farms Nursery
9448 Mayfield Road
P.O. Box 6
Chesterland, OH 44026
(216) 729-7232

Catalog $1.00

A good listing of herbs (24 thymes, 16 sages), scented geraniums, perennials, hosta, and ivies.

MISCELLANEOUS

Montrose Nursery
P.O. Box 957
Hillsborough, NC 27278
(919) 732-7787

This nursery specializes in cyclamen raised from seed (about ten species and special selections); also less common perennials, such as Helleborus argutifolius, Heuchera americana 'Dale's Strain', Heuchera × 'Montrose Ruby', and Ipomoea batatas 'Blackie'.

Western Hills Nursery
16250 Coleman Valley Road
Occidental, CA 95465
(707) 874-3731

No mail order, but their diverse and eclectic selection and a display garden make a visit worthwhile. The casual groupings are an inducement to wander and find unexpected treasure such as a sedge from New

Zealand and two variegated elderberries.

NATIVE PLANTS - SOUTHWESTERN

Plants of the Southwest
930 Baca Street
Santa Fe, NM 87501
(505) 983-1548

Catalog $1.50

A superb selection of plants and seeds native to the Southwest; catalog is a good reference.

Yucca Do at Peckerwood
  Gardens
FM 359, P.O. Box 655
Waller, TX 77484
(409) 826-6363

Mail-order nursery supplying plants native to Texas and the Southwest as well as northern Mexico, and also a few nonnative, choice exotics (for example, agaves, hesperaloes, and yuccas).

PEONY

The New Peony Farm
Box 18105
St. Paul, MN 55118
(612) 457-8994

An excellent source for older cultivars as well as new introductions; catalog contains useful descriptions (such as "fragrant" or "strong stems").

TROPICAL

Glasshouse Works Greenhouses
Church Street
P.O. Box 97
Stewart, OH 45778
(614) 662-2142

Lists many tropical genera, including but not restricted to Acalypha, Begonia, Codiaeum, Plectranthus, Aeonium, Agave, Aloe, and Sansevieria, as well as ferns, ivies, and some perennials and shrubs.

Stallings Nursery
910 Encinitas Blvd.
Encinitas, CA 92024
(619) 753-3079

Catalog $3.00, refundable with first order

The mild coastal climate of north San Diego County, permits the outdoor cultivation of a wide range of subtropical perennials, vines, shrubs, and trees, including an especially notable list of Phormium, several bananas, and a nice selection of bamboo.

WOODY PLANTS

Forestfarm
990 Tetherow Road
Williams, OR 97544
(503) 846-6963

Catalog $2.00

A good place to look for unusual (and familiar) woody plants, including 15 different species of Eucalyptus, 9 Arctostaphylos, some perennials and grasses.

Heronwood Nursery
7530 288th St. N.E.
Kingston, WA 98346
(206) 297-4172

Offers less common trees, shrubs, vines, perennials, ground covers, grasses, and sedges; lovely selection of Asiatic species; many plants are Zone 6 or 7.

$\mathscr{S}$UGGESTED $\mathscr{R}$EADING

Bailey, Liberty Hyde, and Ethel Zoe Bailey; revised and expanded by the staff of the L. H. Bailey Hortorium. 1976. *Hortus Third.* New York: Macmillan Publishing Co.

Bartels, Andreas. 1987. *Gardening with Dwarf Trees and Shrubs.* Portland, Oregon: Timber Press.

Brooklyn Botanic Gardens. 1978. *Handbook on Ground Covers and Vines.* Plants & Gardens, vol. 32, no. 3. Brooklyn, New York: Brooklyn Botanic Garden.

Bryan, John E. 1989. *Bulbs,* vol. I and II. Portland, Oregon: Timber Press.

Clark, David E., ed. 1979. *Sunset New Western Gardening Book.* Menlo Park, California: Lane Publishing Co.

Clausen, Ruth R., and Nicolas H. Ekstrom. 1989. *Perennials for American Gardens.* New York: Random House.

Cox, Jeff, and Marilyn Cox. 1985. *The Perennial Garden: Color Harmonies through the Seasons.* Emmaus, Pennsylvania: Rodale Press.

Crockett, James Underwood. 1971. *Annuals.* New York: Time-Life Books.

De Wolfe, Gordon P., Jr., ed. 1987. *Taylor's Guide to Ground Covers, Vines, and Grasses.* New York: Houghton Mifflin Co.

——.1987. *Taylor's Guide to Shrubs.* New York: Houghton Mifflin Co.

——.1988. *Taylor's Guide to Trees.* New York: Houghton Mifflin Co.

Elmore, Francis H. 1976. *Shrubs and Trees of the Southwest Uplands*. Tuscon, Arizona: Southwest Parks and Monuments Association.

Fish, Margery. 1980. *Ground Cover Plants*. London: Faber & Faber.

Flint, Harrison L. 1983. *Landscape Plants for Eastern North America, Exclusive of Florida and the Immediate Gulf Coast*. New York: John Wiley & Sons.

Foster, F. Gordon. 1964. *The Gardener's Fern Book*. Princeton, New Jersey: D. Van Nostrand Co.

Grounds, Roger. 1990. *Ornamental Grasses*. London: David and Charles.

Hightshoe, Gary L. 1987. *Native Trees, Shrubs, and Vines for Urban and Rural America: A Planting Design Manual for Environmental Designers*. New York: Van Nostrand Reinhold Co.

Kaye, Reginald. 1968. *Hardy Ferns*. London: Faber and Faber.

Madson, John. 1985. *Where the Sky Began*. Santa Fe, NM: Sierra Club.

Ortho Books. 1981. *All about Annuals*. San Francisco: Chevron Chemical Co.

———.1982. *All about Groundcovers*. San Francisco: Chevron Chemical Co.

Ottesen, Carole. 1989. *Ornamental Grasses: The Amber Wave*. New York: McGraw-Hill Publishing Co.

Perl, Phillip. 1977. *Ferns*. Alexandria, Virginia: Time-Life Books.

Phillips, Judith. 1987. *Southwestern Landscaping with Native Plants*. Santa Fe, New Mexico: Museum of New Mexico Press.

Phillips, Roger, and Martyn Rix. 1989. *Shrubs*. New York: Random House.

Reinhardt, Thomas A., Martina Reinhardt, and Mark Moskowitz. 1989. *Ornamental Grass Gardening*. Los Angeles, California: HP Books.

Schmidt, R. Marilyn. 1983. *Gardening on the Eastern Seashore*. 2nd edition, 1989. New Jersey: Barnegat Light Press.

Smith, J. Robert, with Beatrice S. Smith. 1980. *The Prairie Garden*. Madison, Wisconsin: The University of Wisconsin Press.

Still, Steven M. 1988. *Herbaceous Ornamental Plants*. 3rd edition. Champaign, Illinois: Stipes Publishing Co.

Symonds, George W.D. 1973. *The Shrub Identification Book*. New York: William Morrow & Co.

———.1977. *The Tree Identification Book*. New York: William Morrow & Co.

Thomas, Graham Stuart. 1990. *Perennial Garden Plants*. Portland, OR: Timber Press.

———.1984. *Plants for Ground-Cover*. London: J. M. Dent & Sons Ltd.

Wyman, Donald. 1990. *Trees for American Gardens*. New York: MacMillan Publishing Co.

———.1969. *Shrubs and Vines for American Gardens*. New York: Macmillan Publishing Co.

GLOSSARY

Abscission. The natural separation of a leaf or flower from the plant.

Acaulescent. Stemless plants, or plants with very short stems.

Annual. A plant that completes its life cycle, from germination to maturation and death, within one season. *See also* Biennial, Perennial

Architectural foliage. Bold, coarse, large-scale foliage.

Basal. At the base.

Biennial. A plant whose life cycle extends over two seasons; usually germinates and develops top growth and roots in one season and flowers, fruits, and dies in the next. *See also* Annual, Perennial

Black frost. The first frost in fall that is hard enough to turn foliage black (28°F or lower).

Bulb. A swollen food storage organ arising from modified stem tissue with distinct internal structure, usually underground. Some examples of true bulbs are onions, daffodils, and tulips. *See also* Corm, Tuber, Rhizome

Chlorophyll. The green pigment found in leaves and necessary for photosynthesis.

Compound leaf. With more than one blade (usually referred to as leaflets) attached to each petiole.

Cordate leaf. Heart-shaped, with the petiole attached at the cleft of the heart.

Corm. A short, fleshy, erect, underground stem, replaced each year. Some examples of corms are gladiolus and crocus. *See also* Bulb, Tuber, Rhizome

Cotyledon. The leaves that first emerge upon germination. Also called *seed leaves*.

Crenate margin. With small, rounded teeth on the leaf edge.

Crosier. A curled end of an emerging fern frond, shaped like a shepherd's crook.

Crown. *See* Root crown

Culm. The stem of monocots such as grasses and sedges.

Cultivar. A horticultural variety that originated in gardens and continues under cultivation; different from the species. *See also* Genus, Species, Variety

Cuneate leaf. Wedge-shaped, with the narrowest portion of the triangle at the point of attachment.

Deadhead. Removal of spent flowers.

Deciduous. Plants with leaves that separate naturally from the plant after the growing season.

Dentate margin. A leaf edge with sharp, spreading teeth at right angles to the margin.

Denticulate margin. Small dentate teeth.

Dicot. Plants with two seed leaves, usually with branched or netlike veins.

Ensiform leaf. Swordlike with a pointed tip.

Entire margin. Smooth edged.

Evergreen. Plants that keep leaves beyond the growing season, never dropping all of them at the same time.

Falls. The three outer, often drooping segments of an iris blossom.

Fastigiate. With clustered, erect branches, usually narrowing toward the top.

Genus. A closely related group of plants, including one or more species and having certain obvious structural characteristics in common. *See also* Cultivar, Species

Glaucous. Covered with a fine white, gray, or pale blue, often waxy, bloom or powder.

Habit. The overall appearance and manner of growth of a plant.

Hastate leaf. Shaped like an arrow with pointed, flaring basal lobes.

Humus. Decayed organic matter, valuable for good soil structure.

Hybrid. Offspring of two distinctly different parents (of different cultivars, varieties, species, or genera).

Indumentum. A hairy covering.

Laciniate margin. A leaf edge that is cut into narrow, pointed lobes.

Lanceolate leaf. Lance-shaped, several times longer than broad, and widest toward the base.

Linear leaf. Narrow and elongated, with nearly parallel sides.

Lobed margin. A leaf edge with the space between serrations or waves extending at least one-third of the way toward the center of the leaf.

Margin. Leaf edge.

Monocot. Plants with only one seed leaf, with parallel veins; these include grasses, sedges, irises, lilies, cannas, and palms.

Oblong leaf. Like an elongated circle, with sides nearly parallel through most of length.

Obovate leaf. Egg-shaped, with the point of attachment at the narrow end.

Oval leaf. Egg-shaped, with the broader portion in the middle.

Ovate leaf. Egg-shaped, with the point of attachment at the broad end.

Palmate leaf. Arising from a central point, like the fingers on a hand.

Pedatisect leaf. Having leaflets arranged palmately, with the side lobes cut into two or more segments.

Peltate leaf. A circular leaf with the petiole attached within the circumference on the lower leaf surface.

Perennial. A plant that lives for three or more years. *See also* Annual, Biennial

Petiole. The means by which a leaf is attached to a twig; leaf stalk.

Photosynthesis. The process by which green leaves use the energy of sunlight to manufacture sugar and starch from carbon dioxide and nutrients.

Pinnate leaf. Arranged along a central axis, like the barbs on a feather.

Procumbent. Trailing or lying flat (but not rooting along the trailing part).

Pubescent. Covered with short, soft, fine, but not dense, hairs.

Rhizome. An underground or rootlike stem (usually horizontal) that serves as a food storage organ, and from which spring true roots and stems of new plants. An example of a rhizome is Solomon's seal. *See also* Bulb, Corm, Tuber

Root crown. The portion of the plant at or just below the surface of the ground where the stem emerges from the root.

Rootstock. An underground stem or rhizome.

Rosette. A cluster of leaves usually radiating from the root crown.

Runner. A long, slender, trailing stem that may take root and produce new plants wherever its leaf and bud parts contact the soil.

Sagittate leaf. Arrowlike, with sharp basal lobes pointing downward.

Scurfy. Covered with tiny scales.

Seed leaf. *See* Cotyledon

Semideciduous. Plants that remain green during the winter but lose their leaves at the beginning of the second growing season.

Semievergreen. Plants that keep their leaves in milder areas of their range and lose their leaves where winters are more severe.

Serrate margin. With a sawtooth edge; pointed teeth often curve forward.

Shrub. A plant with woody branches but with several stems instead of a single trunk like that of a tree.

Simple leaf. With only one blade.

Spatulate leaf. Oblong with the outer tip rounded and the narrower portion at the point of attachment.

Species. A group of plants comprising a subdivision of a genus and consisting of individuals that breed together and produce offspring like themselves. *See also* Genus, Cultivar

Specimen plant. A superb example of a plant featured as a focal point in the landscape or design.

Subspecies. A distinct subdivision of a species, ranking between a species and a cultivar or variety. *See also* Species

Sunscald. A plant injury caused by excessive heat and light in summer or cold and light in summer.

Tomentum. A dense covering of short, soft, matted, woolly hairs.

Tree. A woody plant, usually with a single main trunk and crowned at the top with spreading branches.

Tuber. A short, swollen stem or branch, usually underground, with buds or "eyes"; serves as a storage organ. An example of a tuber is dahlia. *See also* Bulb, Corm, Rhizome

Twice-serrate margin. With a coarsely toothed edge, the teeth of which are additionally serrated.

Variety. A subdivision of a species, but with differences too slight to constitute another species. *See also* Cultivar, Species

Winter burn. A condition in which the tips and edges of broad-leaved evergreens turn brown and look scorched; caused by the loss of water from the leaves when the ground is frozen. Plants located in exposed, windy areas are particularly at risk.

Woolly. Covered with soft, long, curly, matted hairs.

KEY TO COMMON NAMES OF PLANTS

COMMON NAME	BOTANICAL NAME	PLANT TYPE
absinthe	*Artemisia absinthium* 'Lambrook Silver'	Perennials
Adam's-needle	*Yucca smalliana* *Yucca filamentosa*	Perennials
aeonium	*Aeonium* spp.	Perennials
African sumac	*Rhus lancea*	Shrubs
ajuga	*Ajuga reptans*	Ground Covers
Alabama fothergilla	*Fothergilla monticola*	Shrubs
Albrecht azalea	*Rhododendron albrechtii*	Shrubs
Algerian ivy	*Hedera canariensis*	Vines
Allegany serviceberry	*Amelanchier laevis*	Trees
Alleghany spurge	*Pachysandra procumbens*	Ground Covers
aloe	*Aloe* spp.	Perennials
Alphonse Karr bamboo	*Bambusa glaucescens* 'Alphonse Karr'	Trees
alumroot	*Heuchera* spp.	Perennials
American aloe	*Agave americana*	Perennials
American arborvitae	*Thuja* spp.	Shrubs
American elderberry	*Sambucus canadensis*	Shrubs
American smokebush	*Cotinus americanus*	Trees
American wild ginger	*Asarum canadense*	Ground Covers
Amur maple	*Acer ginnala*	Trees
Andromeda	*Pieris japonica*	Shrubs
Arnold's promise	*Hamamelis* x *intermedia* 'Arnold's Promise'	Shrubs
arrow bamboo	*Pseudosasa japonica* *(Arundinaria japonica)*	Trees
arrowwood	*Viburnum dentatum*	Shrubs
astilbe	*Astilbe* spp.	Perennials

COMMON NAME	BOTANICAL NAME	PLANT TYPE
aucuba	*Aucuba japonica*	Shrubs
azalea	*Rhododendron (Azalea)* spp.	Shrubs
bamboo	*Arundinaria* spp.	Trees
	Phyllostachys spp.	
	Pseudosasa spp.	
banana yucca	*Yucca baccata*	Perennials
baneberry	*Actaea pachypoda*	Perennials
basil	*Ocimum basilicum*	Annuals
bayberry	*Myrica pensylvanica*	Shrubs
beach wormwood	*Artemisia stellerana*	Perennials
bearberry	*Arctostaphylos* spp.	Ground Covers
	Arctostaphylos uva-ursi	
bearberry cotoneaster	*Cotoneaster dammeri*	Ground Covers
	(Cotoneaster humifusus)	
bear grass	*Yucca smalliana*	Perennials
bear's-breech	*Acanthus montanus*	Perennials
	Acanthus mollis	
beech	*Fagus sylvatica*	Trees
beefsteak plant	*Acalypha wilkesiana*	Annuals
	Iresine herbstii	
	Perilla frutescens	
bergenia	*Bergenia* spp.	Perennials
bishop's weed	*Aegopodium podagraria*	Ground Covers
black bamboo	*Phyllostachys nigra*	Trees
black cherry	*Prunus serotina*	Trees
black chokeberry	*Aronia melanocarpa*	Shrubs
black cohosh	*Cimicifuga racemosa*	Perennials
black gum	*Nyssa sylvatica*	Trees
black haw	*Viburnum prunifolium*	Shrubs
black-leaved cranesbill	*Geranium sessiliforum*	Perennials
	var. *nigrum*	
black-leaved sweet potato	*Ipomomea batatas* 'Blackie'	Annuals
black locust	*Robinia pseudoacacia*	Trees
black mondo grass	*Ophiopogon planiscapus*	Ground Covers
	'Arabicus'	
black oak	*Quercus velutina*	Trees
black snakeroot	*Cimicifuga racemosa*	Perennials
bleeding-heart	*Dicentra* spp.	Perennials
	Dicentra spectabilis	
blood banana	*Musa velutina* 'Zebrina'	Trees
	(Musa acuminata)	
bloodleaf	*Iresine herbstii*	Annuals
bloodroot	*Sanguinaria canadensis*	Perennials

COMMON NAME	BOTANICAL NAME	PLANT TYPE
blue Atlas cedar	*Cedrus atlantica* 'Glauca'	Trees
blueberry	*Vaccinium* spp.	Shrubs
blue box	*Eucalyptus baueriana*	Trees
blue flag	*Iris versicolor*	Perennials
blue gum	*Eucalyptus globulus*	Trees
blue lilyturf	*Liriope muscari*	Ground Covers
blue Lyme grass	*Elymus arenarius*	Grasses
blue oat grass	*Helictotrichon sempervirens*	Grasses
blue sage	*Salvia clevelandii*	Shrubs
blue taro	*Xanthosoma violaceum*	Perennials
blue yucca	*Yucca baccata*	Perennials
Boston ivy	*Parthenocissus tricuspidata*	Vines
Bowle's golden grass	*Milium effusum* 'Aureum'	Grasses
Bowle's golden sedge	*Carex stricta (elata)* 'Bowle's Golden'	Grasses
box blueberry	*Vaccinium ovatum*	Shrubs
box-leaved holly	*Ilex crenata*	Shrubs
bramble	*Rubus calycinoides*	Ground Covers
British Columbia wild ginger	*Asarum caudatum*	Ground Covers
broad beech fern	*Thelypteris hexagonoptera*	Ferns
buffalo currant	*Ribes odoratum*	Shrubs
bugbane	*Cimicifuga* spp.	Perennials
bugleweed	*Ajuga reptans*	Ground Covers
bull-bay magnolia	*Magnolia grandiflora*	Trees
burning bush	*Euonymus alata*	Shrubs
	Kochia scoparia var. *trichophylla*	Annuals
bushman's-poison	*Acokanthera oppositifolia*	Shrubs
caladium	*Caladium* x *hortulanum*	Perennials
California bayberry	*Myrica californica*	Shrubs
California fuschia	*Zauschneria cana*	Shrubs
California live oak	*Quercus agrifolia*	Trees
canna	*Canna* x *generalis*	Perennials
caraway thyme	*Thymus herba-barona*	Ground Covers
cardoon	*Cynara cardunculus*	Perennials
Carolina rhododendron	*Rhododendron carolinianum*	Shrubs
cast-iron plant	*Aspidistra elatior*	Perennials
castor bean	*Ricinus communis*	Annuals
catalpa	*Catalpa bignonioides*	Trees
Catawba rhododendron	*Rhododendron catawbiense*	Shrubs
century plant	*Agave* spp., *Agave americana*	Perennials
chain fern	*Woodwardia virginica*	Ferns
cheddar pink	*Dianthus gratianopolitanus*	Perennials

COMMON NAME	BOTANICAL NAME	PLANT TYPE
chenille plant	*Acalyphy hispida*	Annuals
cherry	*Prunus* spp.	Trees
cherry plum	*Prunus cerasifera*	Trees
Chinese juniper	*Juniperus chinensis*	Shrubs
Chinese mahonia	*Mahonia lomariifolia*	Shrubs
Chinese rice paper plant	*Tetrapanax papyriferus*	Shrubs
Chinese witch-hazel	*Hamamelis mollis*	Shrubs
chokeberry	*Aronia* spp.	Shrubs
Christmas fern	*Polystichum acrostichoides*	Ferns
Christmas rose	*Helleborus niger*	Perennials
cinnamon fern	*Osmunda cinnamomea*	Ferns
climbing hydrangea	*Hydrangea anomola* spp. *petiolaris*	Vines
clivia	*Clivia miniata*	Perennials
clove carnation	*Dianthus caryophyllus*	Perennials
clove currant	*Ribes odoratum*	Shrubs
clumping giant timber bamboo	*Bambusa oldhamii* (*Sinocalamus oldhamii*)	Trees Trees
coast leucothoe	*Leucothoe axillaris (catesbei)*	Shrubs
coast live oak	*Quercus agrifolia*	Trees
cohosh	*Actaea pachypoda*	Perennials
coleus	*Coleus blumei*	Annuals
Colorado blue spruce	*Picea pungens* 'Glauca'	Trees
common deerberry	*Vaccinium stamineum*	Shrubs
common juniper	*Juniperus communis*	Shrubs
common peony	*Paeonia lactiflora* *Paeonia officinalis*	Perennials
common sage	*Salvia officinalis*	Shrubs
common witch-hazel	*Hamamelis virginiana*	Shrubs
copperleaf	*Acalypha wilkesiana*	Annuals
coral aloe	*Aloe striata*	Perennials
coralbells	*Heuchera* x *brizoides*	Perennials
Corsican hellebore	*Helleborus lividus* ssp. *corsicus*	Perennials
cotoneaster	*Cotoneaster* spp.	Ground Covers
cottage pink	*Dianthus plumarius*	Perennials
cowberry	*Vaccinium vitis-idaea*	Ground Covers
crab apple	*Malus* spp.	Trees
creeping cotoneaster	*Cotoneaster adpressus*	Ground Covers
creeping juniper	*Juniperus* spp. *Juniperus horizontalis*	Shrubs
creeping lilyturf	*Liriope spicata*	Ground Covers
creeping mahonia	*Mahonia repens*	Ground Covers
creeping phlox	*Phlox stolonifera*	Ground Covers

COMMON NAME	BOTANICAL NAME	PLANT TYPE
creeping thyme	*Thymus praecox (serpyllum)*	Ground Covers
creeping willow	*Salix repens*	Shrubs
crested iris	*Iris cristata*	Perennials
crocodile-jaws	*Aloe humilis*	Perennials
croton	*Codiaeum variegatum*	Shrubs
currant	*Ribes* spp.	Shrubs
cushionbush	*Calocephalus brownii*	Perennials
cut-leaf stephanandra	*Stephanandra incisa*	Shrubs
cyclamen	*Cyclamen* spp.	Perennials
dagger plant	*Yucca aloifolia*	Perennials
David viburnum	*Viburnum davidii*	Shrubs
daylilies	*Hemerocallis* spp.	Perennials
desert mahonia	*Mahonia fremontii*	Shrubs
dianthus	*Dianthus* spp.	Perennials
doll's-eyes	*Actaea pachypoda*	Perennials
dragon's-eye pine	*Pinus densiflora 'Oculus-draconis'*	Trees
drooping leucothoe	*Leucothoe fontanesiana (catesbei)*	Shrubs
dusty-miller	*Artemisia stellerana*	Perennials
	Senecio cineraria	Annuals
Dutchman's-breeches	*Dicentra cucullaria*	Perennials
Dutchman's-pipe	*Aristolochia durior (macrophylla)*	Vines
dwarf fern-leaf bamboo	*Arundinaria disticha (Bambusa disticha)*	Ground Covers
dwarf fothergilla	*Fothergilla gardenii*	Shrubs
dwarf gold-stripe bamboo	*Arundinaria viridistriata*	Ground Covers
dwarf white-stripe bamboo	*Arundinaria variegata (Sasa variegata)*	Ground Covers
eastern redbud	*Cercis canadensis*	Trees
eastern red cedar	*Juniperus virginiana*	Shrubs
	Juniperus virginiana	Trees
eastern white cedar	*Thuja occidentalis*	Shrubs
elderberry	*Sambucus nigra* spp.	Shrubs
elephant-ear	*Xanthosoma sagittifolium*	Perennials
English holly	*Ilex aquifolium*	Trees
English ivy	*Hedera helix*	Vines
English yew	*Taxus baccata*	Trees
epimedium	*Epimedium* spp.	Ground Covers
eucalyptus	*Eucalyptus* spp.	Shrubs
	Eucalyptus spp.	Trees

COMMON NAME	BOTANICAL NAME	PLANT TYPE
euonymus	*Euonymus* spp.	Vines
European elder	*Sambucus nigra*	Shrubs
European ginger	*Asarum europaeum*	Ground Covers
European hazel	*Corylus avellana*	Shrubs
evergreen shield fern	*Dryopteris marginalis*	Ferns
false cypress	*Chamaecyparis* spp.	Shrubs
false goatsbeard	*Astilbe biternata*	Perennials
false hellebore	*Veratrum viride*	Perennials
false spirea	*Filipendula* spp.	Perennials
fennel	*Foenicum vulgare*	Perennials
fern-leaf bamboo	*Bambusa glaucescens* 'Fernleaf' *(Bambusa disticha)*	Trees
fernleaf peony	*Paeonia tenuifolia*	Perennials
filbert	*Corylus* spp., *Corylus maxima*	Shrubs
five-leaf akebia	*Akebia quinata*	Vines
golden hop vine	*Humulus lupulus* 'Aureus'	Vines
flame nettle	*Coleus blumei*	Annuals
florists' cyclamen	*Cyclamen persicum*	Perennials
flowering dogwood	*Cornus florida*	Trees
flowering fern	*Osmunda* spp.	Ferns
foamflower	*Tiarella cordifolia*	Ground Covers
fothergilla	*Fothergilla* spp.	Shrubs
fountain bamboo	*Sinarundinaria nitida*	Trees
fountain grass	*Pennisetum alopecuroides*	Grasses
foxberry	*Vaccinium vitis-idaea*	Ground Covers
fragrant sumac	*Rhus aromatica*	Shrubs
fringed bleeding-heart	*Dicentra eximia*	Perennials
fringe tree	*Chionanthus virginicus*	Trees
full-moon maple	*Acer japonicum*	Trees
gardener's-garters grass	*Phalaris arundinacea* 'Picta'	Grasses
garden sage	*Salvia officinalis*	Shrubs
geranium	*Pelargonium* x *hortorum*	Annuals
giant eulalia grass	*Miscanthus sinensis*	Grasses
giant hogweed	*Heracleum mantegazzianum*	Perennials
giant reed grass	*Arundo donax*	Grasses
giant Solomon's-seal	*Polygonatum commutatum* *Polygonatum canaliculatum*	Perennials
giant wood fern	*Dryopteris goldiana*	Ferns
ginger	*Asarum* spp.	Ground Covers
ginkgo	*Ginkgo biloba*	Trees
globe thistle	*Echinops ritro*	Perennials
goatsbeard	*Aruncus dioicus*	Perennials
golden bamboo	*Phyllostachys aurea* *(Phyllostachys bambusoides*	Trees

COMMON NAME	BOTANICAL NAME	PLANT TYPE
	var. *aurea*)	
golden-eardrops	*Dicentra chrysantha*	Perennials
golden-feather	*Chrysanthemum parthenium* 'Aureum', *Matricaria eximia*	Annuals
golden feverfew	*Chrysanthemum parthenium* 'Aureum', *Matricaria eximia*	Annuals
golden goddess bamboo	*Bambusa glaucescens* 'Golden Goddess'	Trees
golden hop vine	*Humulus lupulus* 'Aureus'	Vines
golden-tooth aloe	*Aloe nobilis*	Perennials
golden wood millet	*Milium effusum* 'Aureum'	Grasses
Goldie's fern	*Dryopteris goldiana*	Ferns
goldmoss stonecrop	*Sedum acre*	Ground Covers
goutweed	*Aegopodium podagraria*	Ground Covers
greater periwinkle	*Vinca major*	Ground Covers
greater wood rush	*Luzula sylvatica*	Grasses
green-and-gold crown aloe	*Aloe nobilis*	Perennials
griselinia	*Griselinia lucida* 'Variegata'	Shrubs
gunnera	*Gunnera manicata*	Perennials
Harriman's yucca	*Yucca harrimaniae*	Perennials
hart's-tongue fern	*Phyllitis scolopendrium*	Ferns
hay-scented fern	*Dennstaedtia punctilobula*	Ferns
hazel	*Corylus* spp.	Shrubs
heart-leaved bergenia	*Bergenia cordifolia*	Perennials
heaths and heathers	*Erica* spp., *Calluna* spp.	Shrubs
hedgehog agave	*Agave stricta*	Perennials
hedgehog aloe	*Aloe humilis*	Perennials
hellebore	*Helleborus* spp.	Perennials
hen-and-chicks	*Echeveria* spp.	Perennials
	Sempervivum spp.	Perennials
highbush blueberry	*Vaccinium corymbosum*	Shrubs
Hinoki false cypress	*Chamaecyparis obtusa*	Shrubs
hobblebush	*Viburnum alnifolium*	Shrubs
holly	*Ilex* spp.	Shrubs
honey locust	*Gleditsia tricanthos*	Trees
horse chestnut	*Aesculus hippocastanum*	Trees
horseshoe geranium	*Pelargonium* x *hortorum*	Annuals
hosta	*Hosta* spp.	Perennials
Indian bean tree	*Catalpa bignonioides*	Trees
inkberry	*Ilex glabra*	Shrubs
interrupted fern	*Osmunda claytoniana*	Ferns
iris	*Iris* spp.	Perennials
ivy	*Hedera* spp.	Vines

COMMON NAME	BOTANICAL NAME	PLANT TYPE
ivy-leaved cyclamen	*Cyclamen hederifolium*	Perennials
jaburan lilyturf	*Ophiopogon jaburan*	Ground Covers
Japanese autumn fern	*Dryopteris erythrosora*	Ferns
Japanese barberry	*Berberis thunbergii*	Shrubs
Japanese blood grass	*Imperata cylindrica* 'Red Baron'	Grasses
Japanese bugbane	*Cimicifuga japonica* var. *acerina*	Perennials
Japanese crimson glory vine	*Vitis coignetiae*	Vines
Japanese holly	*Ilex crenata*	Shrubs
Japanese holly fern	*Cyrtomium falcatum*	Ferns
Japanese iris	*Iris ensata*	Perennials
Japanese leucothoe	*Leucothoe keiskei*	Shrubs
Japanese maple	*Acer palmatum*	Trees
Japanese painted fern	*Athyrium goeringianum* 'Pictum'	Ferns
Japanese sedge	*Carex morrowii*	Grasses
Japanese timber bamboo	*Phyllostachys bambusoides*	Trees
Japanese viburnum	*Viburnum japonicum*	Shrubs
Japanese wind-combed grass	*Hakonechloa macra*	Grasses
jeweled aloe	*Aloe distans*	Perennials
Joseph's coat	*Amaranthus tricolor*	Annuals
Judas tree	*Cercis canadensis*	Trees
juniper	*Juniperus* spp.	Shrubs
	Juniperus spp.	Trees
Kamchatka bugbane	*Cimicifuga simplex*	Perennials
Kashgar tamarix	*Tamarix hispida*	Shrubs
kerria	*Kerria japonica*	Shrubs
King Ferdinand agave	*Agave fernandi-regis*	Perennials
kirengeshoma	*Kirengeshoma palmata*	Perennials
kolomikta actinidia	*Actinidia kolomikta*	Vines
Kruse's mallee	*Eucalyptus kruseana*	Shrubs
kuma bamboo grass	*Sasa veitchii*	Ground Covers
Labrador violet	*Viola labradorica*	Perennials
lace aloe	*Aloe aristata*	Perennials
lady fern	*Athyrium filix-femina*	Ferns
lady's-mantle	*Alchemilla mollis*	Perennials
lamb's-ears	*Stachys byzantina* (*Stachys lanata*)	Ground Covers
large fothergilla	*Fothergilla major*	Shrubs
lavender	*Lavandula angustifolia*	Shrubs
lavender-cotton	*Santolina chamaecyparissus*	Shrubs

COMMON NAME	BOTANICAL NAME	PLANT TYPE
leadplant	*Amorpha canescens*	Shrubs
leadwort	*Plumbago larpentae*	Ground Covers
	(Ceratostigma plumbaginoides)	
leatherleaf mahonia	*Mahonia bealei*	Shrubs
leatherleaf viburnum	*Viburnum rhytidophyllum*	Shrubs
lemon thyme	*Thymus* x *citriodus*	Ground Covers
Lenten rose	*Helleborus orientalis*	Perennials
lesser periwinkle	*Vinca minor*	Ground Covers
lettuce	*Lactuca sativa*	Annuals
leucothoe	*Leucothoe* spp.	Shrubs
licorice plant	*Helichrysum petiolatum*	Shrubs
	(Gnaphalium lanatum)	
lily-of-the-valley	*Convallaria majalis*	Ground Covers
lilyturf	*Liriope* spp., *Liriope muscari*	Ground Covers
linden viburnum	*Viburnum dilatatum*	Shrubs
ling heather	*Calluna vulgaris*	Shrubs
lingonberry	*Vaccinium vitis-idaea*	Ground Covers
little bluestem	*Schizachyrium scoparium*	Grasses
	(Andropogon scoparius)	
Little Sur manzanita	*Arctostaphylos edmundsii*	Ground Covers
locust	*Robinia pseudoacacia*	Trees
longleaf mahonia	*Mahonia nervosa*	Shrubs
loquat	*Eriobotrya japoica*	Trees
lords-and-ladies	*Arum italicum*	Perennials
Lord's-candlestick	*Yucca gloriosa*	Perennials
lowbush blueberry	*Vaccinium angustifolium*	Shrubs
lungwort	*Pulmonaria saccharata*	Perennials
magnolia	*Magnolia grandiflora*	Trees
mahonia	*Mahonia* spp.	Shrubs
	Mahonia spp.	Ground Covers
maidenhair fern	*Adiantum pedatum*	Ferns
maiden pink	*Dianthus deltoides*	Perennials
manzanita	*Arctostaphylos* spp.	Ground Covers
maple	*Acer* spp.	Trees
maple-leaf viburnum	*Viburnum acerifolium*	Shrubs
marginal shield fern	*Dryopteris marginalis*	Ferns
mayapple	*Podophyllum peltatum*	Perennials
meadow rue	*Thalictrum speciosissimum*	Perennials
mescal agave	*Agave parryi*	Perennials
Mexican bush sage	*Salvia leucantha*	Shrubs
milk thistle	*Silybum marianum*	Annuals
mondo grass	*Ophiopogon* spp.	Ground Covers
	Ophiopogon japonicus	

COMMON NAME	BOTANICAL NAME	PLANT TYPE
moss pink	*Phlox subulata*	Ground Covers
mother-in-law's-tongue	*Sansevieria trifasciata*	Perennials
mother-of-thyme	*Thymus praecox (serpyllum)*	Ground Covers
mountain acanthus	*Acanthus montanus*	Perennials
mountain cranberry	*Vaccinium vitis-idaea*	Ground Covers
mustard	*Brassica juncea*	Annuals
myrobalan plum	*Prunus cerasifera*	Trees
myrtle	*Vinca minor*	Ground Covers
nannyberry	*Viburnum lentago*	Shrubs
necklace cotoneaster	*Cotoneaster conspicuus* var. *decorus*	Ground Covers
net-leaved willow	*Salix reticulata*	Shrubs
New Zealand flax	*Phormium tenax*	Perennials
Nichol's willow-leafed peppermint gum	*Eucalyptus nicholli*	Trees
Nippon lily	*Rohdea japonica*	Perennials
Norway maple	*Acer platanoides*	Trees
oak	*Quercus* spp.	Trees
oak-leaf hydrangea	*Hydrangea quercifolia*	Shrubs
octopus agave	*Agave vilmoriniana*	Perennials
Odessa tamarix	*Tamarix ramosissima* (*odessana, pentandra*)	Shrubs
Ohio buckeye	*Aesculus glabra*	Trees
old-field juniper	*Juniperus communis*	Shrubs
oldham bamboo	*Bambusa oldhamii* (*Sinocalamus oldhamii*)	Trees
ophiopogon	*Ophiopogon planiscapus*	Ground Covers
Oregon grape	*Mahonia nervosa*	Shrubs
Oregon grape holly	*Mahonia aquifolium*	Shrubs
Oriental arborvitae	*Platycladus (Thuja) orientalis*	Shrubs
ornamental cabbage	*Brassica oleracea capitata*	Annuals
ornamental kale	*Brassica oleracea acephala*	Annuals
orris	*Iris pallida*	Perennials
ostrich fern	*Matteuccia pensylvanica*	Ferns
our-Lord's-candle	*Yucca whipplei*	Perennials
oxalis	*Oxalis regnellii*	Perennials
pachysandra	*Pachysandra* spp. *Pachysandra terminalis*	Ground Covers
palmate bamboo	*Sasa palmata (Sasa senanensis)* (*Bambusa palmata*)	Trees
Pampas grass	*Cortaderia selloana*	Grasses
paperbark maple	*Acer griseum*	Trees
partridge berry	*Mitchella repens*	Ground Covers
partridge-breast	*Aloe variegata*	Perennials

COMMON NAME	BOTANICAL NAME	PLANT TYPE
peony	*Paeonia* spp.	Perennials
pepperidge	*Nyssa sylvatica*	Trees
perilla	*Perilla frutescens*	Annuals
periwinkle	*Vinca* spp.	Ground Covers
Persian ivy	*Hedera colchica*	Vines
Persian parrotia	*Parrotia persica*	Trees
phlox	*Phlox* spp.	Ground Covers
	Phlox paniculata 'Nora Leigh'	Perennials
pick-a-back plant	*Tolmeia menziesii*	Ground Covers
pin cherry	*Prunus pensylvanica*	Trees
pink-shell azalea	*Rhododendron vaseyi*	Shrubs
pin oak	*Quercus palustris*	Trees
pistachio	*Pistacia chinensis*	Trees
pittosporum	*Pittosporum tobira*	Shrubs
plantain	*Plantago major*	Perennials
plantain-leafed sedge	*Carex plantaginea*	Grasses
plume poppy	*Macleaya cordata*	Perennials
polka-dot plant	*Hypoestes phyllostachya (sanguinolenta)*	Annuals
poverty grass	*Schizacyrium scoparium (Andropogon scoparius)*	Grasses
prairie dock	*Silphium terebinthinaceum*	Perennials
prairie dropseed	*Sporobolus heterolepis*	Grasses
prairie rose	*Rosa setigera*	Shrubs
purple-and-gold-crown aloe	*Aloe mitriformis*	Perennials
purple-crown	*Aloe mitriformis*	Perennials
purple-heart	*Setcreasea pallida* 'Purple Heart'	Perennials
purple hop bush	*Dodonaea viscosa*	Shrubs
purple-leaved sand cherry	*Prunus* x *cistena*	Shrubs
purple sage	*Salvia leucophylla*	Shrubs
quaking aspen	*Populus tremuloides*	Trees
queen-of-the-meadow	*Filipendula ulmaria*	Perennials
Queen Victoria agave	*Agave victoriae-reginae*	Perennials
rattlesnake-master	*Eryngium yuccafolium*	Perennials
red baneberry	*Actaea rubra*	Perennials
red chokeberry	*Aronia arbutifolia*	Shrubs
red fountain grass	*Pennisetum setaceum*	Grasses
redleaf rose	*Rosa rubrifolia (glauca)*	Shrubs
red maple	*Acer rubrum*	Trees
red oak	*Quercus rubra (Quercus borealis)*	Trees

COMMON NAME	BOTANICAL NAME	PLANT TYPE
red orach	*Atriplex hortensis*	Annuals
rex begonia	*Begonia rex*	Perennials
rhododendron	*Rhododendron* spp.	Shrubs
rhubarb	*Rheum rhabarbarum*	Perennials
rock cotoneaster	*Cotoneaster horizontalis*	Ground Covers
rock maple	*Acer saccharum*	Trees
Rocky Mountain juniper	*Juniperus scopulorum*	Shrubs
rodgersia	*Rodgersia* spp.	Perennials
Roman wormwood	*Artemisia pontica*	Perennials
rose	*Rosa* spp.	Shrubs
rosebay rhododendron	*Rhododendron maximum*	Shrubs
rosemary	*Rosmarinus officinalis* 'Prostrata'	Ground Covers
round-leaved snow gum	*Eucalyptus perriniana*	Trees
royal azalea	*Rhododendron schlippenbachii*	Shrubs
royal fern	*Osmunda regalis*	Ferns
rue	*Ruta graveolens*	Perennials
rum cherry	*Prunus serotina*	Trees
sacred bamboo	*Nandina domestica*	Shrubs
sage	*Salvia* spp.	Shrubs
	Salvia spp.	Perennials
sagebrush	*Artemisia tridentata*	Perennials
St. Mary's thistle	*Silybum marianum*	Annuals
salt cedar	*Tamarix chinensis*	Shrubs
salt-spray rose	*Rosa rugosa*	Shrubs
sassafras	*Sassafras albidum*	Trees
Savin juniper	*Juniperus sabina*	Shrubs
Sawara false cypress	*Chamaecyparis pisifera*	Shrubs
scarlet oak	*Quercus coccinea*	Trees
Scotch heather	*Calluna vulgaris*	Shrubs
Scotch thistle	*Onopordum acanthium*	Annuals
sea kale	*Crambe maritima*	Perennials
sea tomato	*Rosa rugosa*	Shrubs
sedge	*Carex* spp.	Grasses
sedum	*Sedum* spp.	Ground Covers
senecio	*Senecio cineraria*	Annuals
sensitive fern	*Onoclea sensibilis*	Ferns
shadbush	*Amelanchier laevis*	Trees
sheep's fescue	*Festuca ovina*	Grasses
shield fern	*Polystichum* spp.	Ferns
shining rose	*Rosa nitida*	Shrubs
shining sumac	*Rhus copallina*	Shrubs
short-leaved stonecrop	*Sedum brevifolium*	Ground Covers
Siberian bugloss	*Brunnera macrophylla*	Perennials

COMMON NAME	BOTANICAL NAME	PLANT TYPE
Siberian iris	*Iris sibirica*	Perennials
Siberian meadowsweet	*Filipendula palmata*	Perennials
Siberian tea	*Bergenia crassifolia*	Perennials
Siebold's viburnum	*Viburnum sieboldii*	Shrubs
silver-dollar gum	*Eucalyptus polyanthemos*	Trees
silver-king wormwood	*Artemisia ludoviciana albula*	Perennials
silver-leaved mountain gum	*Eucalyptus pulverulenta*	Trees
silver-leaved pear	*Pyrus salicifolia*	Trees
silver-mound artemisia	*Artemisia schmidtiana*	Perennials
silver-queen wormwood	*Artemisia ludoviciana albula*	Perennials
silver sage	*Salvia argentea*	Perennials
silver-stripe bamboo	*Bambusa glaucescens* 'Silver-stripe'	Trees
silver tree	*Leucodendron argenteum*	Trees
silver-vein creeper	*Parthenocissus henryana*	Vines
single-seed juniper	*Juniperus squamata*	Shrubs
small soapweed	*Yucca glauca*	Perennials
small Solomon's-seal	*Polygonatum biflorum*	Perennials
Smirnow rhododendron	*Rhododendron smirnowii*	Shrubs
smokebush	*Cotinus coggygria*	Shrubs
smooth sumac	*Rhus glabra*	Shrubs
snow gum	*Eucalyptus niphophila*	Trees
snow-on-the-mountain	*Euphorbia marginata*	Annuals
Solomon's-seal	*Polygonatum* spp.	Perennials
sour gum	*Nyssa sylvatica*	Trees
sourwood	*Oxydendrum arboreum*	Trees
southern magnolia	*Magnolia grandiflora*	Trees
southernwood	*Artemisia abrotanum*	Perennials
Spanish-bayonet	*Yucca aloifolia, Yucca baccata*	Perennials
Spanish-dagger	*Yucca gloriosa*	Perennials
spicebush	*Lindera benzoin*	Shrubs
spider aloe	*Aloe humilis*	Perennials
spiny acanthus	*Acanthus spinosissimus*	Perennials
spotted dead nettle	*Lamium maculatum*	Ground Covers
spreading willow-leaf cotoneaster	*Cotoneaster salicifolius*	Ground Covers
spring heath	*Erica carnea*	Shrubs
squirrel corn	*Dicentra canadensis*	Perennials
staghorn sumac	*Rhus typhina*	Shrubs
star magnolia	*Magnolia stellata*	Trees
stephanandra	*Stephanandra incisa*	Shrubs
stinking hellebore	*Helleborus foetidus*	Perennials
stonecrop	*Sedum* spp.	Ground Covers

COMMON NAME	BOTANICAL NAME	PLANT TYPE
stringy stonecrop	*Sedum lineare* (*Sedum sarmentosum*)	Ground Covers
striped sedge	*Carex siderostricta*	Grasses
sugar maple	*Acer saccharum*	Trees
sumac	*Rhus* spp., *Rhus aromatica*	Shrubs
swamp azalea	*Rhododendron viscosum*	Shrubs
swamp maple	*Acer rubrum*	Trees
sweet azalea	*Rhododendron arborescens*	Shrubs
sweetbells	*Leucothoe racemosa*	Shrubs
sweet box	*Sarcococca hookerana* var. *humilis*	Ground Covers
sweetbriar rose	*Rosa eglanteria*	Shrubs
sweet cicely	*Myrrhis odorata*	Perennials
sweetfern	*Comptonia peregrina*	Shrubs
sweet flag	*Acorus calamus*	Perennials
sweet gum	*Liquidambar styraciflua*	Trees
sword fern	*Nephrolepis exaltata*	Ferns
tamarix	*Tamarix* spp.	Shrubs
Texas ranger	*Leucophyllum frutescens*	Shrubs
thimbleberry	*Rubus odoratus*	Shrubs
thyme	*Thymus* spp.	Ground Covers
thyme rock-spray cotoneaster	*Cotoneaster microphyllus* var. *thymifolius*	Ground Covers
tiger aloe	*Aloe variegata*	Perennials
ti plant	*Cordyline australis* 'Atropurpurea'	Trees
torch plant	*Aloe aristata*	Perennials
tuber oat grass	*Arrhenatherum elatius* spp. *bulbosum*	Grasses
tulip tree	*Liriodendron tulipifera*	Trees
tupelo	*Nyssa sylvatica*	Trees
two-row stonecrop	*Sedum spurium*	Ground Covers
umbrella plant	*Peltiphyllum peltatum*	Perennials
Utah agave	*Agave utahensis*	Perennials
variegated corn	*Zea mays japonica folia-variegata*	Grasses
variegated Siberian dogwood	*Cornus alba* 'Argenteo-marginata'	Shrubs
viburnum	*Viburnum* spp.	Shrubs
vinca vine	*Vinca major*	Ground Covers
vine-hill manzanita	*Arctostaphylos densiflora*	Ground Covers
vine maple	*Acer circinatum*	Trees
Virginia creeper	*Parthenocissus quinquefolia*	Vines

COMMON NAME	BOTANICAL NAME	PLANT TYPE
Virginia rose	*Rosa virginiana*	Shrubs
wayfaring tree	*Viburnum lantana*	Shrubs
weigela	*Weigela florida*	Shrubs
western bleeding-heart	*Dicentra formosa*	Perennials
western red cedar	*Juniperus scopulorum*	Trees
western sword fern	*Polystichum munitum*	Ferns
white hellebore	*Veratrum viride*	Perennials
white oak	*Quercus alba*	Trees
white stonecrop	*Sedum album*	Ground Covers
wide-leaf sedge	*Carex plantaginea*	Grasses
wild ginger	*Asarum* spp.	Ground Covers
willow	*Salix* spp.	Shrubs
willow oak	*Quercus phellos*	Trees
Wilson rhododendron	*Rhododendron* **x** *laetevirens*	Shrubs
winter begonia	*Bergenia ciliata*	Perennials
winter creeper	*Euonymus fortunei*	Vines
winter currant	*Ribes sanguineum*	Shrubs
witch-alder	*Fothergilla* spp.	Shrubs
witch-hazel	*Hamamelis* spp.	Shrubs
woodbine	*Parthenocissus* spp. *Parthenocissus quinquefolia*	Vines
woodruff	*Galium odoratum (Asperula odorata)*	Ground Covers
woolly thyme	*Thymus pseudolanuginosus (lanuginosus)*	Ground Covers
woolly willow	*Salix lanata*	Shrubs
wormwood	*Artemisia* spp.	Perennials
Yaku-shima rhododendron	*Rhododendron yakusimanum*	Shrubs
yarrow	*Achillea* **x** *taygeta* 'Moonshine'	Perennials
yautia	*Xanthosoma violaceum*	Perennials
yellow archangel	*Lamiastrum galeobdolon* 'Variegatum'	Ground Covers
yellow flag	*Iris pseudacorus*	Perennials
yellow-groove bamboo	*Phyllostachys aureosulcata*	Trees
yew	*Taxus* **x** *media (Taxus cuspidata* **x** *Taxus baccata)*	Trees
youth-on-age	*Tolmeia menziesii*	Ground Covers
yucca	*Yucca* spp.	Perennials
zonal geranium	*Pelargonium* **x** *hortorum*	Annuals

USDA Zone Map

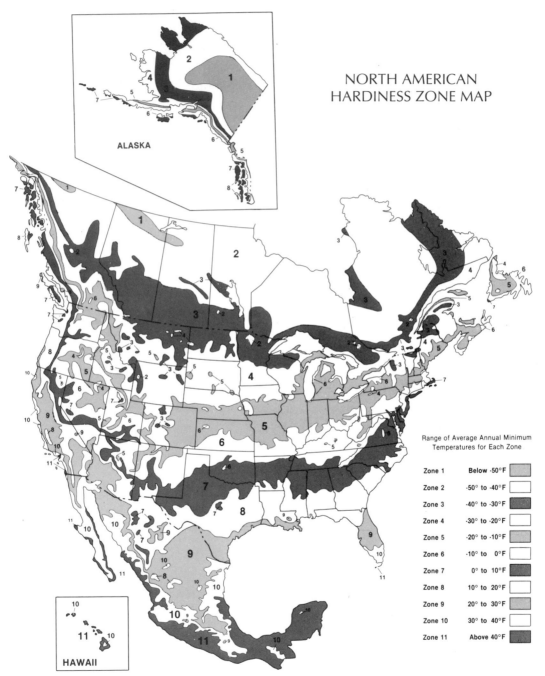

NORTH AMERICAN
HARDINESS ZONE MAP

ALASKA

HAWAII

Range of Average Annual Minimum
Temperatures for Each Zone

Zone 1	Below -50°F
Zone 2	-50° to -40°F
Zone 3	-40° to -30°F
Zone 4	-30° to -20°F
Zone 5	-20° to -10°F
Zone 6	-10° to 0°F
Zone 7	0° to 10°F
Zone 8	10° to 20°F
Zone 9	20° to 30°F
Zone 10	30° to 40°F
Zone 11	Above 40°F

INDEX

Figures in **boldface** indicate illustrations and photographs. A Key to Common Names of Plants can be found on pages 195-209.

Mulch, 185
Musa velutina 'Zebrina', 81
Myrica spp., **43,** 98
Myrrhis odorata, 14, 148

N

Nandina domestica, 98–99, **151**
Native plants of the Southwest,
    sources of, 190
Nephrolepis exaltata, 163–164
Nitrogen, 183
Nymphaea odorata minor, **44**
Nyssa sylvatica, **44,** 81

O

Oblong leaf, 7, **8**
Obovate leaf, 7, **8**
Ocimum basilicum, 177
Onoclea sensibilis, 164
Onopordum acanthium, 177
Ophiopogon spp. and cultivars,
    14, 123–124
Opuntia sp., **116**
Organic matter in soil, 182–183
Osmunda spp., 164–165
Oval, 7, **8**
Ovate leaf, 7, **8**
Oxalis regnellii, 148
Oxydendrum arboreum, 81–82

P

Pachysandra spp. and cultivars,
    36, 124
Paeonia spp. and cultivars, **12,**
    14, 148, 153
    sources of, 190
Palmate leaflet, **8,** 9
Parrotia persica, 82
Parthenocissus spp. and culti-
    vars, **80,** 112, 117
Pelargonium spp. and cultivars,
    152, 177–178
    sources of, 189
Peltate leaf, 7, **8**

Peltiphyllum peltatum, 153
Pennisetum spp., 171
Perennials, **78,** 128–161
    with bold, architectural foli-
        age, 11
    evergreen, 34
    late-flowering, 30
    problems with, 4–5
    for winter interest 32, 35–36
        (table)
Perilla frutescens, 178
Petiole, 7, **7**
Phalaris arundinacea 'Picta',
    171
Phlox spp., 124–125, 153
Phormium tenax, 14, 153–154
Phosphorus, 183
Photosynthesis, 7
Phyllitis scolopendrium, 165
Phyllostachys spp., 68–70
Picea pungens, **77,** 82
Pieris japonica, 35, 99
Pinnate leaflet, **8,** 9
Pinus densiflora 'Oculus-
    draconis', 82
Pistacia chinensis, 82
Pittosporum tobira, 99
Plantago major, 154
Planting, 184–185
Plants. *See also* Leaves
    annuals, 172–179, 188
    combinations of, 5
    container garden, 57–62
    dictionary of, 63–179
    for dry, sandy garden, 51–52
    evergreens, 9, 32–33, 34, 52–
        53
    ferns, 161–166, 189
    grasses, 166–172, 189
    ground covers, 117–128
    key to common names, 195–
        209
    perennials. *See* Perennials
    putting in, 184–185
    for sandy, infertile garden,
        52–54

for seasonal interest, 35–36
    (table)
selecting, 2–3
    for foliage color, 15–25
    for foliage shape, 11–13
    for size, 12
    for shady gardens, 38–40,
        45–49
    for shady slopes, 46–47
    shrubs. *See* Shrub(s)
    sources of, 188–190
    for sunny gardens, 49–50
    trees. *See* Trees
    vines, 110–112, 117
    for wetland gardens, 54–57
Platycladus [Thuja] orientalis,
    99–100
*Plectranthus coleoides mar-
    ginata,* **115**
*Plumbago larpentiae [Cerato-
    stigma plumbaginoides],*
    125
Polygonatum spp. and cultivars,
    154–154
Polystichum spp., 36, **41,** 165
Populus tremuloides, 83
Potassium, 183–184
Prunus spp. and hybrids, 25,
    35, 83, 100
Pseudosasa spp., 68–69
Pulmonaria saccharata, 25, **78,**
    155
Purple
    and blue garden, 49–50
    foliage, 24–25 (table)
Pyrus salicifolia, 83–84

Q

Quercus spp., 35, **41,** 84–85

R

Rabbits, 186–187
Red foliage, 24–25 (table)
Rheum spp., 14, **44, 115,** 155–
    156